LeBrone C. Harris
University of South Florida

James E. Moon
University of South Florida

Study Guide to accompany

Financial Accounting

An Introduction to Concepts, Methods, and Uses

Clyde Stickney
Dartmouth College

Roman Weil
University of Chicago

D1408694

THE DRYDEN PRESS
Harcourt Brace College Publishers

Fort Worth   Philadelphia   San Diego   New York   Orlando   Austin   San Antonio
Toronto   Montreal   London   Sydney   Tokyo

Address for Editorial Correspondence
The Dryden Press, 301 Commerce Street, Suite 3700, Fort Worth, TX 76102

Address for Orders
The Dryden Press, 6277 Sea Harbor Drive, Orlando, FL 32887
1-800-782-4479, or 1-800-433-0001 (in Florida)

ISBN: 0-03-096650-7

Printed in the United States of America

6 7 8 9 0 1 2   023   9 8 7 6 5 4 3

The Dryden Press
Harcourt Brace College Publishers

Contents

Introduction to Business Activities and Overview of Financial Statements and the Reporting Process

Chapter Highlights

1. Firms prepare financial statements for various external users–owners, lenders, regulators. The statements attempt to present in a meaningful way the results of a firm's business activities.

2. Companies establish goals or targets that are the end results toward which the energies of the firm are directed. The company's strategies are the means for achieving the company's goals.

3. The principal sources of funds for a firm are owners and creditors. While owners are not repaid at a particular future date, creditors require that the funds be repaid, often with interest, at a specific date.

4. Funds obtained from owners and creditors are invested in various items needed to carry out the firm's business activities. The funds are invested in various resources in order to generate profit.

5. The balance sheet presents a snapshot, as of a moment in time, of the investing and financing activities of a firm. The balance sheet presents a listing of a firm's assets, liabilities, and shareholders' equity.

6. Assets are economic resources that have the potential or ability to provide future services or benefits to the firm.

7. Liabilities are creditors' claims on the resources that result from benefits previously received by the company. Typically, liabilities require that a specific amount be paid on a specified date.

8. Shareholders' equity is the owners' claim on the assets of the firm. The owners' claim is called a residual interest because owners have a claim on all assets of the firm in excess of those required to meet creditors' claims.

9. Shareholders' equity is generally comprised of two parts: contributed capital and retained earnings. The funds invested by shareholders make up contributed capital. Retained earnings represent the earnings realized by a firm since its formation in excess of dividends distributed to shareholders.

10. The relative mix of assets reflects a firm's investment decisions, and the relative mix of liabilities plus shareholders' equity reflects a firm's financing decisions. Therefore, Assets = Liabilities + Shareholders' Equity or Investing = Financing.

11. The balance sheet presents an overall view of a company's financial position as of a given date and classifies assets and liabilities as being either current or noncurrent.

12. Current assets include cash and assets that are expected to be turned into cash, or sold, or consumed within approximately one year from the date of the balance sheet. Current liabilities include liabilities that are expected to be paid within one year.

13. Noncurrent assets are typically held and used for several years. Noncurrent liabilities and shareholders' equity are a firm's longer-term sources of funds.

14. Assets, liabilities, and shareholders' equity items might have balance sheet values measured on one of two bases: (a) an historical valuation or (b) a current valuation.

15. An historical valuation reflects the acquisition cost of assets or the amounts of funds originally obtained from creditors or owners. A current valuation reflects the current cost of acquiring assets or the current market value of creditors' and owners' claims on a firm.

16. The income statement presents the results of the operating activities of a firm for a period of time. Net income or earnings is the difference between revenues and expenses.

17. Revenues are a measure of the inflows of assets (or reductions in liabilities) from selling goods and providing services to customers. Expenses are a measure of the outflows of assets (or increases in liabilities) used in generating revenue. Net income results when revenues exceed expenses. When expenses for a period exceed revenues, a firm incurs a net loss.

18. The income statement links the beginning and ending balance sheets through the Retained Earnings account. The amount of net income helps explain the change in retained earnings between the beginning and end of the period.

19. The statement of cash flows reports the net cash flow relating to operating, investing, and financing activities for a period of time. The statement explains the change in cash between the beginning and end of the period and details the major investing and financing activities of the period.

20. For most firms, a primary source of cash is the firm's operating activities. The excess of cash received from customers over the amount of cash paid to suppliers, employees, and others is the amount of cash provided by the firm's operating activities.

21. Investing activities include selling existing noncurrent assets and the acquisition of noncurrent assets.

22. Financing activities include new financing (issuing bonds or common stock) and using cash for dividends and to retire old financing.

23. Every set of published financial statements is supplemented by explanatory notes, which indicate the accounting methods used by the firm and disclose additional information, which elaborates on items presented in the three principal statements. To fully understand a firm's balance sheet, income statement, and statement of cash flows, a careful reading of the notes is required.

24. A certified public accountant, upon the examination of a client's accounting records and procedures, expresses an opinion on the fairness of the client's financial statements.

25. The opinion usually contains three paragraphs. The first paragraph indicates the financial presentations covered by the opinion and indicates that the responsibility for the financial statements rests with management. The second paragraph affirms that auditing standards and practices generally accepted by the accounting profession have been followed unless otherwise noted and described. The opinion expressed by the auditor in the third paragraph regarding the financial statement's fair presentation of financial position and results of operations may be unqualified or qualified.

26. If an auditor cannot express an opinion as to the fairness of the financial statements as a whole, the auditor must issue either a disclaimer of opinion or an adverse opinion.

27. One issue that faces the accounting profession is the question, Who should have the authority for establishing acceptable accounting standards? A governmental body could develop accounting standards and use its legislative power to enforce them. A private sector body would more likely incorporate viewpoints of various preparer and user groups in developing accounting standards but would lack the power to enforce the accounting standards.

28. Another issue that faces the accounting profession is the question, Should standard-setters require uniformity in accounting method across firms or should firms be allowed flexibility in selecting accounting methods?

29. A third issue concerns the approach standard-setting bodies should follow in establishing acceptable accounting methods. One approach requires that financial reports conform to income tax reports, so that the government tax authorities would effectively establish acceptable accounting standards. A second approach to developing accounting standards is a deductive theory-based approach in which a common core of theory would guide the standard-setting process. A third approach recognizes the political nature of the standard-setting process and would select those accounting methods most favored by preparers, users, and others involved with financial accounting reports.

30. Employees of a firm conduct internal audits (a) to assess the capability of the firm's accounting system to accumulate, measure, and synthesize transactional data properly and (b) to assess the operational effectiveness of the firm's accounting system. External audits by independent auditors assess whether the financial statements "present fairly the financial position … and the results of operations and cash flows … in conformity with generally accepted accounting principles."

31. The efficient capital market theory maintains that market prices react quickly and incorporate new information within a day or two of its release to the market. Research suggests that market participants adjust for nonrecurring items and differences in accounting methods among firms and do not interpret financial statement data naively.

32. The Securities and Exchange Commission (SEC) has the legal authority to set acceptable accounting methods, or standards, in the United States. The SEC has delegated most of the responsibility for establishing such standards to the Financial Accounting Standards Board (FASB).

33. The FASB issues its major pronouncements in the form of Statements of Financial Accounting Standards. These pronouncements are referred to as generally accepted accounting principles (GAAP). The FASB follows a combination of the deductive theoretical approach and the political lobbying approach in setting accounting standards.

34. The FASB has developed a conceptual framework to use as a guide for setting accounting standards. One of the components of the conceptual framework is a statement of the objectives of financial reporting. The seven objectives are as follows:
    a. Provide information useful for making investment and credit decisions.
    b. Provide information to help investors and creditors assess the amount, timing, and uncertainty of cash flows.
    c. Provide information about economic resources and claims on those resources.
    d. Provide information about a firm's operating performance.
    e. Provide information about how a firm obtains and uses cash.

f. Provide information for assessing management's stewardship responsibility to owners.

g. Provide explanatory and interpretative information to help users understand the financial information provided.

Questions and Exercises

True/False. **For each of the following statements, place a T or F in the space provided to indicate whether the statement is true or false.**

_____ 1. The first paragraph of the auditor's opinion indicates the financial presentations covered by the opinion and indicates that the responsibility for the financial statements rests with management.

_____ 2. The income statement attempts to present an overall view of a firm's financial position as of a given date.

_____ 3. The terms net income, earnings, and profits are synonymous and are defined as the difference between revenues and expenses for a period.

_____ 4. Retained earnings represents the sum of all prior earnings of the firm in excess of dividends.

_____ 5. Most auditors' opinions are qualified because of uncertainties regarding reduction of assets or outstanding litigation.

_____ 6. A disclaimer of opinion or an adverse opinion occurs when the auditor believes an opinion cannot be expressed as to the fairness of the financial statements as a whole.

_____ 7. The balance sheet presents the results of earnings activity over time.

_____ 8. Financial reporting should provide useful information for making rational investment and credit decisions.

_____ 9. One of the objectives of accounting is to help investors and creditors assess the amount, timing, and uncertainty of cash flows.

_____ 10. Financial accounting is concerned with the preparation of reports that provide information to users external to the firm.

_____ 11. Shareholders' equity is the owners' claim on the assets of the firm.

_____ 12. The two sources of any firm's assets are the firm's creditors and owners.

_____ 13. Noncurrent assets provide firms with long-term productive capacity.

_____ 14. Contributed capital represents the earnings realized by a firm since its formation in excess of dividends distributed to stockholders.

_____ 15. Acquisition of noncurrent assets is an activity that would result in an inflow of cash for a firm.

_____ 16. Current liabilities include liabilities that are expected to be paid within one year.

_____ 17. "Generally accepted accounting principles" are the accounting methods and procedures used by firms in preparing their financial statements.

_____ 18. The statement of cash flows provides information about the operating, financing, and investing activities of a firm.

_____ 19. Issuing bonds or common stock are examples of investing activities that would result in an inflow of cash for a firm.

_____ 20. The Securities and Exchange Commission has the legal authority to establish accounting standards and issues its pronouncements in the form of Statements of Financial Accounting Standards.

Matching. From the list of terms below, select that term which is most closely associated with each of the descriptive phrases or statements that follows and place the letter for that term in the space provided.

a. Assets
b. Balance Sheet
c. Contributed Capital
d. Disclaimer of Opinion or Adverse Opinion
e. Expenses
f. Historical Valuation
g. Income Statement
h. Liabilities

i. Net Income
j. Net Loss
k. Operating Activities
l. Retained Earnings
m. Revenues
n. Shareholders' Equity
o. Statement of Cash Flows
p. Unqualified Opinion

__A__ 1. Economic resources that have the potential or ability to provide future services or benefits to the firm.

__m__ 2. Inflows of assets (or reductions in liabilities) from selling goods and providing services to customers.

__k__ 3. This should be a primary source of cash for most firms.

__l__ 4. This item represents the earnings, or profits, realized by the firm since its formation in excess of dividends distributed to shareholders.

__d__ 5. Such an opinion is given when the auditor feels an opinion cannot be expressed as to the fairness of the financial statements as a whole.

__e__ 6. Outflows of assets (or increases in liabilities) used up in generating revenue.

__O__ 7. This financial statement reports the net cash flows relating to operating, investing, and financing activities for a period of time.

__h__ 8. Creditors' claims on the resources of the company.

__j__ 9. The excess of expenses over revenues for a period.

__n__ 10. Owners' claim on the assets of the company. The owners' claim is called a residual interest.

__f__ 11. Reflects the acquisition cost of assets or the amounts of funds originally obtained from creditors or owners.

__i__ 12. The excess of revenues over expenses for a period.

__c__ 13. Represents a measure of the assets provided by the original shareholder in exchange for an ownership interest in the firm.

___b___ 14. This financial statement presents an overall view of a company's financial position as of a given date.

___c___ 15. This financial statement presents the results of earnings activity over time.

___e___ 16. Such an opinion reports that the statements "present fairly the financial position...and the results of operations and cash flows ... in conformity with generally accepted accounting principles."

Multiple Choice. Choose the best answer for each of the following questions and enter the identifying letter in the space provided.

_____ 1. Evans Company reports total assets and total liabilities of $850,000 and $400,000, respectively, at the conclusion of its first year of business. The company earned $190,000 during the first year and distributed $60,000 in dividends. What was the firm's contributed capital?

   a. $450,000.
   b. $260,000.
   c. $320,000.
   d. $130,000.

_____ 2. Which of the following financial statements provides information about economic resources and claims on those resources?

   a. Income Statement.
   b. Balance Sheet.
   c. Statement of Cash Flows.
   d. All of the above.

_____ 3. During the year, Anna Louise, Inc., sold one of its warehouses for $150,000 cash. This transaction is an example of which of the following:

   a. An investing activity.
   b. A financing activity.
   c. An operating activity.
   d. None of the above.

_____ 4. Which of the following does not describe an expense?

   a. Paid dividends to shareholders.
   b. Cost of merchandise sold.
   c. Salaries earned by employees but not yet paid.
   d. Depreciation for the period on the firm's building.

_____ 5. Which of the following transactions of the Fort Company does not result in an inflow of cash?

   a. Additional common stock was issued.
   b. Additional equipment was acquired.
   c. A long-term note was issued.
   d. A tract of land was sold.

_____ 6. Which of the following assets is not a current asset?

    a. Cash.
    b. Land.
    c. Merchandise Inventory.
    d. Accounts Receivable.

_____ 7. Which of the following financial statements provides information about inflows and outflows of cash?

    a. Income Statement.
    b. Balance Sheet.
    c. Statement of Cash Flows.
    d. All of the above.

_____ 8. Which of the following would not appear on an Income Statement?

    a. Rent Expense.
    b. Salaries Payable.
    c. Sales Revenue.
    d. Cost of Goods Sold.

_____ 9. Revenues are a measure of the inflows of assets (or reductions in liabilities) from selling goods and providing services to customers. Which of the following is not a revenue transaction?

    a. Sold merchandise for cash to a customer.
    b. Sold merchandise on account to a customer.
    c. Delivered weekly magazines to a subscriber, who had paid previously for a one-year's subscription.
    d. Went to the local bank and borrowed money to be used in the business.

_____ 10. Which of the following would not appear on a balance sheet?

    a. Retained Earnings.
    b. Bonds Payable.
    c. Cost of Goods Sold.
    d. Accounts Receivable.

_____ 11. Which of the following transactions of the Corley Company does not result in an outflow of cash?

    a. Purchased a tract of land.
    b. Paid dividends to shareholders.
    c. Reacquired some of the company's common stock.
    d. Long-term debt was issued.

_____ 12. Which of the following is not a current asset?

    a. Patent.
    b. Inventory.
    c. Accounts Receivable.
    d. Cash.

_____ 13. Which of the following equations is incorrect?

    a. Shareholders' Equity = Contributed Capital + Retained Earnings.

    b. Revenues - Expenses = Net Income.

    c. Assets = Liabilities + Shareholders' Equity.

    d. All of the above equations are correct.

_____ 14. Which one of the following liabilities is not a current liability?

    a. Mortgage Payable.

    b. Accounts Payable.

    c. Salaries Payable.

    d. Taxes Payable.

_____ 15. Monroe Corporation's retained earnings increased by $200,000 during the year. Also, during the year, dividends totaling $37,500 were declared and paid to shareholders. What was Monroe Corporation's net income for the year?

    a. $ 37,500.

    b. $162,500.

    c. $200,000.

    d. $237,000.

_____ 16. Which of the following transactions does not result in an inflow of cash?

    a. Sold surplus equipment.

    b. Common stock was issued.

    c. Dividends were distributed to shareholders.

    d. Long-term debt was issued.

_____ 17. Kozar Company reports total assets and total shareholders' equity of $710,000 and $440,000, respectively, at the end of its first year of business. The company reported earnings of $200,000 and distributed dividends of $80,000 during its first year. Also, during the year, the company issued additional shares of stock for $110,000. What are the firm's liabilities at year end and the firm's contributed capital at the beginning of the year, respectively?

    a. $150,000; $330,000.

    b. $160,000; $320,000.

    c. $270,000; $330,000.

    d. $270,000; $210,000.

_____ 18. During the year Vorght Co. issued additional common stock. This transaction is an example of which of the following?

    a. An investing activity.

    b. A financing activity.

    c. An operating activity.

    d. None of the above.

_____ 19. Which of the following approaches does the Financial Accounting Standards Board follow in establishing generally accepted accounting principles?

    a.   Financial reports conform to income tax reports.

    b.   A deductive theory-based approach.

    c.   A political lobbying approach, which selects accounting methods favored by those involved with financial accounting reports.

    d.   Both b and c.

_____ 20. "Claims on the resources that result from benefits previously received by the company, which require that a specified amount be paid on a specified date." This statement describes which of the following?

    a.   Shareholders' Equity.

    b.   Contributed Capital.

    c.   Liabilities.

    d.   Retained Earnings.

Exercises

1. Using the information given, determine the missing amounts in each of the independent cases below:

	a	b	c
Current Assets	$150,000	$_____	$640,000
Noncurrent Assets	$225,000	$400,000	$720,000
Current Liabilities	$ 30,000	$100,000	$_____
Noncurrent Liabilities	$105,000	$200,000	$400,000
Contributed Capital	$_____	$220,000	$280,000
Retained Earnings	$ 60,000	$_____	$600,000
Shareholders' Equity	$_____	$360,000	$_____

2. Using the information given, determine the missing amounts in each of the independent cases below:

	a	b	c
Assets	$_____	$960,000	$400,000
Liabilities	$160,000	$300,000	$190,000
Contributed Capital	$100,000	$_____	$140,000
Retained Earnings 1/1	$_____	$ 0	$ 20,000
Net Income	$ 28,000	$150,000	$ 80,000
Dividends	$ 10,000	$ 72,000	$_____
Retained Earnings 12/31	$ 40,000	$_____	$_____

3. Using the information given, determine the missing amounts from the income statement and retained earnings statement in each of the independent cases below:

	a	b	c
Revenues	$240,000	$540,000	$_____
Expenses	$140,000	$_____	$340,000
Net Income	$_____	$_____	$ 80,000
Retained Earnings 1/1	$ 50,000	$ 90,000	$_____
Net Income	$_____	$108,000	$_____
Dividends	$ 20,000	$_____	$ 64,000
Retained Earnings 12/31	$_____	$138,000	$ 40,000

4. The Lynchburg Corporation began operations in July, Year 1. Total shareholders' equity at that time was $120,000. On December 31, Year 1, the corporation reports assets of $600,000 and liabilities of $384,000.

   a. Determine the amount of shareholders' equity at December 31, Year 1. Has shareholders' equity increased or decreased?

   b. Give several possible explanations for the change in shareholders' equity.

   c. What items make up shareholders' equity?

5. Using the information given, determine the missing amount in each of the independent cases below:

	a	b	c
Inflows of Cash			
Operations	$_____	$ 60,000	$ 90.000
New Financing	$600,000	$170,000	$200,000
Sales of Noncurrent Assets	$120,000	$120,000	$110,000
Outflows of Cash			
Dividends	$ 40,000	$_____	$ 70,000
Reduction in Financing	$360,000	$200,000	$ 80,000
Acquisition of Noncurrent Assets	$200,000	$140,000	$200,000
Increase (Decrease) in Cash	$300,000	$ (40,000)	$_____

6. Cash inflows and cash outflows can fit into one of three categories: (1) operating activities, (2) investing activities, and (3) financing activities. For each of the following transactions, indicate the appropriate category by placing the identifying number in the space provided.

_____   a. Purchased machinery.

_____   b. Sold additional stock to shareholders.

_____   c. Paid mortgage note at maturity date.

_____   d. Paid dividends to shareholders.

_____   e. Borrowed money on a five-year note.

_____   f. Sold a building.

7. The comparative balance sheets for the Farnum Company for Year 1 and Year 2 are presented below:

	Year 1	Year 2
Cash	$100,000	$140,000
Noncurrent Assets	500,000	610,000
Total Assets	$600,000	$750,000
Noncurrent Liabilities	$350,000	$230,000
Contributed Capital	$175,000	$300,000
Retained Earnings	75,000	220,000
Total Shareholders' Equity	$250,000	$520,000
Total Equity	$600,000	$750,000

The company reported earnings of $190,000 in Year 2.

Identify five transactions during Year 2 that either provided or used cash. What was the amount of cash inflow or cash outflow in each transaction? Specify whether the transaction was an operating, financing, or investing activity.

Answers to Questions and Exercises

True/False

1.	T	6.	T	11.	T	16.	T
2.	F	7.	F	12.	T	17.	T
3.	T	8.	T	13.	T	18.	T
4.	T	9.	T	14.	F	19.	F
5.	F	10.	T	15.	F	20.	F

Matching

1.	a	5.	d	9.	j	13.	c
2.	m	6.	e	10.	n	14.	b
3.	k	7.	o	11.	f	15.	g
4.	l	8.	h	12.	i	16.	p

Multiple Choice

1.	c	6.	b	11.	d	16.	c
2.	b	7.	c	12.	a	17.	d
3.	a	8.	b	13.	d	18.	b
4.	a	9.	d	14.	a	19.	d
5.	b	10.	c	15.	d	20.	c

Exercises

1.

	a	b	c
Current Assets	$150,000	$260,000	$640,000
Noncurrent Assets	$225,000	$400,000	$720,000
Current Liabilities	$ 30,000	$100,000	$ 80,000
Noncurrent Liabilities	$105,000	$200,000	$400,000
Contributed Capital	$180,000	$220,000	$280,000
Retained Earnings	$ 60,000	$140,000	$600,000
Shareholders' Equity	$240,000	$360,000	$880,000

2.

	a	b	c
Assets	$300,000	$960,000	$400,000
Liabilities	$160,000	$300,000	$190,000
Contributed Capital	$100,000	$582,000	$140,000
Retained Earnings 1/1	$ 22,000	$ 0	$ 20,000
Net Income	$ 28,000	$150,000	$ 80,000
Dividends	$ 10,000	$ 72,000	$ 30,000
Retained Earnings 12/31	$ 40,000	$ 78,000	$ 70,000

3.

	a	b	c
Revenues	$240,000	$540,000	$420,000
Expenses	$140,000	$432,000	$340,000
Net Income	$100,000	$108,000	$ 80,000
Retained Earnings 1/1	$ 50,000	$ 90,000	$ 24,000
Net Income	$100,000	$108,000	$ 80,000
Dividends	$ 20,000	$ 60,000	$ 64,000
Retained Earnings 12/31	$130,000	$138,000	$ 40,000

4. a.

Assets at 12/31, Year 1	$600,000
Liabilities at 12/31, Year 1	384,000
Shareholders' equity at 12/31, Year 1	$216,000

Shareholders' equity has increased by $96,000 ($216,000 - $120,000) during the 6-month period, July 1 to December 31.

b. The $96,000 increase may be attributable to the company earning net income and paying no dividends or earning net income and paying dividends; or the shareholders may have made additional purchases of the company's stock; or the increase could be attributed to a combination of the above-mentioned changes.

c. Contributed capital represents the assets provided by the shareholders in exchange for an ownership interest in the firm. Retained earnings represents the earnings, or profits, realized by the firm since its formation in excess of dividends distributed to shareholders.

5.

	a	b	c
Inflows of Cash			
Operations	$180,000	$ 60,000	$ 90,000
New Financing	$600,000	$170,000	$200,000
Sales of Noncurrent Assets	$120,000	$120,000	$110,000
Outflows of Cash			
Dividends	$ 40,000	$ 50,000	$ 70,000
Reduction in Financing	$360,000	$200,000	$ 80,000
Acquisition of Noncurrent Assets	$200,000	$140,000	$200,000
(Decrease) in Cash	$300,000	$ (40,000)	$ 50,000

6.

  a. 2
  b. 3
  c. 3
  d. 3
  e. 3
  f. 2

14

7.

1.	($110,000)	Purchased a noncurrent asset, use of cash, investing activity.
2.	($120,000)	Paid liabilities, use of cash, financing activity.
3.	$125,000	Issued stock, source of cash, financing activity.
4.	$190,000	Net income, source of cash, operating activity.
5.	($ 45,000)	Paid distribution to owners, use of cash, financing activity.
	$ 40,000	Increase in cash during Year 2.

Chapter 2

Balance Sheet: Presenting the Investments and Financing of a Firm

Chapter Highlights

1. The balance sheet is one of the three principal financial statements. It derives its name from the fact that it shows the following balance, or equality:

$$\text{Assets} = \text{Liabilities} + \text{Shareholders' Equity}$$

The firm's resources (the assets) must equal the firm's claims on the resources (the liabilities and shareholders' equity).

2. Assets are resources that have the potential for providing a firm with future economic benefits. The resources recognized as assets are those (a) for which the firm has acquired rights to their use in the future through a past transaction or exchange, and (b) for which the firm can measure or quantify the future benefits with a reasonable degree of precision. Assets are future benefits; not all future benefits are assets.

3. A monetary amount must be assigned to each asset on the balance sheet. Methods for determining this amount include (a) acquisition or historical cost, (b) current replacement cost, (c) current net realizable value, and (d) present value of future net cash flows.

4. The acquisition, or historical, cost is the amount of cash payment (or cash equivalent value) made in acquiring an asset.

5. Current replacement cost (an entry value) represents the amount required currently to acquire the rights to receive future benefits from the asset.

6. Net realizable value (an exit value) is the net amount of cash (selling price less selling costs) that the firm would receive currently if it sold each asset separately.

7. The future benefits from an asset come from the asset's ability to generate future cash receipts or reduce future cash expenditures. A final way to express the valuation of an asset is in terms of the asset's present value, representing today's value of the stream of future cash flows. Because cash can earn interest over time, the present value is worth less than the sum of the cash amounts to be received or saved over time.

8. Financial statements prepared by publicly held firms are based primarily on one of two valuation methods: one for monetary assets and one for nonmonetary assets. Monetary assets, such as cash and

17

accounts receivable, are shown at their current cash or cash-equivalent value. Nonmonetary assets, such as merchandise inventory, land, buildings, and equipment, are stated at acquisition cost and in some cases are adjusted downward to reflect the services of the assets that have been consumed. The use of acquisition cost is supported by three important accounting concepts or conventions: (a) the going concern concept, (b) the objectivity concept, and (c) the conservatism convention.

9. The going concern concept assumes the firm is to remain in operations long enough for all of its current plans to be carried out.

10. Objectivity refers to the ability of several independent measures to come to the same conclusion about the valuation of an asset.

11. Conservatism has evolved as a convention to justify acquisition cost valuations. Acquisition cost generally provides more conservative valuations of assets (and measures of earnings) relative to other methods. Many accountants feel that the possibility of misleading financial statements users will be minimized when assets are stated at lower rather than higher amounts.

12. The classification of assets within the balance sheet varies widely from firm to firm, but the principal asset categories are usually (a) current assets, (b) investments, (c) property, plant, and equipment, and (d) intangible assets. Current assets include cash and other assets that are expected to be realized in cash or sold or consumed during the normal operating cycle. Investments include primarily long-term investments in securities of other firms. Property, plant, and equipment includes the tangible, long-lived assets used in a firm's operations and generally not acquired for resale. Intangibles are long-lived assets that lack physical substances such as patents, trademarks, franchises, and goodwill.

13. A liability is an obligation that arises when a firm receives benefits or services and in exchange promises to pay the provider of those goods or services a reasonably definite amount at a reasonably definite future time.

14. Most liabilities are monetary in nature, requiring payments of specific amounts of cash. Those monetary liabilities due within one year or less are stated at the amount of cash expected to be paid to discharge the liability. Those liabilities with due dates extending more than one year into the future are stated at the present values of the future cash outflows. Liabilities that are discharged by delivering goods or rendering services are nonmonetary items and are stated at the amount of cash received.

15. Liabilities in the balance sheet are typically classified in one of the following categories: (a) current liabilities, (b) long-term debt, and (c) other long-term liabilities. Current liabilities are obligations expected to be paid or discharged during the normal operating cycle (they are usually paid using current assets). Long-term debt are those obligations having due dates more than one year from the balance sheet date. Obligations that do not fit in current liabilities or long-term debt are classified as other long-term liabilities.

16. The owners' (shareholders') equity, or interest, in a firm is a residual interest, since the owners have a claim only against those assets not required to meet the claims of creditors. Since owners' equity is a residual interest, its valuation on the balance sheet reflects the valuation of assets and liabilities.

17. The owners' (shareholders') equity section for a corporation is divided into two sections, contributed capital and retained earnings. Contributed capital represents amounts shareholders have provided for an interest in the firm (that is, common stock). Retained earnings are earnings subsequently realized by the firm in excess of dividends declared.

18. Contributed capital is usually further disaggregated into the par or stated value of the shares and amounts contributed in excess of par value or stated value. The par or stated value of a share of stock is a somewhat arbitrary amount assigned to comply with corporation laws of each state.

19. Firms organized as sole proprietorships or partnerships do not make a distinction between contributed capital and retained earnings in their balance sheet. The balance sheet reports a capital account for each owner containing their share of capital contributions plus their share of earnings in excess of distributions.

20. The balance sheet provides a constant equality between total assets and total equities (liabilities plus owners' equity). Any single transaction has a dual effect in maintaining this equality by either of the following:
    a. An increase in both an asset and a liability or shareholders' equity;
    b. A decrease in both an asset and a liability or shareholders' equity;
    c. An increase in one asset and a decrease in another asset; or
    d. An increase in one liability or shareholders' equity and a decrease in another liability or shareholders' equity.

21. A practical approach to accumulating information about each balance sheet item is to use a device known as an account. The most useful form of an account for textbook problems and examinations is the T-account, which simply accumulates the increases and decreases in each account, as well as their balances. The form of a T-account is shown below.

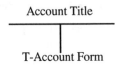

T-Account Form

22. The following rules have been developed for recording transactions using individual T-accounts for each asset and equity account.
    a. Increases in assets are entered on the left side and decreases in assets are entered on the right side. The normal balance in an asset account is on the left.
    b. Increases in liabilities and shareholders' equity are entered on the right side and decreases in liabilities and shareholders' equity are entered on the left side. The normal balance in a liability and a shareholders' equity account is on the right.

23. Instead of using the terms "left" and "right" when referring to the effect of transactions upon various accounts, we use the terms "debit" and "credit." The debit (or charge) refers to nothing more than the entry on the left side of an account, whereas credit refers to an entry on the right side of an account. In terms of balance sheet categories,

    a. Debit indicates:
       Increases in an asset;
       Decreases in a liability or a shareholders' equity item.
    b. Credit indicates:
       Decreases in an asset;
       Increases in a liability or a shareholders' equity item.

24. In order to maintain equality of the balance sheet equation, the amounts debited to various accounts for each transaction must equal the amounts credited. At the end of each period the sum of balances in accounts with debit balances must equal the sum of balances in accounts with credit balances.

25. The accounting system designed around this recording framework generally involves the following operations:

a. Journalizing each transaction in the general journal, referred to as the book of original entry. The standard journal entry format is

---

Date Account Debited .... Amount Debited
      Account Credited .... Amount Credited
      Explanation of transaction or event being journalized.

---

b. Periodic posting of journal entries to the general ledger, a book, or a record of individual accounts.

c. Preparing a listing of each of the accounts in the general ledger with their balances as of a particular date. This listing is called a trial balance and serves as a check on the mathematical accuracy of the manner in which the double-entry recording framework has been applied.

d. Making adjusting and correcting entries to various accounts in the trial balance. Primarily, this involves the recognition of unrecorded events that help to determine the financial position at the end of the period and net income for the period.

e. Preparing financial statements from a trial balance after adjusting and correcting entries.

26. The preparation of a balance sheet requires that you recognize and understand the meaning of a large list of account titles that are commonly used. Careful attention should be given to this discussion in the text.

27. The balance sheet reflects the effects of a firm's investing and financing decisions. A reasonable balance should exist between the term structure of assets and the term structure of liabilities plus shareholders' equity. Term structure refers to the length of time that must elapse before an asset becomes cash or a liability or stockholders' equity requires cash. The proportion of short- versus long-term financing should bear some relation to the proportion of current versus noncurrent assets.

28. The format and terminology of the balance sheet in many foreign countries differ from that used in the United States. Other countries accounting practice includes reporting some accounts seldom appearing on balance sheets in the United States and recognizing revaluation of assets not allowed in the United States.

Questions and Exercises

True/False. **For each of the following statements, place a T or F in the space provided to indicate whether the statement is true or false.**

_____ 1. In measuring net realizable value, we generally assume that the asset is not being sold at a distress price.

_____ 2. The valuation basis selected by a firm depends upon the purpose of the financial report being prepared.

_____ 3. Whenever a firm develops a good reputation over many years of operations, it is acceptable to assign a value to this resource and classify it as goodwill on the balance sheet.

_____ 4. A trial balance is used to check the arithmetic accuracy of the dual-entry recording procedure.

_____ 5. All assets found on a balance sheet are recorded at their historical cost.

_____ 6. The balance sheet derives its name from the fact that it shows the following balance, or equality:

$$\text{Assets} + \text{Liabilities} = \text{Owners' Equity.}$$

_____ 7. Assets are only resources used by the firm for which legal title is held.

_____ 8. Land is a good example of a nonmonetary asset.

_____ 9. A company is considered to be a going concern only if it is expected to last forever.

_____ 10. The operating cycle for most companies is one year or less.

_____ 11. Depreciable assets such as buildings and machinery appear on the balance sheet at acquisition cost adjusted downward to reflect services consumed by the firm since acquisition.

_____ 12. Replacement cost and net realizable value are opposite approaches to determining the current value of an asset: replacement cost refers to an asset's exit value, and net realizable value refers to an asset's entry value.

_____ 13. Net realizable value is defined as the net amount of cash that could be realized from the sale of an asset.

_____ 14. The only accounts found in the investments section of the balance sheet are for the investments in the securities of other firms.

_____ 15. Intangibles are long-term assets that lack physical substance.

_____ 16. The present value of $20,000 to be received in one year at 10 percent is an amount greater than $20,000.

_____ 17. Even though no errors have been detected in the processing of accounting data, correcting or adjusting entries may be needed at the end of a period.

_____ 18. The T-account, which serves the purpose of accumulating increases and decreases for each balance sheet item, uses the following simple rules: all increases are recorded on the left, and all decreases are recorded on the right.

_____ 19. The term "debit" refers to the left-hand side of a T-account for both assets and liabilities.

21

_____ 20. Interest receivable on 10-year bonds would represent the total interest to be received over the 10-year period.

_____ 21. The present value of future cash flows should be less than the total of the future cash flows.

_____ 22. Cash and accounts receivable are examples of monetary assets.

_____ 23. Unexecuted contracts, sometimes called executory contracts, generally do not result in recording an asset but always result in recording a liability.

_____ 24. Convertible bonds payable allow the holder to convert or "trade in" the bonds for shares of common stock.

_____ 25. Common stock is the same as preferred stock except the latter is issued only by companies with preferred credit ratings.

_____ 26. Balance sheet equality requires firms to balance the term structure of their financing with the term structure of their investments.

_____ 27. The par value of stock is the same as its market value.

_____ 28. The term "charge" can be used interchangeably with "debit."

_____ 29. As long as a partnership has always been profitable, there will be a credit balance in the retained earnings account.

_____ 30. The process of posting is transferring the amounts from T-accounts to the journal affected by the transaction.

_____ 31. If the debits and credits in a trial balance are not equal, a possible explanation is that a current asset was improperly classified as an investment.

_____ 32. Conservatism in accounting refers to the ability of several independent appraisers to come to the same conclusion about the valuation of an asset.

_____ 33. The general ledger is also known as the "book of original entry."

_____ 34. Some resources of a firm provide future economic benefits but are not capable of being reasonably measured or quantified and, therefore, are not classified as assets on the balance sheet.

_____ 35. The historical cost of an asset always represents its future economic value to the firm.

_____ 36. A lease transaction is an example of an unexecuted contract, which often is not recognized as a liability at the time of the agreement between the lessor and the lessee.

_____ 37. A balance sheet prepared for a sole proprietorship or partnership contains a contributed capital account and a retained earnings account for each owner.

_____ 38. A liability represents any obligation taken on by a firm.

_____ 39. Liabilities that will be discharged by the rendering of goods or services are considered nonmonetary liabilities and are stated at the amount of cash received.

_____ 40. Since owners' equity is a residual interest in the firm's assets, its valuation is dependent upon the valuations assigned to the assets and liabilities within the balance sheet.

_____ 41. Accumulated depreciation does not represent a fund set aside to replace fixed assets after they have been fully depreciated.

_____ 42. Retained earnings represent the cumulative amount of cash available for dividends.

_____ 43. Liability accounts are increased by debits, decreased by credits, and normally have a resulting debit balance.

_____ 44. A basic rule underlying the balance sheet equation is that total debits must always equal total credits.

_____ 45. Since the accounts in the general ledger and the journal entries within the general journal both report the same transactions, it is not necessary to maintain both a general ledger and a general journal.

_____ 46. Only specifically identifiable intangible assets acquired from other entities are recognized as assets.

_____ 47. An example of an account included in the "other long-term liability" section is deferred income taxes.

_____ 48. The more specialized a firm's assets the more difficulty there is in determining either their replacement cost or net realizable value, because a well-organized secondhand market for these items may not exist.

_____ 49. The present value of future cash flows approach to assigning values to balance sheet items is likely to be employed with current liabilities such as accounts payable and taxes payable.

_____ 50. A piece of land acquired for use should be classified as property, plant, and equipment.

_____ 51. For an obligation to be treated as a liability, it is necessary that it can be estimated with a reasonable degree of accuracy.

_____ 52. Current liabilities are usually paid from assets classified as current.

_____ 53. Treasury shares are usually shown as a deduction from the total of the other shareholders' equity accounts on the balance sheet.

_____ 54. If a firm accounts for the assets in a conservative manner, it is less likely that net income will be overstated.

_____ 55. All transactions have a dual effect upon the balance sheet equation, since both an asset and an equity account are affected in equal amounts in every transaction.

_____ 56. The format of the balance sheet in the United States is the same as the format of the balance sheet in the United Kingdom.

_____ 57. Some liabilities due within one year are not classified as current liabilities.

_____ 58. In a common size balance sheet each balance sheet item is expressed as a percentage of either total assets or total liabilities plus stockholders' equity.

Matching

1. From the list of terms below, select the term most closely associated with each of the descriptive phrases or statements that follows and place the letter for that term in the space provided.

a.	Accounts Payable	n.	Marketable Securities
b.	Accounts Receivable	o.	Merchandise Inventory
c.	Accumulated Depreciation	p.	Mortgage Payable
d.	Advances from Customers	q.	Notes Receivable
e.	Cash	r.	Organization Costs
f.	Common Stock	s.	Patents
g.	Deferred Income Taxes	t.	Preferred Stock
h.	Finished Goods Inventory	u.	Premium on Preferred Stock
i.	Goodwill	v.	Prepaid Insurance
j.	Income Taxes Payable	w.	Retained Earnings
k.	Interest Payable	x.	Rent Received in Advance
l.	Interest Receivable	y.	Treasury Shares
m.	Leasehold	z.	Work-in-Process Inventory

_____ 1. The right to use property owned by someone else.

_____ 2. The estimated and unpaid liability for current income taxes.

_____ 3. Amounts paid for various fees incurred in organizing a corporation.

_____ 4. Amounts due from customers, for which the claim is in the form of a written promise to pay.

_____ 5. The shares originally issued and outstanding that have been reacquired from the owners.

_____ 6. The financial obligation of the company associated with a loan that accrues with the passage of time.

_____ 7. A residual claim of owners having certain preferences relative to other owners' claims.

_____ 8. A type of liquid asset, an example of which is a demand deposit.

_____ 9. A right granted to exclude others from manufacturing, using, or selling a certain process or device.

_____ 10. The balance in this account is the amount owed to the company by its customers.

_____ 11. Payments received for goods or services to be furnished to customers in the future.

_____ 12. The amount of income taxes postponed for payments to future years.

_____ 13. The amount of proceeds from the sales of Preferred Stock in excess of the par value.

_____ 14. Cumulative amount of net income earned by a business since its inception in excess of dividends declared.

_____ 15. Amounts owed for goods or services acquired under an informal credit agreement.

_____ 16. Stock and bonds that can readily be converted into cash.

24

_____ 17. Partially completed manufactured products.

_____ 18. Recorded only when another business enterprise is acquired.

_____ 19. An example of long-term debt.

_____ 20. Insurance premiums paid for future coverage.

_____ 21. The amount subtracted from the cost of a fixed asset to get net book value.

_____ 22. Amounts received for the par value of a firm's voting stock.

_____ 23. Goods on hand that have been purchased for resale.

2.   For the list of accounts below, select the balance sheet category in which that account should be classified.

a.	Current Assets	f.	Long-Term Debt
b.	Investments	g.	Other Long-Term Liabilities
c.	Property, Plant, and Equipment	h.	Capital Stock
d.	Intangible Assets	i.	Contributed Capital in Excess of Par Value
e.	Current Liabilities	j.	Retained Earnings

_____ 1. Accounts Payable

_____ 2. Accounts Receivable

_____ 3. Accumulated Depreciation

_____ 4. Additional Paid-in Capital

_____ 5. Advances from Customers

_____ 6. Advances to Suppliers

_____ 7. Bonds Payable

_____ 8. Buildings

_____ 9. Cash

_____ 10. Common Stock

_____ 11. Convertible Bonds Payable

_____ 12. Deferred Income Taxes

_____ 13. Equipment

_____ 14. Finished Goods Inventory

_____ 15. Furniture and Fixtures

_____ 16. Goodwill

_____ 17. Income Taxes Payable

_____ 18. Interest Receivable

_____ 19. Investment in Stock

_____ 20. Land

_____ 21. Leasehold

_____ 22. Marketable Securities

_____ 23. Merchandise Inventory

_____ 24. Mortgage Payable

_____ 25. Notes Payable (due in 3 years)

_____ 26. Notes Receivable (due in 6 months)

_____ 27. Organization Costs

_____ 28. Patents

_____ 29. Preferred Stock

_____ 30. Prepaid Insurance

_____ 31. Prepaid Rent

_____ 32. Raw Materials Inventory

_____ 33. Rent Received in Advance

_____ 34. Retained Earnings

_____ 35. Supplies Inventory

_____ 36. Treasury Shares

_____ 37. Work-in-Process Inventory

3. From the list of terms below, select the term that is most closely associated with each of the descriptive phrases or statements that follows and place the letter for that term in the space provided.

a.	Acquisition Cost	k.	Going Concern
b.	Charge	l.	Journal Entry
c.	Conservatism	m.	MonetaryAassets
d.	Credit	n.	Nonmonetary Assets
e.	Current Net Realizable Value	o.	Objectivity
f.	Current Replacement Cost	p.	Par or Stated Value
g.	Debit	q.	Present Value
h.	Executory Contract	r.	T-account
i.	General Journal	s.	Term Structure of Assets and Liabilities
j.	General Ledger	t.	Trial Balance

_____   1. An entry on the right side of an account.

_____   2. A word use instead of "debit," both as a noun and as a verb.

_____   3. Record an entry on the left side of an account.

_____   4. A stock's somewhat arbitrary face amount assigned to comply with corporation laws.

_____   5. A useful form of an account for textbooks, problems, and examinations.

_____   6. The book of original entry.

_____   7. A record of each transaction in the general journal.

_____   8. A list of each account in the general ledger with its balance at a particular date.

_____   9. The name for the formal ledger containing all of the financial statement accounts.

_____   10. The amount of cash or cash equivalent payment in acquiring an asset.

_____   11. An entry value, the amount currently required to acquire the rights to receive future benefits from an asset.

_____   12. An exit value, the amount obtainable if the firm currently disposed of an asset.

_____   13. An amount fixed in terms of dollars by statute or contract.

_____   14. Examples include merchandise inventory, land, buildings, and equipment.

_____   15. A firm will remain in operation long enough to carry out all of its current plans.

_____   16. Today's value of a stream of future cash flows.

_____   17. The length of time that must elapse before assets become cash or a liabilities require cash.

_____   18. The ability of several independent measures to come to the same conclusion about the evaluation of an asset.

_____   19. The reporting of assets at lower rather than higher amounts.

_____   20. Unexecuted contract, an exchange of promises.

Multiple Choice. **Choose the best answer for each of the following questions and enter the identifying letter in the space provided.**

_____ 1. The balance in all asset accounts combined is $100,000 on

December 1. During December the following transactions took place.
Purchase of $10,000 of inventory for cash.
Purchase of $15,000 of machinery on account.
Retirement of $20,000 in bonds with cash.

What is the combined December 31 balance in the asset accounts?

a. $ 95,000.
b. $115,000.
c. $105,000.
d. $ 80,000.

_____ 2. The balance sheet reflects the application of various valuation methods. Which of the methods listed below may be used on a balance sheet that follows generally accepted accounting principles?

a. Acquisition cost.
b. Current cash-equivalent value.
c. Present value of future cash flows.
d. All of the above.

_____ 3. What account below would not be found on the balance sheet of a corporation?

a. Premium on Common Stock.
b. Retained Earnings.
c. Investment in Ladner Co. Stock.
d. Holstrum, Capital.

_____ 4. Which of the journal entries below is incorrectly recorded?

a.	Jan. 1:	Cash	$33,000	
		Investment in X Co. Stock		$33,000
		Sales of an investment for cash.		
b.	Jan. 2:	Prepaid Insurance	$ 750	
		Cash		$ 750
		Paid in Advance for a 1-year insurance policy.		
c.	Jan. 3:	Accounts Receivable	$ 1,200	
		Merchandise Inventory		$ 1,200
		Returned defective merchandise for credit. The merchandise has not yet been paid for.		
d.	Jan. 4:	Machinery	$30,500	
		Notes Payable		$30,500
		Gave a 1-year note to acquire machinery.		

_____ 5. All of the assets listed below are nonmonetary assets except one. Which one is not a nonmonetary asset?

    a. Accounts receivable.
    b. Land.
    c. Inventory.
    d. Patent.

_____ 6. The concept of present value

    a. Can be simply defined as value today of a stream of future cash flows.
    b. Implies that the value of receiving cash today will be less than the value of receiving it in the future.
    c. Is employed extensively in the valuation of assets under current generally accepted accounting principles.
    d. Determines the minimum amount that a buyer would be willing to pay for an asset.

_____ 7. Different balance sheet items employ different valuation methods. Which valuation application below is not generally accepted?

    a. A major line of inventory has increased in value substantially above its cost and has been restated to its current replacement cost.
    b. Machinery is stated at its historical cost less the estimated amount of benefits consumed to date.
    c. Cash is received for goods to be delivered next month. The liability is stated at the amount of cash received and not the cost of goods to be delivered.
    d. Common stock is stated at the amount at which it was originally sold.

_____ 8. Mary Corp. has assets and liabilities of $30,000 and $24,000, respectively. If Mary issues an additional $3,000 of stock for cash, what will be the balance in shareholders' equity following this transaction?

    a. $30,000.
    b. $27,000.
    c. $ 9,000.
    d. $33,000.

_____ 9. Which of the statements below is incorrect concerning the rules of debit and credit?

    a. Debits are always recorded on the left.
    b. Debits reduce shareholders' equity.
    c. Assets have debit balances.
    d. Credits always mean decreases.

    29

10. From the following list of selected account balances, determine the total for the shareholders' equity section of the balance sheet for Bullard Co.:

Investment in Stock of Donald Co.	$ 2,500
Retained Earnings	5,000
Cash (in special bank account for payment of dividends)	3,000
Note Payable to Suppliers	2,000
Common Stock	10,000
8% Preferred Stock	7,500

   a. $20,500.
   b. $22,500.
   c. $24,500.
   d. $25,500.

11. A debit balance is normal for all of the following accounts except

   a. Preferred Stock.
   b. Treasury Shares.
   c. Investment in Stock.
   d. All of the above have normal debit balances.

12. The following are account titles for liabilities except

   a. Advances to Suppliers.
   b. Advances from Tenants.
   c. Rent Received in Advance.
   d. Advances from Customers.

13. From the list of accounts below, determine the amount that would be properly classified as property, plant, and equipment.

Land Used in Business	$100,000
Machinery Leased from Others (no liability has been recorded)	60,000
Accumulated Depreciation	(80,000)
Inventories	124,000
Land Held for Future Plant Site	40,000
Building	200,000
Investment in Stock of Construction Company	50,000

   a. $220,000.
   b. $360,000.
   c. $260,000.
   d. $280,000.

14. Which of the following would cause the accounting equation to no longer balance?

   a. Recording a purchase on account at the wrong amount.
   b. Recording a 1994 purchase in 1995 instead.
   c. Posting the credit for a cash purchase at the wrong amount.
   d. All of the above.

_____ 15. The following entry was made on June 15 for Nash Co.

| Jun. 15 | Machinery | $ 17,000 | |
| | Accounts Payable | | $ 17,000 |

This entry was made for which of the transactions?

a. Payment for purchase of machinery.
b. Sale of machinery.
c. Depreciation of machinery.
d. Purchase of machinery.

_____ 16. All of the following operations are considered to be a part of the accounting process leading to financial statement preparation except

a. Journalizing transactions.
b. Posting to the general ledger.
c. Adjusting accounts.
d. Auditing statements.

_____ 17. All of the following would normally be classified as a current liability account except

a. Accounts Payable.
b. Interest Payable.
c. Rent Received in Advance.
d. All of the above would be classified as a current liability.

_____ 18. The Dorn Corporation failed to record the purchase of inventory on account at the end of 1995. In which of the following ways is the balance sheet misstated?

a. Assets and liabilities are both understated.
b. Assets are understated and liabilities are overstated.
c. Assets and shareholders' equity are both understated.
d. Assets, liabilities, and shareholders' equity are all correctly stated.

_____ 19. Which equation below does not represent an acceptable presentation of the balance sheet equation?

a. Assets - Liabilities = Owners' Equity.
b. Assets = Liabilities + Capital Stock + Capital Contributed in Excess of Par Value + Retained Earnings.
c. Assets = Equities.
d. All of the above represent acceptable presentations of the balance sheet equation.

_____ 20. Which of the liabilities below would be accounted for at the present value of future cash payments?

a. Accounts Payable.
b. Bonds Payable.
c. Income Taxes Payable.
d. Advances from Customers.

_____ 21. The Van Petten Company is interested in disposing of one of its subsidiaries and trying to decide upon the maximum price it might be able to charge. Which valuation method below would likely be used?

    a. Acquisition Cost.
    b. Net Realizable Value.
    c. Present Value.
    d. Replacement Cost.

Exercises

1. Indicate the effect of each transaction below on the balance sheet equation. After each transaction is properly recorded, compute new subtotals for the Assets, Liabilities, and Owners' Equity, being sure to maintain the equality of the equation. Use the following format:

Transaction Number	Assets	=	Liabilities	+	Owner's Equity
Example	$+500,000				$+500,000
Subtotal	$ 500,000				$ 500,000

Example: Issued 3,000 shares of $100 par value common stock for $500,000 cash.

a. Purchased for $400,000 cash a building to be used for office space.

b. Received $1,000 for a magazine subscription to be delivered to customers over the next year.

c. Paid $2,100 in advance for one year of rent.

d. Paid $750 to an advertising agency for a promotional campaign which will start in one month.

e. Bought $30,000 of merchandise inventory on account.

f. Paid $12,000 to the supplier for inventory purchase in (e) and gave a note for the remaining $18,000.

g. Loaned $3,500 to an officer and accepted his 90-day note.

h. Bought $5,500 of merchandise for cash.

i. Borrowed $5,000 from the bank.

j. Ten shares of $100 par value common stock are issued in settlement of an account payable of $2,000.

k. The company agrees to buy four trucks 6 months from now for $60,000.

2.   Below is a list of balance sheet account titles that may be needed in recording the transactions that follow. For each transaction, select those accounts that would be used in journalizing and place the letters accompanying the account title in the appropriate columns for debit and credit.

a. Accounts Payable
b. Notes Payable
c. Rent Received in Advance
d. Capital Stock
e. Additional Paid-in Capital
f. Retained Earnings
g. Marketable Securities

h. Cash
i. Notes Receivable
j. Merchandise Inventory
k. Supplies Inventory
l. Prepaid Insurance
m. Machinery and Equipment
n. Organization Costs

Transaction	Account Debited	Account Credited
Example: Bought inventory for cash.	j	h
1. Paid the lawyers in company stock for the legal work performed in organizing the company		
2. Advanced money to an officer and received a 90-day note as recognition of the debt.		
3. A 120-day note was given to the bank for a loan.		
4. Purchased stock of another company as a temporary use of cash.		
5. Sold stock purchased in previous transaction (no. 2 above).		
6. Acquired supplies for cash.		
7. Purchased merchandise on open account.		
8. Purchased for cash a 1-year insurance policy for $300.		
9. Received a 1-year advance from tenants for rental property.		
10. Owners invested $20,000 cash in the company in exchange for 2,000 shares of stock having a par value of $5.		
11. Machinery and equipment were bought on open account.		
12. Paid off the creditors for inventory purchases.		

3.   Set up in T-account form the balances for the following list of accounts for Ball Company at January 1, 1995.

For each transaction listed (a–g), make the appropriate journal entry and post each entry to the proper T-accounts. Following these two steps prepare an unadjusted trial balance at month-end.

Cash	$ 60,000
Notes Receivable	18,000
Merchandise Inventory	100,000
Land	30,000
Building	140,000
Accounts Payable	40,000
Notes Payable	32,000
Interest Payable	1,600
Bonds Payable	40,000
Common Stock, $100 Par Value	160,000
Premium on Common Stock	40,000
Retained Earnings	34,400

a. The note receivable of $18,000 was collected.

b. The note for $32,000 and the related accrued interest of $1,600 were paid on January 2.

c. The January 1 balance in Accounts Payable was paid during the month of January.

d. Issued $160,000 of bonds at face value and used the proceeds to pay for an addition to the building.

e. Merchandise inventory costing $60,000 was acquired with payment of $32,000 in cash and the remainder due in 30 days on open account.

f. The plot of land costing $30,000 was sold for $30,000.

g. Sold an additional 800 shares of common stock for $125 per share.

4. Indicate whether or not each of the following items should be recognized as a liability for the organization. Indicate the correct answer by placing a "Yes" or "No" in the space provided.

_____ 1. Unpaid income taxes from the current year.

_____ 2. The obligation to pay workers for services already rendered.

_____ 3. The burden of having a senile president.

_____ 4. The obligation of the president to pay for his son's traffic fines.

_____ 5. The expectation of replacing worn out equipment.

_____ 6. An agreement to purchase inventory in the following year.

_____ 7. An agreement to publish and ship magazines next year for cash already received.

_____ 8. The obligation to pay dividends from income earned next year.

_____ 9. The obligation to pay interest next year on bonds that were issued on the balance sheet date.

_____ 10. The obligation to repay a loan made in the current year and due in 5 years.

5. Indicate whether or not each of the following items should be recognized as an asset. Indicate the correct answer by placing a "Yes" or "No" in the space provided.

_____ 1. Cash received from subscribers for publications to be shipped next year.

_____ 2. The benefit to the firm of its employees receiving advanced college degrees.

_____ 3. The goodwill paid for when acquiring another business enterprise.

_____ 4. A union agreement that promises a higher quality of performance in the upcoming year.

_____ 5. A piece of machinery worth $1,000, purchased originally for use, but subsequently retired from use and awaiting sale.

_____ 6. Shares of the company's own stock purchased back from the original shareholders.

_____ 7. Cash held in a fund by our trustee, to be used to retire bonds in 5 years.

_____ 8. The value to be derived by the firm from having a key location for selling its product.

_____ 9. Costs incurred to develop a new patent.

_____ 10. Interest to be received for the previous 6 months on a long-term note receivable.

6.   From the list of account balances below, prepare in proper form a balance sheet for Doug's Memorial Park.

Trial Balance
December 31, 1995

	Dr.	Cr.
Cash	$ 3,000	
Marketable Securities	16,000	
Accounts Receivable	41,000	
Building	50,000	
Notes Payable (due in one year)		$ 26,000
Patent	8,000	
Building–Accumulated Depreciation		10,000
Property Taxes Payable		6,000
Accounts Payable		29,000
Retained Earnings		77,800
Common Stock		50,000
Bonds Payable		80,000
Inventory	30,000	
Land	100,000	
Investment in IBM Stock	28,000	
Investments in Florida Power Bonds	12,000	
Prepaid Insurance	1,000	
Withheld Income Tax		2,200
Capital Contributed in Excess of Par Value		23,000
Goodwill	15,000	
	$304,000	$304,000

Answers to Questions and Exercises

True/False

1.	T	13.	T	25.	F	37.	F	49.	F
2.	T	14.	F	26.	F	38.	F	50.	T
3.	F	15.	T	27.	F	39.	T	51.	T
4.	T	16.	F	28.	T	40.	T	52.	T
5.	F	17.	T	29.	F	41.	T	53.	T
6.	F	18.	F	30.	F	42.	F	54.	T
7.	F	19.	T	31.	F	43.	F	55.	F
8.	T	20.	F	32.	F	44.	T	56.	F
9.	F	21.	T	33.	F	45.	F	57.	T
10.	T	22.	T	34.	T	46.	F	58.	T
11.	T	23.	F	35.	F	47.	T		
12.	F	24.	T	36.	T	48.	T		

Matching

1.
1.	m	6.	k	11.	d	16.	n	21.	c
2.	j	7.	t	12	g	17.	z	22.	f
3.	r	8.	e	13.	u	18.	i	23.	o
4.	q	9.	s	14.	w	19.	p		
5.	y	10.	b	15.	a	20.	v		

2.
1.	e	11.	f	21.	d or c	31.	a	
2.	a	12.	g	22.	a	32.	a	
3.	Reduction of c	13.	c	23.	a	33.	e	
4.	i	14.	a	24.	f	34.	j	
5.	e	15.	c	25.	f	35.	a	
6.	a	16	d	26.	a	36.	Reduction of (h,i,j)	
7.	f	17.	e	27.	d	37.	a	
8.	c	18.	a	28.	d			
9.	a	19.	b	29.	h			
10.	h	20.	c	30.	a			

3.
1.	d	5.	r	9.	j	13.	m	17.	s
2.	b	6.	i	10.	a	14.	n	18.	o
3.	g	7.	l	11.	f	15.	k	19.	c
4.	p	8.	t	12.	e	16.	q	20.	h

Multiple Choice

1.	a	6.	a	11.	a	16.	d	21.	c
2.	d	7.	a	12.	a	17.	d		
3.	d	8.	c	13.	a	18.	a		
4.	c	9.	d	14.	c	19.	d		
5.	a	10.	b	15.	d	20.	b		

Exercises

1.

Transaction Number	Assets	=	Liabilities	+	Owners' Equity
Example	$500,000				$500,000
Subtotal	$500,000	=			$500,000
a.	+400,000				
	−400,000				
Subtotal	$500,000	=			$500,000
b.	+ 1,000		+ 1,000		
Subtotal	$501,000	=	$ 1,000	+	$500,000
c.	+ 2,100				
	− 2,100				
Subtotal	$501,000	=	$ 1,000	+	$500,000
d.	+ 750				
	− 750				
Subtotal	$501,000	=	$ 1,000	+	$500,000
e.	+ 30,000		+30,000		
Subtotal	$531,000	=	$31,000	+	$500,000
f.	− 12,000		−30,000		
			+18,000		
Subtotal	$519,000	=	$19,000	+	$500,000
g.	+ 3,500				
	− 3,500				
Subtotal	$519,000	=	$19,000	+	$500,000
h.	+ 5,500				
	− 5,500				
Subtotal	$519,000	=	$19,000	+	$500,000
i.	+ 5,000		+ 5,000		
Subtotal	$524,000	=	$24,000	+	$500,000
j.			− 2,000		+ 2,000
Subtotal	$524,000	=	$22,000	+	$502,000
k. (no effect)					
Total	$524,000	=	$22,000	+	$502,000

2.

	Account Debited	Account Credited
1.	n	d (possibly e as well)
2.	i	h
3.	h	b
4.	g	h
5.	h	g
6.	k	h
7.	j	a
8.	l	h
9.	h	c
10.	h	d, e
11.	m	a
12.	a	h

3.

			Dr.	Cr.
a.	Cash		18,000	
	Notes Receivable			18,000
	To record note collection.			
b.	Notes Payable		32,000	
	Interest Payable		1,600	
	Cash			33,600
	Paid note and interest.			
c.	Accounts Payable		40,000	
	Cash			40,000
	Paid balance in accounts payable.			
d.	Cash		160,000	
	Bonds Payable			160,000
	Issued bonds payable.			
	Building		160,000	
	Cash			160,000
	Paid for building addition.			
e.	Merchandise Inventory		60,000	
	Cash			32,000
	Accounts Payable			28,000
	Purchased merchandise inventory.			
f.	Cash		30,000	
	Land			30,000
	Sold land.			
g.	Cash		100,000	
	Common Stock			80,000
	Premium on Common Stock			20,000
	Sold 800 shares of common stock.			

Cash			
Bal.	60,000	33,600	(b)
(a)	18,000	40,000	(c)
(d)	160,000	160,000	(d)
(f)	30,000	32,000	(e)
(g)	100,000		
Bal.	102,400		

Notes Receivable			
Bal.	18,000	18,000	(a)
Bal.	0		

Merchandise Inventory		
Bal.	100,000	
(e)	60,000	
Bal.	160,000	

Land			
Bal	30,000	30,000	(f)
Bal.	0		

Building		
Bal.	140,000	
(d)	160,000	
Bal.	300,000	

Accounts Payable			
(c)	40,000	40,000	Bal.
		28,000	(e)
		28,000	Bal.

Notes Payable			
(b)	32,000	32,000	Bal.
		0	Bal.

Interest Payable			
(b)	1,600	1,600	Bal.
		0	Bal.

Bonds Payable			
		40,000	Bal.
		160,000	(d)
		200,000	Bal.

Common Stock $100 Par Value			
		160,000	Bal.
		80,000	(g)
		240,000	Bal.

Premium on Common Stock			
		40,000	Bal.
		20,000	(g)
		60,000	Bal.

Retained Earnings			
		34,400	Bal.
		34,400	Bal.

Ball Company
Trial Balance
January 31, 1995

	Debits	Credits
Cash	$102,400	
Merchandise Inventory	160,000	
Building	300,000	
Accounts Payable		$ 28,000
Bonds Payable		200,000
Common Stock		240,000
Premium on Common Stock		60,000
Retained Earnings		34,400
	$562,400	$562,400

4.

1. Yes	4. No	7. Yes	10. Yes
2. Yes	5. No	8. No	
3. No	6. No	9. No	

5.

1. Yes	4. No	7. Yes	10. Yes
2. No	5. Yes	8. No	
3. Yes	6. No	9. No	

6.

Doug's Memorial Park
Balance Sheet
December 31, 1995

Assets

Current Assets			
Cash		$ 3,000	
Marketable Securities		16,000	
Accounts Receivable		41,000	
Inventory		30,000	
Prepaid Insurance		1,000	$ 91,000
Investments			
Investment in Stock		$ 28,000	
Investment in Bonds		12,000	40,000
Property, Plant, & Equipment			
Land		$100,000	
Building	$ 50,000		
Accumulated Dep.	(10,000)	40,000	140,000
Intangibles			
Patent		$ 8,000	
Goodwill		15,000	23,000
Total Assets			$294,000

Liabilities

Current Liabilities			
Accounts Payable		$ 29,000	
Notes Payable		26,000	
Property Taxes Payable		6,000	
Withheld Income Tax		2,200	$ 63,200
Long-Term Debt			
Bonds Payable			80,000
Total Liabilities			$143,200

Shareholders' Equity

Common Stock		$ 50,000	
Capital Contributed in			
Excess of Par Value		23,000	
Retained Earnings		77,800	
Total Shareholders' Equity			$150,800
Total Liabilities and Shareholders' Equity			$294,000

Chapter 3

Income Statement: Reporting the Results of Operating Activities

Chapter Highlights

1. The income statement provides a measure of the operating performance of a firm for a particular period of time. Net income is produced when revenues exceed expenses. A loss results when expenses exceed revenues.

2. Revenues measure the net assets (assets less liabilities) that flow into a firm when goods are sold or services are rendered.

3. Expenses measure the net assets that a firm consumes in the process of generating revenues.

4. Most companies use the calendar year as the time span for preparing financial statements for distribution to stockholders and potential investors.

5. Other companies use a natural business year for their accounting period. A natural business year ends when most earnings activities of the firm have been substantially completed.

6. Interim reports are reports of performance for periods shorter than a year. These reports do not eliminate the need to prepare annual reports but are prepared as indicators of progress during the year.

7. The cash basis and the accrual basis are two approaches for measuring operating performance.

8. A company applying the cash basis recognizes revenues when cash is received from customers and recognizes expenses when cash is expended for merchandise, salaries, insurance, taxes, and similar items. The cash basis of accounting is subject to two important criticisms. First, the cost of the efforts required in generating revenues are not adequately matched with those revenues. Second, the cash basis postpones unnecessarily the time when revenue is recognized.

9. Some companies use a modified cash basis, which is the same as a cash basis except that long-lived assets (buildings, equipment, etc.) are treated as assets (not expenses) when purchased. A portion of the asset's acquisition cost is recognized as an expense over several accounting periods as the asset's services are consumed.

10. The accrual basis of accounting typically recognizes revenues when goods are sold or services are rendered. It reports costs as expenses in the period when the revenues that they help produce are recognized. Thus accrual accounting attempts to match expenses with associated revenues.

11. Costs that cannot be closely identified with specific revenues are treated as expenses of the period in which services of an asset are consumed and the future benefits of an asset disappear.

12. Accrual accounting focuses on the inflows of net assets from operations, and the use of net assets in operations regardless of whether those inflows and outflows currently produce or use cash.

13. The accrual basis provides a superior measure of operating performance compared to the cash basis because (a) revenues more accurately reflect the results of sales activity and (b) expenses are associated more closely with reported revenues.

14. Under the accrual basis, revenue is recognized when the following two criteria have been met: (a) a firm has performed all, or a substantial portion, of the services it expects to provide and (b) the firm has received either cash, a receivable, or some other asset susceptible to reasonably precise measurement. For most companies, revenues are recognized at the point of sale.

15. The amount of revenue recognized is measured by the cash or cash-equivalent value of other assets received from customers. The gross revenue for some companies needs to be adjusted for amounts estimated to be uncollectible, discounts for early payment, and for charges included, which represent financing costs for delayed payments.

16. Expenses measure the assets consumed in generating revenue. Assets are unexpired costs. Expenses are expired costs.

17. Asset expirations associated directly with revenues are expenses in the period when a firm recognizes revenues. This treatment is called the matching convention.

18. Asset expirations not clearly associated with revenues become expenses of the period when a firm consumes services in operations. These expenses are called period expenses. Most selling and administrative costs receive this treatment.

19. The cost of merchandise sold is generally the easiest to associate directly with revenue. For a merchandising firm, such as a department store, the acquisition cost (product cost) of inventory is an asset until it is sold, at which time it becomes an expense. A manufacturing firm incurs costs (product costs) of direct materials, direct labor, and manufacturing overhead in producing its product. Manufacturing overhead is a mixture of indirect costs, which providess the capacity to produce the product. Manufacturing overhead often includes items such as plant utilities, property taxes and insurance on the factory, and depreciation on the factory plant and equipment. In both the merchandising firm and the manufacturing firm, product costs are expended when revenues are generated from the sale of the product.

20. Net Income, or earnings, for a period measures the excess of revenues (net asset inflows) over expenses (net asset outflows) from selling goods and providing services.

21. Dividends measure the net assets distributed to shareholders. Dividends are not expenses.

22. The Retained Earnings account on the balance sheet measures the cumulative excess of earnings over dividends since the firm began operations.

23. Revenues and expenses could be recorded directly in the Retained Earnings account. However, to facilitate the preparation of the income statement, individual revenue and expense accounts are maintained during the accounting period.

24. At the end of each period, the balances in the revenue and expense accounts are transferred to Retained Earnings. After the transfer, each revenue and expense account will have a zero balance, and Retained

Earnings will be increased (or decreased) by the amount of net income (or net loss) for the period. The process of transferring the balances in revenue and expense accounts to retained earnings is referred to as the closing process.

25. Revenue and expense accounts are called temporary accounts because they accumulate amounts for only a single accounting period. Balance sheet accounts, which are not closed each period, are called permanent accounts and reflect the cumulative changes in each account from the time the firm was first organized.

26. Revenues increase owners' equity and have credit account balances. Conversely, expenses decrease owners' equity and have debit account balances.

27. The six steps in the accounting process are (a) journalizing entries, (b) posting entries to the general ledger, (c) preparing a trial balance, (d) journalizing adjusting entries, (e) journalizing closing entries, and (f) preparing financial statements.

28. The third step in the accounting process is the preparation of the trial balance. Since it is prepared at the end of the accounting period before adjusting and closing entries, it is called an unadjusted trial balance.

29. At the end of the accounting period, entries are prepared that adjust or correct balances in the general ledger accounts in order to match all revenues and expenses for the proper reporting of net income and financial position. Examples of adjusting entries include adjusting for insurance that has expired, adjusting for salaries that have been earned but not paid, or recording interest payable or interest receivable.

30. Depreciation accounting is a cost-allocation procedure whereby the cost of a long-lived asset is allocated to the periods in which services are received and used. The charge made to the current operations for the portion of the cost of such assets consumed during the current period is called depreciation.

31. A widely used method of allocating the acquisition cost of a long-lived asset to the period of benefit is the straight-line method. Under this procedure, an equal portion of the acquisition cost less estimated salvage value is allocated to each period of the asset's estimated useful life.

32. In recording depreciation for a period, the account Accumulated Depreciation is credited. Accumulated Depreciation is a contra account and appears on the balance sheet as a deduction from the asset to which it relates. The balance in the Accumulated Depreciation account represents the cumulative depreciation on the asset since acquisition. The use of the contra account enables the financial statements to indicate both the acquisition cost of the assets in use and the portion of that amount that has previously been recognized as an expense. Showing both acquisition cost and accumulated depreciation amounts separately provides a rough indication of the relative age of the firm's long-lived assets.

33. An adjusted trial balance is a trial balance of the general ledger accounts after adjusting entries are made. The income statement can be prepared from information in the adjusted trial balance.

34. The closing process transfers the balances in the temporary revenue and expense accounts to Retained Earnings. Closing entries reduce the balances in all temporary accounts to zero.

35. An alternative closing procedure uses a temporary "Income Summary" account. Individual revenue and expense accounts are first closed to the Income Summary account. The balance in the Income Summary account, representing net income for the period, is then closed to Retained Earnings.

36. A post-closing trial balance is prepared after closing entries and shows revenue and expense accounts with zero balances and balance sheet accounts at their end-of-the-period balances. The post-closing trial balance provides information for preparing the balance sheet.

Questions and Exercises

True/False. **For each of the following statements, place a T or F in the space provided to indicate whether the statement is true or false.**

_____ 1. Net income is produced when revenues exceed expenses.

_____ 2. Expenses measure the net assets used in the process of generating revenue.

_____ 3. The balance in a revenue account is closed to Retained Earnings by a debit to the revenue account.

_____ 4. Permanent accounts that reflect the cumulative changes in each account from the time the firm was first organized appear on the income statement.

_____ 5. Revenues - Expenses - Dividends = Net Income.

_____ 6. Revenues reflect an increase in owners' equity and are recorded as credits.

_____ 7. Depreciation accounting attempts to adjust the ledger account balances for long-lived assets to equate to their current market value.

_____ 8. The balance in the Accumulated Depreciation account represents the cumulative depreciation on the asset since acquisition.

_____ 9. For accounting purposes the cash-basis income statement provides the most meaningful measure of operating performance during a particular period, because cash flow is the most objective measure of a company's performance.

_____ 10. The major difference between the cash basis and the accrual basis is in expense recognition, because revenues are the same for both methods.

_____ 11. The adjusted trial balance is prepared from information in the income statement and balance sheet.

_____ 12. Product costs are recorded as expenses of the period in which the services are consumed, since these costs rarely create assets with future benefits.

_____ 13. The balance in an expense account is closed to Retained Earnings by a credit to the expense account.

_____ 14. Dividends represent distributions of earnings and decrease owners' equity.

_____ 15. The Depreciation Expense account reflects the cumulative depreciation on the asset since acquisition.

_____ 16. The Parker Company recorded the purchase of a 1-year insurance policy on July 1, Year 1, by debiting Prepaid Insurance. On December 31, Year 1, the company should prepare an adjusting entry that debits Insurance Expense and credits Prepaid Insurance for the amount of the expired insurance.

_____ 17. Assets may be referred to as unexpired costs, while expenses may be referred to as expired costs.

_____ 18. Product costs represent only the costs of raw material for a manufacturing firm.

_____ 19. Assets = Liabilities + Contributed Capital + Revenues - Expenses - Dividends.

_____ 20. Assets = Liabilities + Contributed Capital + Retained Earnings.

_____ 21. The income statement provides a measure of the operating performance of the firm for a particular period of time.

_____ 22. Expenses measure the net assets (assets less liabilities) that flow into a firm when goods are sold or services are rendered.

_____ 23. A natural business year for a company is always the one that coincides with the calendar year.

_____ 24. Expenses cause a decrease in owners' equity and are recorded as credits.

_____ 25. Under the accrual basis of accounting, revenue is recognized in the period when the cash is received as opposed to when the sale is made.

Matching. **From the list of terms below, select that term that is most closely associated with each of the descriptive phrases or statements that follows and place the letter for that term in the space provided.**

a.	Accrual Basis	k.	Matching Convention
b.	Accumulated Depreciation	l.	Natural Business Year
c.	Adjusted Trial Balance	m.	Owners' Equity
d.	Cash Basis	n.	Period Expenses
e.	Closing Process	o.	Permanent Accounts
f.	Contra Accounts	p.	Post-Closing Trial Balance
g.	Depreciation	q.	Posting
h.	Dividends	r.	Product Costs
i.	Expenses	s.	Revenues
j.	Journalizing	t.	Temporary Accounts
		u.	Unadjusted Trial Balance

_____ 1. These accounts reflect the cumulative changes in each account from the time the firm was first organized.

_____ 2. A measure of the inflow of net assets from selling goods and providing services.

_____ 3. A trial balance prepared at the end of the accounting period after adjusting entries are made.

_____ 4. Recognizes revenues and expenses as cash flows (inflow and outflow) take place.

_____ 5. A measure of the outflow of net assets that are used or consumed, in the process of generating revenues.

_____ 6. The year ends when most earnings activities of a firm have been substantially completed.

_____ 7. A manufacturing firm's cost of producing its product.

_____ 8. The process of transferring entries in the general journal to the accounts in the general ledger.

_____ 9. The charge made to the current operations for the portion of cost of long-lived assets consumed during the current period.

_____ 10. The balance in this account reflects the cumulative depreciation of an asset since acquisition.

_____ 11. The basis that recognizes revenues upon the completion of a critical event in the earnings process.

_____ 12. Asset expirations associated directly with revenues are expenses in the period when a firm recognizes revenues.

_____ 13. A trial balance prepared at the end of the accounting period before adjusting and closing entries.

_____ 14. Asset expirations not clearly associated with revenues become expenses of the period when a firm consumes services in operations.

_____ 15. Contributed Capital plus Retained Earnings.

_____ 16. The process of transferring the balances in revenue and expense accounts to retained earnings.

_____ 17. The process of recording transactions in the general journal or in a special journal.

_____ 18. These accounts accumulate amounts for only a single accounting period.

_____ 19. This account represents distributions of earnings to shareholders of the firm.

_____ 20. Deduction or valuation accounts that accumulate amounts that are subtracted from another account.

_____ 21. A trial balance which shows revenue and expense accounts with zero balances and balance sheet accounts at their end-of-the-period balances.

Multiple Choice. Choose the best answer for each of the following questions and enter the identifying letter in the space provided.

_____ 1. Which of the following is a permanent account (balance sheet account)?

    a. Accumulated Depreciation.
    b. Advances from Customers.
    c. Both (a) and (b) are permanent accounts.
    d. Neither (a) nor (b) are permanent accounts.

_____ 2. Moos Company purchased some equipment on July 1, Year 1, for $80,000. The equipment has an estimated useful life of 10 years and an estimated salvage value of $5,000. Moos computes depreciation on a straight-line basis. How much depreciation should be recorded for Year 1?

    a. $8,000.
    b. $7,500.
    c. $4,000.
    d. $3,750.

_____ 3. Daniel Company purchased a 1-year insurance policy on April 1, Year 1, for $6,000. The amount of prepaid insurance reported on the balance sheet and the amount of insurance expense reported on the income statement at December 31, Year 1, are, respectively

    a. $1,500; $4,500.
    b. $4,500; $1,500.
    c. $2,000; $4,000.
    d. $4,000; $2,000.

_____   4. Which of the following transactions did not result in revenue being reported?

    a. Sold merchandise for cash.
    b. Sold merchandise on account.
    c. Collected an account receivable.
    d. All of the above transactions would result in revenue being reported.

_____   5. Sandi Company has just completed its first year of operations in Year 1. The company distributed dividends of $25,000. If the ending balance of Retained Earnings on 12/31, Year 1, is $35,000 and the company had revenues of $200,000 from Year 1 sales, the company's Year 1 expenses totaled

    a. $175,000.
    b. $165,000.
    c. $140,000.
    d. None of the above.

_____   6. On December 26, Year 1, Diamond Company hired three salesclerks to begin work immediately on an after-Christmas sale. The clerks were paid on January 9, Year 2. Disregarding amounts, what entry should have been made on December 31, Year 1?

    a. Debit Salary Expense and credit Salary Payable.
    b. Debit Salary Expense and credit Cash.
    c. Debit Salary Payable and credit Cash.
    d. Debit Salary Payable and credit Salary Expense.

_____   7. Wilson Company reported a balance in Accounts Receivable of $81,000 on 1/1, Year 2. During Year 2, Wilson collected $255,000 from its customers who had purchased on account. On 12/31, Year 2, Wilson reported a balance in Accounts Receivable of $42,500. How much was Wilson's credit sales for Year 2?

    a. $216,500.
    b. $259,000.
    c. $293,500.
    d. $297,500.

_____   8. Which of the following accounts in <u>not</u> an expense?

    a. Depreciation.
    b. Sales Salaries.
    c. Dividends Declared.
    d. Delivery Expense.

_____   9. The normal balances in Depreciation Expense and its related Accumulated Depreciation accounts are

    a. Debit and credit, respectively.
    b. Credit and debit, respectively.
    c. Both have debit balances.
    d. Both have credit balances.

_____ 10. Joanne Company reported total shareholders' equity of $450,000 on 12/31, Year 1, of which $360,000 represented contributed capital. If revenues, expenses, and dividends during Year 2 were $1,000,000, $860,000, and $60,000, respectively, how much additional capital was contributed by shareholders if total shareholders' equity is $580,000 on 12/31, Year 2?

    a. $50,000.
    b. $80,000.
    c. $130,000.
    d. $410,000.

_____ 11. Windland Company completed its second year of operations in Year 2. On 1/1, Year 2, the balance in Retained Earnings was $168,000. During the year, the company declared and paid a dividend of $130,000 to shareholders. The company reported net earnings of $210,000 in its Year 2 income statement. What was the 12/31, Year 2 balance in Retained Earnings?

    a. $378,000.
    b. $340,000.
    c. $298,000.
    d. $248,000.

_____ 12. In preparing its Year 1 adjusting entries, the Yiengst Company neglected to adjust rental fees received in advance for the amount of rental fees earned during Year 1. As a result of this error:

    a. Year 1 net income is understated, the balance in retained earnings is understated, and liabilities are overstated.
    b. Year 1 net income is overstated, the balance in retained earnings is overstated, and liabilities are correctly stated.
    c. Year 1 net income is understated, the balance in retained earnings is understated, and liabilities are understated.
    d. None of the above.

_____ 13. The account Accumulated Depreciation reflects

    a. Depreciation for the current accounting period only.
    b. Cumulative depreciation on the asset since acquisition.
    c. The amount of depreciation that can be taken in future periods.
    d. None of the above.

_____ 14. In preparing its Year 1 adjusting entries, the Schrieber Company neglected to adjust prepaid insurance for the amount of insurance expired during Year 1. As a result of this error

    a. Year 1 net income is understated, the balance in retained earnings is understated, and assets are understated.
    b. Year 1 net income is overstated, the balance in retained earnings is overstated, and assets are correctly stated.
    c. Year 1 income is overstated, the balance in retained earnings is overstated, and assets are overstated.
    d. None of the above.

_____ 15. All of the following are temporary accounts and should be closed during the closing process except

    a. Prepaid Insurance.
    b. Cost of Goods Sold.
    c. Sales Revenue.
    d. Depreciation.

_____ 16. La Palme, Inc., publishes a monthly sports magazine. On July 1, Year 1, the company sold 1,000 2-year subscriptions for $100 each. On December 31, Year 1, the amount reported as a liability on the balance sheet and the amount reported as revenue on the income statement are, respectively

    a. $-0-; $100,000.
    b. $25,000; $75,000.
    c. $50,000; $50,000.
    d. $75,000; $25,000.

_____ 17. Which of the following accounts is <u>not</u> closed during the closing process?

    a. Wage Expense.
    b. Interest Revenue.
    c. Utility Expense.
    d. Accumulated Depreciation.

_____ 18. Firms may prepare reports of performance

    a. Using the calendar year as the accounting period.
    b. Using a natural business year as the accounting period.
    c. For interim periods.
    d. Answers (a), (b), and (c) above are correct under appropriate circumstances.

_____ 19. All of the following are examples of period expenses except

    a. Administrative costs.
    b. Inventory costs.
    c. Accounting costs.
    d. Selling costs.

_____ 20. Temporary revenue and expense accounts may be closed

    a. Individually by separate entries to Retained Earnings.
    b. In a single entry to Retained Earnings.
    c. To a temporary "Income Summary" account.
    d. By any of the above 3 methods.

_____ 21. During the year, Boger's inventory account balance increased from $52,000 to $63,000. During the year, the company made payments to creditors for inventory purchases totaling $305,000 and the company reported Cost of Goods Sold of $319,000 on its income statement. How much inventory was purchased during the year?

    a. $330,000.
    b. $316,000.
    c. $305,000.
    d. $319,000.

_____ 22. C. L. May, an attorney, collects a retainer fee from all of her new clients. At the beginning of the year, the Unearned Retainer Fee account had a balance of $12,000. May collected additional retainer fees totaling $47,000 from her clients during the year. Her year-end balance sheet reports an $8,000 balance in the Unearned Retainer Fee account. How much of the retainer fees were earned by May during the year?

    a. $59,000.
    b. $55,000.
    c. $43,000.
    d. $51,000.

_____ 23. At the beginning of the year, Dusell reported a $3,600 balance in its Prepaid Insurance account. At year-end, the company reported Insurance Expense of $4,500 in its income statement and a balance of $1,900 in the Prepaid Insurance account. What was the cost of the additional insurance that was purchased during the year?

    a. $4,500.
    b. $6,200.
    c. $2,800.
    d. $6,400.

_____ 24. At the beginning of the year, Toto owed $29,000 to its creditors for inventory purchases. At year-end, the company owed $18,300. During the year, Toto made payments totaling $97,000 to its creditors for inventory purchases. What was the cost of the additional inventory that was purchased during the year?

    a. $115,300.
    b. $ 86,300.
    c. $107,300.
    d. $ 78,700.

_____ 25. At the beginning of the year, Jellybean reported Accounts Receivable of $19,500. During the year, the company had credit sales totaling $144,000. At year-end, the Accounts Receivable balance was $4,000 higher than the beginning balance. How much cash was collected on the accounts during the year?

    a. $148,000.
    b. $144,000.
    c. $140,000.
    d. $136,000.

Exercises

1. Electric Appliance Shop began operations on January 1, Year 4. The owners invested $16,000 and the company borrowed $10,000 from a bank. The bank loan is due on January 1, Year 6, with interest at 12 percent per year.

    On January 1, the company paid $9,000 for a one-year lease of a building. Also, on January 1 the company purchased a one-year insurance policy for $1,800. The company purchased $20,000 of inventory on account on January 2. On January 10 a payment of $12,000 was made to the supplier. At the end of January, inventory costing $6,000 was still on hand.

    During January, cash sales totaled $30,000 and sales to customers on account totaled $22,000. During January, $8,000 was collected from customers who bought on credit.

    Other costs paid in cash during January were as follows: salaries, $10,400; utilities, $3,000; supplies, $1,200.

    a. Prepare an accrual basis income statement for January.

    b. Prepare a cash basis income statement for January.

2.   Indicate whether the following accounts are temporary or permanent by placing either a "T" for temporary or a "P" for permanent to the left of the letter in the space provided.

_____   a.   Retained Earnings

_____   b.   Cost of Goods Sold

_____   c.   Accumulated Depreciation

_____   d.   Advances from Tenants

_____   e.   Sales

_____   f.   Depreciation Expense

_____   g.   Prepaid Insurance

_____   h.   Bonds Payable

_____   i.   Work in Process

_____   j.   Raw Materials

_____   k.   Accounts Receivable

_____   l.   Salaries Payable

_____   m. Salespersons' Commissions

_____   n.   Finished Goods

_____   o.   Interest Revenue

_____   p.   Additional Paid-in Capital

_____   q.   Insurance Expense

_____   r.   Delivery Expense

_____   s.   Dividends Payable

_____   t.   Common Stock

3. The adjusted trial balance for Miller Corporation on December 31, Year 1, is reproduced below (accounts listed alphabetically):

Miller Corporation
Adjusted Trial Balance
12/31 Year 1

	Dr.	Cr.
Accounts Payable		$ 75,000
Accounts Receivable	$ 250,000	
Advertising Expense	15,000	
Cash	140,000	
Common Stock		250,000
Cost of Goods Sold	1,250,000	
Interest Revenue		25,000
Inventory	375,000	
Rent Expense	60,000	
Retained Earnings		562,500
Salaries Expense	450,000	
Salaries Payable		2,500
Sales		1,625,000
	$2,540,000	$2,540,000

a. Prepare the necessary closing entries.

b. What is the amount of the company's reported net income (or loss) for the year?

4. The following is a partial listing of the Boyd Company's unadjusted and adjusted trial balances. From the information given, reconstruct the adjusting entries.

	Unadjusted Trial Balance		Adjusted Trial Balance	
	Dr.	Cr.	Dr.	Cr.
Prepaid Insurance	$ 3,000		$ 1,380	
Supplies on Hand	1,260		540	
Interest Receivable			210	
Building	156,000		156,000	
Accumulated Depreciation		$24,000		$28,000
Advances from Tenants		2,400		1,600
Rent Payable				4,000
Salaries Payable				1,800
Insurance Expense			1,620	
Supplies Expense			720	
Depreciation Expense			4,000	
Salaries Expense	20,000	21,800		
Rent Expense	12,000		16,000	
Interest Revenue				210
Rent Revenue				800

5. Assume that the accrual basis of accounting is used and revenue is recognized at the time goods are sold or services rendered. Indicate in the space provided the dollar amount of revenue recognized in the month of January. (Each case is independent of the others.)

_____ a. In January, a company sold its product for a sales price totaling $400,000, of which $270,000 was collected in January, $100,000 collected in February, and the remainder in March.

_____ b. A theatrical company sells $120,000 of season tickets to its plays, which will be given the second Saturday in each month for 10 months beginning in January Also, the company sells $30,000 of tickets for January's play.

_____ c. The Laker Gators, a pro football team, receives $1,500,000 as its portion of the gate receipts for the playoffs held in the previous December.

_____ d. DJP, Inc., an owner of office buildings, collected $2,000,000 in January for office rental fees. Each tenant pays 4 months rental three times a year.

_____ e. On January 1, a company loans $500,000 to a customer. The customer agrees to repay the $500,000 plus 12 percent interest (total of $560,000) on December 31.

6. Assume that the accrual basis of accounting is used and that revenue is recognized at the time goods are sold or services are rendered. Indicate the amount of expense recognized during the month of September in each of the following situations.

_____ a. During September, a wholesale company purchased $900,000 of its product for resale. A portion, $150,000, was the cost of goods ordered by its customers in August to be delivered in September. Customers placed orders and received goods with a cost to the wholesale company of $450,000 in September. In September, customers ordered goods with a cost of $225,000 to be delivered in October. The remaining portion of September's purchases was maintained for future press orders.

_____ b. A manufacturing firm has two insurance policies covering its property against casualty events. Each policy covers a 6-month period. On August 15, the premium for the first policy, $2,400, is paid to cover the period August 15 through February 15. On September 1, the second policy's premium, $1,920, is paid to cover the period September 1 through February 28.

_____   c.   A pro football team incurred in September a cost of $180,000 for an advertising campaign that will produce full-page ads in local papers, as follows: two in September, three in October, two in November, and one in December.

_____   d.   A swimming pool company purchased concrete supplies totaling $45,000 in August. At the end of August there were still unused supplies totaling $37,500, and at the end of September there were unused supplies totaling $7,500. The remaining $7,500 was used in October.

_____   e.   An accounting firm leases its office space. Every 6 months, on September 1 and March 1, the firm is required to pay $210,000 under the lease contract.

63

_____ f. Sales commissions for a cosmetics company are based on a percentage of each sales dollar generated by the sales staff. The commission is paid at the end of each 3-month period. In September $150,000 was paid for July, August, and September sales. Sales related to commissions for the 3-month period were as follows: July, $375,000; August, $525,000; September, $600,000.

7. Determine the missing amounts in each of the following independent cases:

	a	b	c	d
Assets	$	$410,000	$580,000	$350,000
Liabilities	$270,000	$	$320,000	$125,000
Contributed Capital	$184,000	$125,000	$	$150,000
Beginning Retained Earnings	$	$ 60,000	$150,000	$ 50,000
Revenues	$600,000	$390,000	$	$325,000
Expenses	$420,000	$350,000	$430,000	$
Dividends	$ 80,000	$	$ 25,000	$ 35,000
Ending Retained Earnings	$160,000	$ 55,000	$120,000	$

Answers to Questions and Exercises

True/False

1.	T	6.	T	11.	F	16.	T	21.	T
2.	T	7.	F	12.	F	17.	T	22.	F
3.	T	8.	T	13.	T	18.	F	23.	F
4.	F	9.	F	14.	T	19.	F	24.	F
5.	F	10.	F	15.	F	20.	T	25.	F

Matching

1.	o	6.	l	11.	a	16.	e	21.	p
2.	s	7.	r	12.	k	17.	j		
3.	c	8.	q	13.	u	18.	t		
4.	d	9.	g	14.	n	19.	h		
5.	i	10.	b	15.	m	20.	f		

Multiple Choice

1.	c	6.	a	11.	d	16.	d	21.	a
2.	d	7.	a	12.	a	17.	d	22.	d
3.	a	8.	c	13.	b	18.	d	23.	c
4.	c	9.	a	14.	c	19.	b	24.	b
5.	c	10.	a	15.	a	20.	d	25.	c

Exercises

1. a.

Electric Appliance Shop
Income Statement
For Month Ending January 31, Year 4

Sales Revenue		$52,000
Less Expenses:		
Cost of Goods Sold	$14,000	
Salaries	10,400	
Utilities	3,000	
Supplies	1,200	
Rent	750	
Insurance	150	
Interest	100	
Total Expenses		29,600
Net Income		$22,400

1. b.

Electric Appliance Shop
Income Statement
For Month Ending January 31, Year 4

Sales Revenue		$38,000
Less Expenses:		
Cost of Goods Sold	$12,000	
Salaries	10,400	
Utilities	3,000	
Supplies	1,200	
Rent	9,000	
Insurance	1,800	
Total Expenses		37,400
Net Income		$ 600

2.

a.	P	f.	T	k.	P	p.	P
b.	T	g.	P	l.	P	q.	T
c.	P	h.	P	m.	T	r.	T
d.	P	i.	P	n.	P	s.	P
e.	T	j.	P	o.	T	t.	P

3. a.

	Dr.	Cr.
Sales Revenue	1,625,000	
Interest Revenue	25,000	
Retained Earnings		1,650,000
To close revenue accounts.		
Retained Earnings	1,775,000	
Advertising Expense		15,000
C ost of Goods Sold		1,350,000
Salaries Expense		450,000

Alternatively, the revenue and expense accounts may be closed to the Income Summary account, and then the Income Summary account is closed to Retained Earnings.

b. The reported net loss is $125,000 ($1,625,000 + $25,000 - $15,000 - $1,250,000 - $60,000 - $450,000).

4.

		Dr.	Cr.
a.	Insurance Expense	1,620	
	Prepaid Insurance		1,620
	To record expired insurance.		
b.	Supplies Expense	720	
	Supplies on Hand		720
	To record supplies used.		
c.	Interest Receivable	210	
	Interest Revenue		210
	To record interest earned and receivable.		
d.	Depreciation Expense	4,000	
	Accumulated Depreciation		4,000
	To record depreciation expense.		
e.	Advances from Tenants	800	
	Rent Revenue		800
	To record rent revenue earned.		
f.	Rent Expense	4,000	
	Rent Payable		4,000
	To record rent expenses.		
g.	Salaries Expense	1,800	
	Salaries Payable		1,800
	To record salaries expense.		

5. a. $400,000.
    b. $ 42,000.
    c. -0-
    d. $500,000.
    e. $ 5,000.

6. a. $600,000.
    b. $ 720.
    c. $ 45,000.
    d. $ 30,000.
    e. $ 35,000.
    f. $ 60,000.

7.

	a	b	c	d
Assets	$614,000	$410,000	$580,000	$350,000
Liabilities	$270,000	$230,000	$320,000	$125,000
Contributed Capital	$184,000	$125,000	$140,000	$150,000
Beginning Retained Earnings	$ 60,000	$ 60,000	$150,000	$ 50,000
Revenues	$600,000	$390,000	$425,000	$325,000
Expenses	$420,000	$350,000	$430,000	$265,000
Dividends	$ 80,000	$ 45,000	$ 25,000	$ 35,000
Ending Retained Earnings	$160,000	$ 55,000	$120,000	$ 75,000

Chapter 4

Income Statement:
Extending the Accrual Concept

Chapter Highlights

1. Under the accrual basis of measuring income, revenue is recognized when all, or a substantial portion, of the services expected to be provided have been performed and cash, or another asset whose cash equivalent value can be objectively measured, has been received. Expenses are recognized in the period when related revenues are recognized or in the period when goods or services are consumed in operations.

2. Most merchandising firms recognize revenue in the period when they sell goods. They then match expenses either directly with the revenue or with the period when the firm consumes goods or services.

3. Merchandising firms acquire inventory in finished form ready for sale. At the time of sale, the cost of items sold is transferred from the asset account, Merchandise Inventory, to the expense account, Cost of Goods Sold.

4. Manufacturing firms incur costs for direct materials, direct labor, and manufacturing overhead to convert raw materials into finished products. Manufacturing costs are treated as product costs (assets) and are accumulated in various inventory accounts. At the time of sale, the cost of items sold is transferred from the asset account, Finished Goods Inventory, to the expense account, Cost of Goods Sold.

5. Manufacturing firms maintain separate inventory accounts for product costs incurred at various stages of completion. The Raw Materials Inventory account includes the cost of raw materials purchased but not yet transferred to production. The Work-in-Process Inventory account accumulates the costs incurred in producing units during the period. The balance in the Work-in-Process Inventory account indicates the product costs incurred thus far on units not yet finished as of the date of the balance sheet. The Finished Goods Inventory account includes the total manufacturing cost of units completed but not yet sold.

6. Both merchandising and manufacturing firms incur various selling and administrative costs, which they treat as period expenses. Period expenses are expenditures associated with the generation of revenue within an accounting period, which are not directly associated with the product. These costs are expenses of the period when the firm consumes the services.

7. The application of accrual accounting involves both timing and measurement issues. Timing issues relate to when a firm recognizes the revenues and expenses. Measurement issues relate to the amount of revenue and expense recognized.

69

8. The general principles for <u>when</u> a firm recognizes revenue (the timing issue) are that a firm (a) must have provided all or a substantial portion of the services it expects to perform for customers, and (b) be able to measure the amounts of revenues and expenses with reasonable precision. The general principle for <u>when</u> a firm recognizes expenses is matching asset expirations either with particular revenues or with the accounting period when the firm consumes goods and services in operations.

9. The general principles for the <u>amount</u> of revenue and expense recognized (the measurement issue) are that (a) revenues should equal the present value of the amount of cash a firm expects to receive from customers for goods or services sold, and (b) expenses should equal the amount of cash a firm has expended or expects to expend to generate the revenues.

10. Contractors engaged in long-term construction projects may recognize revenue using the percentage-of-completion method or the completed-contract method.

11. Under the percentage-of-completion method, a portion of the total contract price is recognized as revenue each period. Corresponding proportions of the total estimated costs of the contract are recognized as expenses. Thus, the percentage-of-completion method follows the accrual basis of accounting because expenses are matched with related revenues.

12. Under the completed-contract method, revenue is recognized when the project is completed and sold. The total costs of the project are expensed in the period when revenue is recognized.

13. Firms whose products require aging usually recognize revenue at the completion of the aging process when the product is sold. A proper matching of expenses with revenues requires these firms to capitalize as part of the cost of the aging assets all expenditures during the aging process. Such costs become expenses at the time of sale when revenue is recognized.

14. When substantial uncertainty exists at the time of sale regarding the amount of cash or cash equivalent value of assets that a firm will ultimately receive from customers, it delays the recognition of revenues and expenses until it receives cash. Such sellers recognize revenue at the time of cash collection using either the installment method or the cost-recovery-first method. Generally accepted accounting principles permit the seller to use the installment method and the cost-recovery-first method only when cash collection is highly uncertain.

15. The installment method is similar to the cash basis of accounting, in that revenue is recognized as cash is received. Unlike the cash basis of accounting, the installment method attempts to match expenses with revenues. Revenue is recognized as the periodic cash collections are received, and costs incurred in generating the revenue are matched as closely as possible with the revenue.

16. The cost-recovery-first method is appropriate when there is great uncertainty about cash collection. Under this method, costs of generating revenues are matched dollar for dollar with cash receipts until all such costs are recovered. When cumulative cash receipts exceed total costs, profit will be reported on the income statement.

17. In evaluating a firm's profitability, the nature of income items must be considered. Does the income item result from the firm's primary operating activity or from an activity incidental or peripheral to the primary operating activities? Is the income item recurring or nonrecurring?

18. Firms use different reporting formats in their income statements. The multiple-step format presents several subtotals before reporting the amount of net income for the period. In the single-step format the

computation of net income results from a signal step - the subtraction of total expenses and losses from total revenues and gains.

19. In contrast to the multiple-step format, the single-step format does not distinguish between revenues and expenses related to a firm's primary operating activities and income from activities peripherally related to operations.

20. Depending on the nature of a firm's income for the period, the income statement may contain some or all of the following sections or categories: (a) income from continuing operations; (b) income, gains, and losses from discontinued operations; (c) extraordinary gains and losses; and (d) adjustments for changes in accounting principles.

21. "Income from Continuing Operations" reflects the revenues, gains, expenses, and losses from the continuing areas of business activity of a firm and includes income derived from a firm's primary business activities as well as from activities peripherally related to operations.

22. If a firm sells a major division or segment of its business during the year or contemplates such a sale within a short time after the end of an accounting period, any income, gains, and losses related to the segment should be disclosed separately and reported below income from continuing operations. The separate disclosure in a section titled "Income, Gains and Losses from Discontinued Operations" alerts the financial statement reader that the firm does not expect this source of income to continue.

23. Extraordinary gains and losses are presented in a separate section of the income statement and are reported net of their tax effect. For an item to be classified as extraordinary, it must meet both of the following criteria: (a) unusual in nature and (b) infrequent in occurrence.

24. A firm that changes its principles, or methods, of accounting during the period must disclose in some cases the effects of the change on current and prior years' net income in a separate section titled "Adjustments for Changes in Accounting Principles."

25. "Earnings per Share" must be shown in the body of the income statement by publicly held firms in order to receive an unqualified accountant's opinion. Earnings per share is conventionally calculated by dividing net income minus preferred stock dividends by the average number of common shares outstanding during the accounting period.

26. If a firm has securities outstanding that can be converted to or exchanged for common stock, it may be required to present two sets of earnings per share amounts, primary earnings per share and fully diluted earnings per share.

27. The quality of a firm's earnings, depends, in part, upon (a) the significance of the estimates that were required in measuring revenues and expenses and (b) the items that make up income. The financial statement user must consider the recurring or nonrecurring nature of various income items in assessing a firm's past operating performance and predicting its likely future performance.

28. Common size income statements (a) express each expense and net income as a percentage of revenues and (b) permit a financial statement user to analyze changes or differences between revenues, expenses, and net income.

29. Financial statement users can employ common size income statements in time series analysis and cross section analysis.

30. Time series analysis compares common size income statements for two or more periods. Such comparisons may reveal trends that would help the statement reader interpret and analyze the firm's operations.

31. Cross section analysis involves using common size income statements to compare two or more firms. Such analysis provides information about the different strategies that firms follow.

Questions and Exercises

True/False. **For each of the following statements, place a T or F in the space provided to indicate whether the statement is true or false.**

_____ 1. The Work-in-Process account is debited for the cost of direct labor services used.

_____ 2. Product costs represent only the costs of raw materials for a manufacturing firm.

_____ 3. The balance in the Raw Materials account represents manufacturing cost incurred on uncompleted units.

_____ 4. The Finished Goods account accumulates the costs incurred in producing units during the period.

_____ 5. For an item to qualify as extraordinary, it must be both unusual in nature and infrequent in occurrence.

_____ 6. Generally accepted accounting principles permit the installment method and the cost-recovery-first method only when substantial uncertainty exists about cash collection.

_____ 7. A contractor would not use the percentage-of-completion method to recognize revenues if is substantial uncertainty regarding the total cost of the project.

_____ 8. The Finished Goods account is credited for the cost of units completed during the period.

_____ 9. The Cost of Goods Sold account is debited for the total manufacturing cost of units completed and transferred to the storeroom.

_____ 10. The Finished Goods account is debited for the cost of units sold during the period.

_____ 11. A common format of the single-step income statement distinguishes between revenues and expenses related to a firm's primary operating activities and income from activities peripherally related to operations.

_____ 12. Earnings per share data should be considered as supplementary and therefore disclosed only at the discretion of management.

_____ 13. The percentage-of-completion method of revenue recognition allows firms with long-term construction contracts to recognize a portion of the total contract price, based on the degree of completion of the work, during each accounting period of the life of the contract.

_____ 14. The installment method of revenue recognition allows a firm to take a cash sale and recognize revenue from the sale equally over a 3- to 5-year period in the future.

_____ 15. The completed contract method of recognizing revenue is the same as the completed sale basis.

_____ 16. Gains or losses on sale of a segment of a business should not be disclosed in a separate classification on the income statement.

_____ 17. The Raw Materials account includes the cost of raw materials purchased but not yet transferred to production.

_____ 18. The cost-recovery-first method of income recognition matches costs of generating revenues dollar for dollar with cash receipts until all such costs are recovered.

_____ 19. The balance in the Finished Goods account represents the total manufacturing cost of units completed but not sold.

_____ 20. The Raw Materials account is credited for the total manufacturing cost of units completed and transferred to the storeroom.

_____ 21. When materials are issued to producing departments, the Work-in-Process account is debited.

_____ 22. In assessing the quality of a firm's earnings, one factor to consider is the recurring or nonrecurring nature of various income items.

_____ 23. Common size income statements express revenues and expenses as a percentage of net income.

_____ 24. "Income from Continuing Operations" includes only income derived from a firm's primary business activities.

_____ 25. One form of a multiple-step income statement distinguishes between revenues and expenses related to a firm's primary operating activities and income from activities peripherally related to operations.

Matching. Indicate whether each of the following transactions and events should be classified within the income statement as (a) income from continuing operations; (b) income, gains, and losses from discontinued operations; or (c) extraordinary items.

_____ 1. Gain on sale of the company's only division for manufacturing sports equipment.

_____ 2. Losses during the year up to the time of sale of the division in (1).

_____ 3. President's salary during the year.

_____ 4. Loss on damages from a tidal wave that hit the company's factory in Key West, Florida.

_____ 5. The cost of goods sold during the year.

_____ 6. Loss on factory and equipment in a South American country when confiscated by the government of that country.

_____ 7. Interest received on short-term investments.

_____ 8. Loss on decline in the market value of several inventory items.

_____ 9. Gain on the sale of the vice-president's company automobile.

_____ 10. Loss from sale of investment in preferred stock.

Matching. **Indicate whether each of the following expenditures should be classified as (a) direct material; (b) direct labor; (c) manufacturing overhead; (d) selling expense; (e) administrative expense; or (f) none of the above.**

_____   1. Salary of the sales vice-president.

_____   2. Cost of paint for the final glossy finish on the product.

_____   3. Salary of the company president.

_____   4. Cost of oil and gasoline for sales staff cars.

_____   5. Sales commissions paid on each sale of the product.

_____   6. Cost of cleaning supplies used to remove grease in the factory.

_____   7. Salary of the painter of the product.

_____   8. Cost of service contract for the maintenance of the computer.

_____   9. Cost of pamphlets that are distributed to advertise the product.

_____   10. The factory supervisor's salary (person in charge of the assembly-line workers).

_____   11. Depreciation on the company's computer.

_____   12. Electricity cost for the office building.

_____   13. Raw materials for the product.

_____   14. Depreciation of the factory equipment.

_____   15. Cost of normal maintenance for machinery in the factory.

_____   16. Salary of the company controller.

_____   17. Insurance costs on factory building.

_____   18. Wages paid to assembly-line workers.

_____   19. Cost of legal fees.

_____   20. Salary of vice-president for production.

Multiple Choice. **Choose the best answer for each of the following questions and enter the identifying letter in the space provided.**

_____   1. Cole Corporation purchased land on December 31, Year 1, for $20,000. The land had a fair market value of $24,000 one year later. On July 1, Year 3, the land was sold for $30,000. Which of the following statements is true?

a. The land was carried on the books at $20,000 on December 31, Year 2.
b. A $10,000 gain was recorded on July 1, Year 3, when the land was sold.
c. There was an unrealized holding gain of $4,000 as of December 31, Year 2.
d. All of the above statements are true.

2. Which of the following costs would not be included as an element of manufacturing overhead?

   a. Depreciation on factory machinery.
   b. Insurance on factory building.
   c. Raw materials.
   d. Supervisory labor.

3. The earnings process for a manufacturing firm includes which of the following?

   a. Completion of production.
   b. Collection of cash.
   c. Acquisition of raw materials, plant, and equipment.
   d. All of the above.

4. If a reasonable estimate of the amount of cash to be received can be made, when should revenue be recognized?

   a. At the time of sale.
   b. At the time of cash collection.
   c. At the time of cash collection, using the cost-recovery-first method.
   d. None of the above.

5. Which of the following is not a product cost?

   a. Depreciation on plant machinery.
   b. Salary of the production vice-president.
   c. Insurance associated with the delivery equipment.
   d. Property taxes associated with the factory building.

The Deland Construction Company began construction of an office building early in Year 1. The project, which was completed during Year 3, incurred costs as follows:

Year	Costs Incurred
1	$2,000,000
2	$2,500,000
3	$1,500,000

The contract price for the construction of the building was $9,000,000.

Assuming that Deland follows the completed contract method, use the information above in answering Questions 6 and 7.

6. How much revenue would Deland recognize in Year 1 on the office building contract?

   a. $3,000,000.
   b. $2,000,000.
   c. $1,000,000.
   d. -0-

_____   7. How much income would Deland recognize in Year 3 on the office building contract?

   a. $ 750,000.
   b. $1,500,000.
   c. $2,250,000.
   d. $3,000,000.

_____   8. Which of the following items would not appear on an Income Statement?

   a. Income from continuing operations.
   b. The effects of a change in accounting principles.
   c. The correction of a prior year's error.
   d. An extraordinary loss.

_____   9. The Orange Bottling Company owned a professional baseball team, which it sold on June 30, Year 1, for a gain of $36 million. This transaction is an example of which of the following?

   a. Income from Continuing Operations.
   b. Extraordinary gain.
   c. Gain from a discontinued operation.
   d. A change in accounting principle.

_____   10. The Work-in-Process account would not be debited for which of the following items?

   a. Direct labor costs.
   b. Manufacturing overhead costs.
   c. Selling and administrative costs.
   d. Costs of raw materials put into production.

The Pugh Company signed a contract late in Year 1 to construct a bridge for the Florida Department of Transportation. The contract price was $42,000,000. The schedule below summarizes the costs during the 3-year construction period:

Year	Construction Costs Incurred
2	$10,000,000
3	$15,000,000
4	$ 5,000,000

Assuming that Pugh follows the percentage-of-completion method, use the information above in answering Questions 11–13.

_____   11. How much income would Pugh recognize in Year 2 on the bridge contract?

   a. $ 4,000,000.
   b. $10,000,000.
   c. $12,000,000.
   d. $14,000,000.

_____ 12. How much income would Pugh recognize in Year 3 on the bridge contract?

    a. $21,000,000.
    b. $12,000,000.
    c. $10,000,000.
    d. $ 6,000,000.

_____ 13. How much income would Pugh recognize in Year 4 on the bridge contract?

    a. -0-
    b. $ 2,000,000.
    c. $ 7,000,000.
    d. $12,000,000.

_____ 14. Which of the following is not a period expense?

    a. Salary of the sales vice-president.
    b. Salaries of factory custodial employees.
    c. Salaries of administrative clerical personnel.
    d. Salaries of employees who deliver the finished product to customers.

_____ 15. Which of the following is the correct sequence of cost flows for a manufacturing firm?

    a. Work in Process, Finished Goods, Cost of Goods Sold, Raw Materials.
    b. Raw Materials, Work in Process, Finished Goods, Cost of Goods Sold.
    c. Cost of Goods Sold, Raw Materials, Work in Process, Finished Goods.
    d. Finished Goods, Work in Process, Raw Materials, Cost of Goods Sold.

_____ 16. The Zerbini Company reported a loss when a foreign government expropriated the assets of Zerbini's division in that country. The foreign government did not compensate Zerbini for the assets taken. This transaction is an example of which of the following?

    a. Loss from continuing operations.
    b. Extraordinary loss.
    c. Loss from a discontinued operation.
    d. A change in accounting principle.

_____ 17. Which of the following is not an inventory account?

    a. Work in Process.
    b. Cost of Goods Sold.
    c. Raw Materials.
    d. Finished Goods.

Columbus Land Development Company sold a residential lot to Mr. James for $50,000. The cost assigned to the lot by Columbus was $20,000. The contract calls for five annual payments of $10,000. Each payment was received, on time, at the end of each of the 5 years. Use the information above in answering Questions 18–20.

_____ 18. If Columbus recognizes income under the installment method, how much income would Columbus recognize in Year 1?

    a. $50,000.
    b. $30,000.
    c. $10,000.
    d. $ 6,000.

_____ 19. If Columbus recognizes income under the cost-recovery-first method, how much income would Columbus recognize in Year 2?

    a. -0-.
    b. $ 6,000.
    c. $10,000.
    d. $12,000.

_____ 20. If Columbus recognizes income under the cost-recovery-first method, how much income would Columbus recognize in Year 3?

    a. -0-.
    b. $ 6,000.
    c. $10,000.
    d. $18,000.

_____ 21. On January 1, Year 3, Fettig Company purchased some machinery for $500,000. The machinery had a 10-year life; a salvage value of $50,000; and was depreciated using straight-line depreciation. In Year 6, Fettig decided to switch from straight-line depreciation to the double declining balance method of depreciation. This is an example of which of the following?

    a. Extraordinary item.
    b. Discontinued operation.
    c. Change in accounting principle.
    d. Correction of an error.

The following information relates to Questions 22 and 23. At the beginning of the year, Stanley Company reported balances in Work-in-Process Inventory and Finished Goods Inventory, respectively, of $145,000 and $85,000. During the year, materials, labor, and overhead costs totaling $565,000 were added to production. Products costing $510,000 were transferred to finished goods during the year. At the end of the year, the balance in Finished Goods Inventory is $60,000.

_____ 22. What is the ending balance in the Work-in-Process Inventory account?

    a. $200,000.
    b. $185,000.
    c. $ 85,000.
    d. $120,000.

_____ 23. What amount should Stanley report as Cost of Goods Sold for the year?

    a. $595,000.
    b. $485,000.
    c. $565,000.
    d. $535,000.

The following information relates to Questions 24–27. Choose the answer to each question from the following four choices:

    a. Primary operating activity, which is recurring.
    b. Primary operating activity, which is nonrecurring.
    c. A recurring activity, which is peripheral to primary operations.
    d. A nonrecurring activity, which is peripheral to primary operations.

_____ 24. A manufacturing firm sold a parcel of land next to one of its warehouses.

_____ 25. A fast food restaurant chain sold a division that operated movie theaters.

_____ 26. A professional soccer team paid a signing bonus to one of its new players.

_____ 27. A Florida hotel chain's properties located on the "Emerald Coast" were destroyed when the area was devastated by an earthquake.

_____ 28. In assessing the quality of a firm's earnings, one factor to consider is the recurring or nonrecurring nature of various income items. Which of the following items would be considered in predicting a firm's future earnings performance?

    a. A loss which resulted from a hurricane.
    b. A gain on the sale of a discontinued operation.
    c. Losses reported by a fashion merchandising chain that resulted from style changes.
    d. A loss which resulted from an expropriation of the firm's assets located in a foreign country.

_____ 29. You are reviewing an annual report that presents the following common size income statements for a 3-year period:

	Year 1	Year 2	Year 3
Sales	100%	100%	100%
Cost of Goods Sold	(62%)	(65%)	(67%)
Selling and Administrative Expense	(18%)	(16%)	(15%)
Income before Taxes	20%	19%	18%

Which of the following statements is true?

a. The increasing "Cost of Goods Sold" percentage may indicate that the company has experienced difficulty in maintaining its markup on its merchandise.

b. The decreasing "Selling and Administrative Expense" percentage indicates that the company has been able to reduce its operating expenses as a percentage of sales over the 3-year period.

c. The increasing "Cost of Goods Sold" more than offsets the decreasing "Selling and Administrative Expenses."

d. All of the above statements are true.

_____ 30. Elmo Gibb, Inc., retired some of its outstanding bond obligations during the year. The company recorded a "Gain on Retirement of Bonds" of $750,000. How should this gain be reported on the company's income statement?

a. As part of income from continuing operations.

b. As a gain from discontinued operations.

c. As an extraordinary item.

d. As an adjustment for a change in accounting principles.

Exercises

1. The Howadel Company has completed its first year in business. Given the incomplete information in the four T-accounts below, answer the following questions.

Raw Materials Inventory		Work-in-Process Inventory	
		Labor 75,000	
		Overhead 36,000	
Balance 12/31 15,000		Balance 12/31 21,000	

Finished Goods Inventory		Cost of Goods Sold	
	120,000	120,000	
Balance 12/31 15,000			

a. Determine the amount of goods finished during the period and transferred to Finished Goods Inventory.

$ _____

b. Determine the amount of raw materials transferred to Work-in-Process Inventory during the period.

$ _____

81

c. Determine the amount of raw materials purchased during the period.

$ _____

d. Record all journal entries for the company's manufacturing activities during the period. Assume that the $36,000 overhead cost relates to depreciation on the factory building.

2. Given the following accounts and balances for Roberts Company for the year ending December 31, Year 5, prepare (a) a multiple-step income statement and (b) a single-step income statement.

Administrative Expense	$ 35,000
Cost of Goods Sold	115,000
Dividend Income	4,000
Gain on Sale	3,000
Income Tax Expense	20,000
Interest Expense	6,000
Interest Income	2,000
Loss on Sale	7,000
Sales Revenue	250,000
Selling Expenses	46,000

3.   On February 1, Year 1, Manley Construction Company contracted to build a portion of interstate high-way at a contract price of $45 million. A schedule of actual cash collections and contract costs for the 3-year contract is as follows:

Year 1	Cash Collections	Cost Incurred
1	$ 6,000,000	$ 8,000,000
2	23,000,000	18,000,000
3	16,000,000	10,000,000
	$45,000,000	$36,000,000

Contract costs on the 3-year project totaled $36 million and a $9 million profit was earned on the project.

Calculate the amount of net income (or profit) for each of the 3 years under the following revenue recognition methods:

(a) percentage-of-completion method.

(b) completed contract method.

(c) installment method.

(d) cost-recovery-first method.

4.   Marcks Company reported the following for the year ending December 31, Year 3:

Adjustment Gain for a Change in Accounting Principles (net of tax)	$ 100,000
Administrative Expenses	1,500,000
Cost of Goods Sold	12,000,000
Gain on Sale of Division (net of tax)	900,000
Loss from Expropriation of Assets by Foreign Government (net of tax)	500,000
Loss from Operations of Division Sold (net of tax)	700,000
Sales	20,000,000
Selling Expenses	2,500,000

The company's "Income from Continuing Operations" is taxed at a 30 percent rate.

Prepare an income statement for Marcks Company for the year ending December 31, Year 3.

Answers to Questions and Exercises

True/False

1.	T	6.	T	11.	F	16.	F	21.	T
2.	F	7.	T	12.	F	17.	T	22.	T
3.	F	8.	F	13.	T	18.	T	23.	F
4.	F	9.	F	14.	F	19.	T	24.	F
5.	T	10.	F	15.	T	20.	F	25.	T

Matching

1.	b	4.	c	7.	a	10.	a
2.	b	5.	a	8.	a		
3.	a	6.	c	9.	a		

Matching

1.	d	6.	c	11.	e	16.	e
2.	a	7.	b	12.	e	17.	c
3.	e	8.	e	13.	a	18.	b
4.	d	9.	d	14.	c	19.	e
5.	d	10.	c	15.	c	20.	c

Multiple Choice

1.	d	7.	d	13.	b	19.	a	25.	b
2.	c	8.	c	14.	b	20.	c	26.	a
3.	d	9.	c	15.	b	21.	c	27.	d
4.	a	10.	c	16.	b	22.	a	28.	c
5.	c	11.	a	17.	b	23.	d	29.	d
6.	d	12.	d	18.	d	24.	c	30.	c

Exercises

1.

Raw Materials Inventory		
Purchased	60,000	
		45,000
Balance 12/31	15,000	

Work-in-Process Inventory		
Materials	45,000	
Labor	75,000	
Overhead	36,000	135,000
Balance 12/31	21,000	

Finished Goods Inventory		
	135,000	120,000
Balance 12/31	15,000	

Cost of Goods Sold	
120,000	

a. $135,000.
b. $ 45,000.
c. $ 60,000.
d. Journal entries:

		Dr.	Cr.
(1)	Raw Materials Inventory	60,000	
	Cash or Accounts Payable		60,000
	To record purchase of raw materials.		
(2)	Work-in-Process Inventory	45,000	
	Raw Materials Inventory		45,000
	To record cost of raw materials transferred to work-in-process inventory.		
(3)	Work-in-Process Inventory	75,000	
	Cash or Salaries Payable		75,000
	To record salaries of factory workers.		
(4)	Work-in-Process Inventory	36,000	
	Accumulated Depreciation		36,000
	To record depreciation on factory building.		
(5)	Finished Goods Inventory	135,000	
	Work-in-Process Inventory		135,000
	To record cost of completed units transferred to finished goods storeroom.		
(6)	Cost of Goods Sold	120,000	
	Finished Goods Inventory		120,000
	To record cost of goods sold.		

2.   (a)

Roberts Company
Income Statement
For Year Ended December 31, Year 5

Sales Revenue			$250,000
Less Cost of Goods Sold			115,000
Gross Margin			$135,000
Less Operating Expenses:			
Selling	$46,000		
Administrative	35,000		81,000
Operating Income			$ 54,000
Other Income:			
Gain on Sale	$ 3,000		
Interest Income	2,000		
Dividend Income	4,000	$ 9,000	
Other Expenses:			
Interest Expense	$ 6,000		
Loss on Sale	7,000	(13,000)	(4,000)
Income before Taxes			$ 50,000
Income Tax Expense			20,000
Net Income			$ 30,000

(b)

Roberts Company
Income Statement
For Year End December 31, Year 5

Sales Revenue		$250,000
Gain on Sale		3,000
Interest Income		2,000
Dividend Income		4,000
Total Revenue		$259,000
Less Expenses:		
Cost of Goods Sold	$115,000	
Selling	46,000	
Administrative	35,000	
Interest	6,000	
Loss on Sale	7,000	
Income Taxes	20,000	229,000
Net Income		$ 30,000

3.

(a) Percentage-of-completion method:

Year	Incremental Percentage Complete		Revenue Recognized	Expenses Recognized	Net Income
1	8/36	(.222)	$10,000,000	$ 8,000,000	$2,000,000
2	18/36	(.50)	22,500,000	18,000,000	4,500,000
3	10/36	(.277)	12,500,000	10,000,000	2,500,000
	36/36	(1.000)	$45,000,000	$36,000,000	$9,000,000

(b) Completed contract method:

Year	Revenue Recognized	Expenses Recognized	Net Income
1	$ 0	$ 0	$ 0
2	0	0	0
3	45,000,000	36,000,000	9,000,000
	$ 45,000,000	$ 36,000,000	$9,000,000

(c) Installment method:

Year	Cash Collected (= Revenue)	Expense Fraction of Cash Collected	(Fraction × Total Cost)	Net Income
1	$ 6,000,000	6/45	$ 4,800,000	$1,200,000
2	23,000,000	23/45	18,400,000	4,600,000
3	16,000,000	16/45	12,800,000	3,200,000
	$45,000,000	1.0	$36,000,000	$9,000,000

(d) Cost-recovery-first method:

Year	Cash Collected (= Revenue)	Expenses Recognized	Net Income
1	$ 6,000,000	$ 6,000,000	$ 0
2	23,000,000	23,000,000	0
3	16,000,000	7,000,000	9,000,000
	$45,000,000	$36,000,000	$ 9,000,000

4.

Marcks Company

Income Statement

For Year Ending December 31, Year 3

<u>Income from Continuing Operations</u>

Sales	$ 20,000,000
Less Cost of Goods Sold	(12,000,000)
Gross Margin	$ 8,000,000
Less Operating Expenses:	
Administrative Expenses	(1,500,000)
Selling Expenses	(2,500,000)
Income from Continuing Operations before Taxes	$ 4,000,000
Income Taxes	(1,200,000)
Income from Continuing Operations	$ 2,800,000

<u>Income, Gains, and Losses from Discontinued Operations</u>

Loss from Operations of Division Sold (net of tax)	$ (700,000)
Gain on Sale of Division (net of tax)	900,000
Income from Discontinued Operations	$ 200,000
Income before Extraordinary Items and Adjustment for Change in Accounting Principles	$ 3,000,000

<u>Extraordinary Gains and Losses</u>

Loss from Expropriation of Assets (net of tax)	($ 500,000)

<u>Adjustment for Changes in Accounting Principles</u>

Change in Accounting Principle (net of tax)	$ 100,000
Net Income	$ 2,600,000

Statement of Cash Flows: Reporting the Effects of Operating, Investing, and Financing Activities on Cash Flows

Chapter Highlights

1. The statement of cash flows, the third major statement discussed in this text, reports the impact of a firm's operating, investing, and financing activities on cash flows during a period of time.

2. The revenues and expenses reported on the income statement will differ from the cash receipts and disbursements during a period for two principal reasons:

   a. The firm measures net income using the accrual basis of accounting. The recognition of revenues will not necessarily coincide with the receipts of cash from customers, and the recognition of expenses will not necessarily coincide with the disbursements of cash to suppliers, employees, and other creditors.

   b. The firm receives cash and makes cash disbursements not directly related to the process of generating earnings, such as from issuing capital stock or bonds, paying dividends, or purchasing buildings and equipment.

3. The statement of cash flows reports the amount of cash flow from three major activities:

   a. Operations
   b. Investing
   c. Financing

4. The statement of cash flows reports the principal inflows and outflows of cash from each of the major activities.

5. The operation component of the statement reports the net amount of cash generated from selling goods and providing services. Some firms follow the direct method, calculating cash flow from operations by listing all revenues that provide cash and subtracting all expenses that use cash. Most firms follow the indirect method of computing cash flows from operations by adjusting net income for noncash revenues and expenses.

6. The investing component reports the cash received from sales of investments and property, plant, and equipment and the cash paid for acquisition of investments and property, plant, and equipment.

7. Cash received from issuing debt or capital stock and cash paid for dividends and reacquisitions of debt or capital stock is reported in the financing segment of the statement of cash flows.

8. Ambiguities exist for classifying some cash transactions into either operations, investing, and financing activities. For example cash flows from interest and dividend revenues are correctly classified as operating activities. Some accountants might argue for classifying these revenues as investing activities, the classification of the related purchase and sale of investment in securities.

9. Some financing and investment transactions do not directly affect cash but must be disclosed either in the statement of cash flows or in a supplementary schedule. An example of such a transaction is the acquisition of a piece of land by issuing a mortgage.

10. The effects of various transactions on cash might be seen by reexamining the accounting equation. The accounting equation states that

$$\text{Assets} = \text{Liabilities} + \text{Shareholders' Equity}.$$
$$C + NCA = L + SE.$$

If the start-of-the-period and end-of-the-period balance sheets maintain the accounting equation, the following equation must also be valid:

$$\Delta C + \Delta NCA = \Delta L + \Delta SE.$$

Rearranging terms, we obtain the equation for changes in cash.

$$\Delta C = \Delta L + \Delta SE - \Delta NCA.$$

where

Δ – the change in an item, whether positive or negative from the beginning to the end of the period.

C = Cash
L = Liabilities
SE = Shareholders' Equity
NCA = Noncash Assets

The equation for changes in cash states that changes in cash (left-hand side) equal the causes of the changes in liabilities plus the changes in shareholders' equity less the change in noncash assets (right-hand side).

11. The procedures for constructing a statement of cash flows are as follows:
   a. Obtain balance sheets for the beginning and end of the period.
   b. Prepare a T-account work sheet. Start first with a master T-account for cash and show the beginning and ending balances in cash for the period. Also prepare T-accounts for all noncash accounts, showing the beginning and ending balance for these accounts for the period. The master T-account for cash would appear as follows:

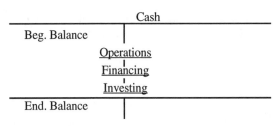

c. Explain the change in the master cash account by explaining the changes in the noncash accounts. Accomplish this by reconstructing, with the T-accounts, the entries originally recorded during the period. As the analytical reconstructing entries are made, changes in cash are indicated in the master cash account as an operations, investing, or financing cash flow item. The offsetting entries reflect the changes in the noncash accounts. In other words, if the reconstructed transactions explain the changes in the right-hand side of the cash equation, they will have explained the changes in cash itself on the left-hand side.

d. Prepare a formal statement of cash flows. Following the most popular format for the statement, the indirect method, the first item disclosed in the statement is the amount of cash generated by operations. This amount is usually derived by starting with net income and (1) adding back to net income the expenses not using cash and (2) deducting revenues not providing cash. A major item of expense that is added back to net income is depreciation expense. Because depreciation is added to net income, some readers of financial statements incorrectly conclude that depreciation expense is a source of cash. The reason an adjustment is needed is that the depreciation expense reduced net income but did not reduce cash. The reported net income understates the cash provided from operations by the amount of depreciation. The adjustment therefore adds back to net income the amount of depreciation expense that was deducted in arriving at net income. Transactions involving noncurrent assets affect cash in one of two ways: (1) cash is used when a noncurrent asset is acquired, and (2) cash is provided when a noncurrent asset is sold.

12. The cash flow from investing and financing activities are reported after cash flow from operations.

13. When a firm sells or purchases assets such as equipment, the cash received or cash disbursed is reported as an investing activity. When a sale generates cash different from the equipment book value, a gain or loss results. In the operations section of the statement of cash flows losses are added back to income and gains are deducted from income to offset their effect on income determination. Making these adjustments allows the gross cash flows of these type transactions to be presented as an investing activity. Other transactions affecting interpretation of the statement of cash flows will be illustrated in subsequent chapters.

14. Most countries outside the United States do not require a statement of cash flows. However, common practice in some countries includes a statement of sources and uses of funds. The definition for "funds" varies, but it usually has a broader definition than "cash." These statements of sources and uses of funds usually consists of a presentation of all sources of funds followed by all uses of funds. The statements do not classify funds-flow items into operations, investing, and financing activities.

15. The statement of cash flows provides information that may be used in the following:
    a. Assessing the impact of operations on liquidity;
    b. Assessing the relation between cash flow from operations, investing, and financing activities.

16. Users find interpreting a statement of cash flows requires an understanding of the economic characteristics of the firm's industry. The interpretation is also enhanced by examining the statement of cash flows over several years.

Questions and Exercises

True/False. For each of the following statements, place a T or F in the space provided to indicate whether the statement is true or false.

_____ 1. Cash flow from operations is always positive unless a company is in bankruptcy.

_____ 2. Cash flow from investing activities include cash received from sales of investments and cash paid for acquisition of property, plant, and equipment.

_____ 3. The statement of cash flows should explain changes in cash and cash equivalents that represent short-term, highly liquid investments.

_____ 4. The statement of cash flows is required in the United States and in most European countries.

_____ 5. The statement of sources and uses of funds is another name for the statement of cash flows.

_____ 6. The cash flow from investing section of the statement of cash flows is the same whether a firm follows the direct or indirect method of computing cash flow from operations.

_____ 7. The indirect method of computing cash flow from operations subtracts cash disbursements to suppliers, employees, and others from cash receipts from customers.

_____ 8. A cash flow for interest expense is shown in the statement of cash flows as a financing activity.

_____ 9. A cash flow for the purchase of marketable securities is shown in the statement of cash flows as an investing activity.

_____ 10. The gain on the sale of equipment is subtracted from net income in the cash flow from operations section of a statement of cash flows.

_____ 11. Since the exchange of a piece of land for a new machine does not involve cash, it should not be included in a statement of cash flows.

_____ 12. The fact that the balance in cash increased over time does not necessarily mean that the cash generated from operations was positive.

_____ 13. Depreciation is added back to net income in a statement of cash flows because it is a source of cash.

_____ 14. One difference between the income statement and the statement of cash flows is that the former is based upon the accrual basis of accounting and the latter is prepared on a cash basis.

_____ 15. If the balance in accounts receivable increases over the year, this means that the sales revenue exceeds the cash receipts.

_____ 16. Cash receipts from operations are the only source of funds for a company.

_____ 17. The declaration of dividends has no effect on cash.

_____ 18. The accounting equation expresses the change in a company's cash in the following manner:

$$\Delta C = \Delta L + \Delta SE + \Delta NCA$$

_____ 19. Cash flow from financing includes cash paid for retirement of debt but does not include cash paid for dividends.

_____ 20. Cash flow from operations includes cash received from sales of services.

_____ 21. A transaction involving an exchange of one piece of land for another piece of land most likely would not be disclosed in the firm's income statement or balance sheet, especially if there were no gain or loss.

_____ 22. It is correct to assume that, if a firm has a loss for a period of time, the firm has also decreased its liquidity.

_____ 23. If the beginning and ending balances in a building T-account are the same, no transactions affecting this account could have taken place during the year.

_____ 24. If the only noncurrent item to change was shareholders' equity, and it decreased, then cash must have increased.

_____ 25. The most important source of cash for successful firms is the return on funds invested in profitable securities.

_____ 26. Like the balance sheet and income statement, the statement of cash flows is generated as a regular output of the firm's record-keeping system.

_____ 27. An increase in accounts payable is added to net income in determining the cash flow from operations.

_____ 28. A decrease in inventory is added to net income in calculating the cash flow from operations.

_____ 29. A reason that revenues and expenses differ from cash receipts and disbursements is that the accrual basis of accounting is used in determining net income.

_____ 30. The statement of cash flows is related to both the balance sheet and the income statement, but also discloses information that is unavailable or only partially available by analysis of the balance sheet and income statements alone.

_____ 31. Accumulated depreciation increased by $10,000 during the year. As long as no depreciable assets have been retired during the year, this increase can be completely attributed to depreciation expense.

_____ 32. A possible explanation for the following analytical entry taken from a T-account work sheet is that bonds were issued for cash:

Cash (Financing)	XX	
Bonds Payable		XX

_____ 33. If a creditor allows a firm to owe money on account, this is effectively a use of cash to the firm.

_____ 34. When all other things remain the same, an increase in noncash assets causes cash to decline.

_____ 35. In determining cash from operations, depreciation expense is added to the net income since it represents a fund of cash set aside during the year for the replacement of long-lived assets.

_____   36. Financing and investing activities that do not directly affect cash do not need to be disclosed.

_____   37. Whenever there are sales on account, the amount of sales revenue will always exceed the amount of cash receipts.

_____   38. The statement of cash flows, although providing useful information to readers, is not considered a major financial statement.

_____   30. One of the most important factors not reported on the balance sheet and income statement is how the operations of the period affected the liquidity of the firm.

_____   40. Dividends are an example of a cash disbursement that did not affect operations.

Matching.

1.   For each transaction below, indicate the effects on cash and noncash accounts and place the letters for your answer in the space provided. The first one is shown as an example:

a	(a)	=	Increase (decrease) in cash
b	(b)	=	Increase (decrease) in liabilities
c	(c)	=	Increase (decrease) in shareholders' equity
d	(d)	=	Increase (decrease) in noncash assets

<u>a,(d)</u>   1. Sale of temporary investments, with no gain or loss.

_____   2. Collect accounts receivable.

_____   3. Paid cash to retire preferred stock.

_____   4. Purchased merchandise inventory on account.

_____   5. Recording of depreciation expense.

_____   6. Receipt of cash for delivery of merchandise next month.

_____   7. Acceptance of a 30-day note for an overdue account receivable.

_____   8. Early retirement of bonds due in 4 years.

_____   9. Prepayment for a 1-year insurance policy.

_____   10. Recognition of accrued interest expense, which is payable in 30 days, on long-term notes.

_____   11. Sale of used equipment with a gain.

_____   12. Pay accounts payable.

_____   13. Issuance of capital stock for cash.

_____   14. Borrowing on a 60-day note payable.

_____   15. Issuance of 10-year bonds.

_____   16. Payment of dividends previously declared.

_____   17. Purchase of equipment for cash.

_____   18. Accrual of income taxes to be paid in following year.

_____   19. Declaration of dividends to be paid in 30 days.

_____   20. Expiration of insurance policy during one year after purchase.

_____   21. Collection of 1-year note receivable from customer.

_____   22. Purchase of a plot of land in exchange for a mortgage payable.

2.   Using the designated letters, classify each of the following cash flows of the current period as either

   a. operating activity.
   b. investing activity.
   c. financing activity.

_____   1. Disbursement of $30,000 to acquire equipment.

_____   2. Receipt of $73,000 from customers for sales made this period.

_____   3. Disbursement of $81,000 for a patent.

_____   4. Disbursement of $6,300 to employees for services performed last period.

_____   5. Receipt of $200,000 from issuing bonds payable.

_____   6. Receipt of $27,000 from customers for sales made last period.

_____   7. Disbursement of $86,000 to merchandise suppliers.

_____   8. Disbursement of $17,000 for insurance for the next 18 months.

_____   9. Disbursement for dividends declared in the current year.

_____   10. Disbursement for acquisition of marketable securities.

3.   For each transaction below, indicate the effects on a statement of cash flows (indirect method) in one of the following ways:

   Cash flows from operations
   a. Net income will be increased or adjusted upward.
   b. Net income will be decreased or adjusted downward.

   Cash flows from investing
   c. Cash received.
   d. Cash paid.

   Cash flows from financing
   e. Cash received.
   f. Cash paid.

97

_____ 1. Purchase of a building for cash.

_____ 2. Paid cash dividends.

_____ 3. Sale of a long-term investment (no gain or loss).

_____ 4. Depreciation on equipment.

_____ 5. Sale of equipment with a gain.

_____ 6. Issuance of preferred stock.

_____ 7. Accounts Receivable increased during the period.

_____ 8. Issuance of long-term debt.

_____ 9. Sale of a building with a loss.

Multiple Choice. **Choose the best answer for each of the following questions and enter the identifying letter in the space provided.**

_____ 1. The Simon Company had a net loss of $160,000 in 1995. The additional facts are also given:

Depreciation expense	$ 30,000
Dividends paid	$ 40,000
Depreciation expense	$ 30,000
Increase in accounts payable	$ 15,000
Issuance of stock	$100,000
Retirement of debt	$ 50,000

What was the amount of cash flow from operations?

a. ($115,000).
b. $205,000.
c. ($ 75,000).
d. $ 65,000.

_____ 2. Referring to the question above, what was the net change in cash for 1995?

a. ($105,000).
b. $ 10,000.
c. $215,000.
d. ($165,000).

_____ 3. During 1995, the Jennings Company had a net income of $100,000. In addition, selected balance sheet accounts showed the following changes:

Accounts Receivable	$ 6,000 increase
Accounts Payable	2,000 increase
Building	8,000 decrease
Accumulated Depreciation	3,000 increase
Bonds Payable	16,000 increase

What was the amount of cash flow from operations?

a. $100,000.
b. $ 99,000.
c. $119,000.
d. $103,000.

_____ 4. The major components of the statement of cash flows include the following:

a. Cash flow from operations, cash flow from investing, and cash flow from financing.
b. Cash flow from operations, other sources of cash, and other uses of cash.
c. Sources of cash from investments, application of cash for financing activities, and other cash transactions.
d. Cash received from customers, cash paid to customers, and other sources of cash.

_____ 5. Which transaction below is presented as a cash flow from financing?

a. Cash paid for investments acquisition.
b. Cash received from sale of property, plant, and equipment.
c. Cash received from customers.
d. Cash paid for dividends.

_____ 6. Which of the following would be an addition to net income in determining cash flow from operations?

a. Increased accounts receivable.
b. Increased merchandise inventory.
c. Increased accounts payable.
d. Decreased notes payable to suppliers.

_____ 7. Which transaction listed below is shown on a statement of cash flow but does not affect cash?

a. Sale of bonds for cash.
b. Exchange of land for stock.
c. Collection of customer accounts.
d. Dividends paid to owners.

_____ 8. During 1995 the Schultz Company had net income of $150,000. In addition, selected additional facts are also given.

Depreciation expense	$ 21,000
Issuance of debt	$120,000
Loss on sale of equipment	$ 23,000
Purchase of building	$110,000
Increase in inventory	$ 12,000

What was the amount of cash flow from operations?

a. $182,000.
b. $171,000.
c. $159,000.
d. $138,000.

_____ 9. Depreciation expense

a. Provides cash from operations.
b. Should be added to net income in determining cash provided by operations.
c. Should be deducted from net income in determining cash provided by operations.
d. Is an example of cash expense.

_____ 10. The method of presenting cash from operations by listing all revenues providing cash followed by all expenses using cash is the

a. Direct method.
b. Operations method.
c. Indirect method.
d. Funds method.

_____ 11. The most popular method of presenting cash from operations in the statement of cash flows is the

a. Direct method.
b. Operations method.
c. Indirect method.
d. Funds method.

_____ 12. During 1995 the Winterline Company had net income of $312,000. In addition, selected additional facts are also given:

Decrease in accounts receivable	$10,000
Gain on sale of building	14,000
Increase in accounts payable	12,000
Issuance of common stock	90,000
Retirement of debt	45,000

What was the amount of cash flow from operations?

a. $334,000.
b. $322,000.
c. $320,000.
d. $324,000.

_____ 13. Cash received from issue of debt is shown as

a. Cash flow from operations.
b. Cash flow from investing.
c. Cash flow from financing.
d. A noncash transaction.

_____ 14. Cash received from sale of investment is shown as

a. Cash flow from operations.
b. Cash flow from investing.
c. Cash flow from financing.
d. A noncash transaction.

_____ 15. Cash paid for dividends is shown as

a. Cash flow from operations.
b. Cash flow from investing.
c. Cash flow from financing.
d. A noncash transaction.

_____ 16. Cash received from sale of services is shown as

a. Cash flow from operations.
b. Cash flow from investing.
c. Cash flow from financing.
d. A noncash transaction.

_____ 17. Cash paid for operating expenses is shown as

a. Cash flow from operations.
b. Cash flow from investing.
c. Cash flow from financing.
d. A noncash transaction.

_____ 18. Bonds Payable had the following balances at the beginning and end of 1995:

January 1	$100,000
December 31	$140,000

In addition $60,000 of bonds were retired in 1995. How much was issued during the year?

a. $100,000.
b. $ 20,000.
c. $160,000.
d. $180,000.

_____ 19. The Marier Company had the following selected amounts taken from its balance sheet.

	Building	Accumulated Depreciation
01/01/95	$800,000	$200,000
12/31/95	$785,000	$225,000

During 1995, a building having a cost of $100,000 was purchased. Was any building sold during the year, and if so, what was its original cost?

a. No, building was sold in 1995.
b. Yes, but its cost cannot be determined.
c. Yes, and its original cost was $85,000.
d. Yes, and its original cost was $115,000.

_____ 20. The balance in the Accumulated Depreciation account was $130,000 on 1/1/95 and $120,000 on 12/31/95. During 1995, an asset costing $100,000 (accumulated depreciation of $80,000) was sold for $20,000. What was the depreciation expense for 1995?

a. $ 10,000.
b. $ 90,000.
c. $110,000.
d. $ 70,000.

_____ 21. Which statement below is true concerning depreciation expense?

a. Depreciation expense increases the expense for a period but does not use cash.
b. Depreciation expense is added back to net income in determining funds from operations because it had originally been subtracted in computing net income but was not a use of cash.
c. Depreciation expense is not a source of funds.
d. All of the above are true.

_____ 22. Which statement below expresses the objective of the statement of cash flows?

a. To report the amount of cash flow from a firm's operating activities.
b. To report the principal inflows and outflows of cash from investing activities.
c. To report the principal inflows and outflows of cash from financing activities.
d. All of the above.

_____ 23. Which of the following would be a deduction from net income in determining cash flow from operations?

    a. Depreciation expense.

    b. Increased accounts receivable.

    c. Decreased accounts receivable.

    d. Increased accounts payable.

_____ 24. During the year 1995, the following changes took place:

Current Liabilities	$75,000 increase
Noncurrent Liabilities	45,000 decrease
Owners' Equity	51,000 decrease
Noncurrent Assets	42,000 increase
Current Assets (other than cash)	18,000 increase

What has been the change in cash for 1995?

    a. ($57,000).

    b. $30,000.

    c. $39,000.

    d. ($81,000).

_____ 25. The following items were found on an income statement: Sales of $600,000, Depreciation Expense of $320,000, Income Taxes of $160,000, and Other Expenses of $100,000. In addition, $80,000 of Common Stock was issued for cash during the year. What was the amount of cash from operations assuming that all noncash working capital balances did not change during the year?

    a. $ 20,000.

    b. $100,000.

    c. $420,000.

    d. $340,000.

_____ 26. Cash paid for land is shown as

    a. Cash flow from operations.

    b. Cash flow from investing.

    c. Cash flow from financing.

    d. A noncash transaction.

_____ 27. Common practice in countries outside the United States, particularly in Europe includes

    a. A statement of cash flows.

    b. A statement of financing activities.

    c. A statement of investing activities.

    d. A statement of sources and uses of funds.

Exercises

1. You are given below a list of several key transactions, along with other relevant information for Phillips Company in 1995. You are to prepare the Statement of Cash Flows for 1995.

    a. Net income for 1995 was $100,000.

    b. Depreciation expense for the year was $25,000, and patent amortization was $500.

    c. Dividends of $18,000 were paid in December.

    d. 10,000 shares of preferred stock were issued for total cash consideration of $350,000.

e. A piece of land was acquired for $20,000.

f. A $2,500 loan was made to one of the company's officers to be repaid in 1997.

g. A long-term investment, having originally cost $1,100, was sold for $1,100.

h. A used piece of equipment was sold for $8,500. It had an original cost of $20,000 and accumulated depreciation of $11,500.

i. The beginning cash balance was $40,000.

j. There were the following changes in other noncash working capital accounts.

Accounts Receivable	$27,000 Increase
Inventory	$16,000 Decrease
Accounts Payable	$11,000 Decrease

2.   Financial Statement dates for Hedgecock Company are presented below for the years ended December 31, 1994, and December 31, 1995.

Hedgecock Company
Comparative Balance Sheets

Assets	1995		1994	
		Year Ended December 31		
Current Assets				
Cash	$ 40,000		$ 42,000	
Accounts Receivable	60,000		34,000	
Inventories	100,000	$200,000	66,000	$142,000
Fixed Assets				
Land	$ 20,000		$ -0-	
Equipment (cost)	20,000		154,000	
Less Accumulated Depreciation	(60,000)	80,000	(64,000)	90,000
Intangibles				
Goodwill		20,000		22,000
Total Asset		$300,000		$254,000

Liabilities				
Current Liabilities				
Accounts Payable	$ 58,000		$ 48,000	
Notes Payable	70,000		-0-	
Interest Payable	2,000	$130,000	2,000	$ 50,000
Long-Term Liabilities				
Notes Payable, due in 1996		-0-		70,000
Total Liabilities		$130,000		$120,000
Shareholders' Equity				
Capital Stock	$ 80,000		$ 50,000	
Retained Earnings	90,000	$170,000	84,000	$134,000
Total Liabilities and Shareholders' Equity		$300,000		$254,000

Hedgecock Company
Income Statement
For the Year Ended December 31, 1995

Sales		$100,000
Deduct Expenses:		
Depreciation	$ 14,000	
Amortization of Goodwill	2,000	
Bad Debts Expense	1,400	
Income Tax	24,000	
Interest Expense	2,600	
Other Expenses	20,000	64,000
Net Income		$ 36,000

Hedgecock Company
Retained Earnings Statement
For the Year Ended December 31, 1995

Retained Earnings 1/1/95	$ 84,000
Plus Net Income	36,000
	120,000
Less Dividends	30,000
Retained Earnings 12/31/95	$ 90,000

Additional Information: There were no purchases of equipment during 1995. Equipment was sold in 1995 for its book value.

Prepare a T-account work sheet and a statement of cash flows for 1995.

3.

Engle Corporation
Statement of Cash Flows
For the Year Ended December 31, 1995

<u>Operations</u>

Net income	$6,000
Depreciation Exp.	700
Changes in Working Capital Accounts	(2,500)
Cash Flow from Operations	$4,200

<u>Investing</u>

Acquisition of Equipment	(2,200)

<u>Financing</u>

Issue of Common Stock	1,500
Change in Cash	3,500
Cash, January 1, 1995	700
Cash, December 31, 1995	$4,200

After preparing this condensed statement of cash flows for 1995, you discover that Engle sold a building on the last day of the year but failed to record it in the accounts or to deposit the check received from the purchases. The building originally cost $100,000 and had accumulated depreciation on $90,000 at the time of sale. Recast the statement of cash flows above assuming the Engle Corporation sold the building for cash in the following amounts (ignore income taxes):

a. $15,000.

b. $ 7,000.

Answers to Questions and Exercises

True/False

1.	F	8.	F	15.	T	22.	F	29.	T	36.	F
2.	T	9.	T	16.	F	23.	F	30.	T	37.	F
3.	T	10.	T	17.	T	24.	F	31.	T	38.	F
4.	F	11.	F	18.	F	25.	F	32.	T	39.	T
5.	F	12.	T	19.	F	26.	F	33.	F	40.	T
6.	T	13.	F	20.	T	27.	T	34.	T		
7.	F	14.	T	21.	T	28.	T	35.	F		

Matching

1.
1.	a,(d)	6.	a,b	11.	a,(d),c	16.	(b),(a)	21.	a,(d)
2.	a,(d)	7.	d,(d)	12.	(b),(a)	17.	d,(a)	22.	d,b
3.	(c),(a)	8.	(b),(a)	13.	a,c	18.	(c),b		
4.	d,b	9.	d,(a)	14.	a,b	19.	(c),b		
5.	(c),(d)	10.	(c),b	15.	a,b	20.	(c),(d)		

2.
1.	b	3.	b	5.	c	7.	a	9.	c
2.	a	4.	a	6.	a	8.	a	10.	b

3.
1.	d	3.	c	5.	c,b	7.	b	9.	c,a
2.	f	4.	a	6.	e	8.	e		

Multiple Choice

1.	a	6.	c	11.	c	16.	a	21.	d	26.	b
2.	a	7.	b	12.	c	17.	a	22.	d	27.	d
3.	b	8.	a	13.	c	18.	a	23.	b		
4.	a	9.	b	14.	b	19.	d	24.	d		
5.	d	10.	a	15.	c	20.	d	25.	d		

Exercises

1.

Phillips Company
Statement of Cash Flows
For the Year Ended December 31, 1995

Operations:		
Net Income	$100,000	
Additions:		
Depreciation Expense Not Using Cash	25,000	
Patent Amortization Not Using Cash	500	
Decreased Merchandise Inventory	16,000	
Subtractions:		
Increased Accounts Receivable	(27,000)	
Decreased Accounts Payable	(11,000)	
Cash Flow from Operations		$103,500
Investing:		
Acquisition of Land	$(20,000)	
Loan to Officer	(2,500)	
Sale of Long-Term Investment	1,100	
Sale of Equipment	8,500	
Cash Flow from Investments		(12,900)
Financing:		
Dividends Paid	$ (18,000)	
Issue Preferred Stock	$350,000	
Cash Flow from Financing		332,000
Net Change in Cash		$422,600
Cash, January 1, 1995		40,000
Cash, December 31, 1995		$462,600

2.

Hedgecock Company
T-Account Work Sheet

Cash

	✓ 42,000		

Operations

(1)	Net Income	36,000	26,000	Accounts Rec. Incr.	(4)
(2)	Depreciation	14,000	34,000	Inventories Incr.	(5)
(3)	Amortization	2,000			
(6)	Accounts Payable Incr.	10,000			

Investing

(9)	Sale of Equipment	16,000	20,000	Acquisition of Land	(8)

Financing

(10)	Sale of Stock	30,000	30,000	Dividends	(7)

	40,000		

Accounts Receivable		Inventories		Land	
✓ 34,000		✓ 66,000			
(4) 26,000		(5) 34,000		(8) 20,000	
60,000		100,000		20,000	

Equipment		Interest Payable		Accounts Payable	
✓ 154,000	34,000 (9)		2,000 ✓		48,000 ✓
					10,000 (6)
120,000			2,000		58,000

Goodwill		Acc. Depreciation		Notes Payable	
22,000	2,000	(9) 18,000	64,000 ✓		70,000✓
			14,000(2)		
20,000			60,000		70,000*

*Reclassified to current liability.

Capital Stock		Retained Earnings	
	50,000 ✓		84,000 ✓
	30,000 (10)	(7) 30,000	36,000 (1)
	80,000		90,000

Hedgecock Company
Statement of Cash Flows
For the Year Ended December 31, 1995

Operations:

Net Income		$36,000	
Additions			
Depreciation	$14,000		
Amortization	2,000		
Accounts Payable Increase	10,000		
Deductions			
Accounts Receivable Increase	(26,000)		
Inventories Increase	(34,000)	(34,000)	
Cash Flow from Operations			$ 2,000

Investing:

Sale of Equipment		$16,000	
Acquisition of Land		(20,000)	
Cash Flow from Investments			(4,000)

Financing:

Sale of Stock		$30,000	
Paid Dividends		(30,000	
Cash Flow from Financing			-0-
Net Decrease in Cash			$ (2,000)
Cash, January 1, 1995			42,000
Cash, December 31, 1995			$40,000

Engle Corporation
Statement of Cash Flows
For Year Ended December 31, 1995

Operations	(a)	(b)
Net Income (includes $5,000 Gains in (a) and $3,000 Loss in (b)	$11,000	$ 3,000
Depreciation	700	700
(Gain) Loss on Sale of Building	(5,000)	3,000
Changes in Working Capital Account	(2,500)	(2,500)
Cash Flow from Operation	$ 4,200	$ 4,200
Investing		
Acquisition of Equipment	(2,200)	(2,200)
Sale of Building	15,000	7,000
Cash Flow from Investing	$12,800	$ 4,800
Financing		
Issue of Common Stock	$ 1,500	$ 1,500
Changes in Cash	18,500	10,500
Cash, January 1, 1995	700	700
Cash, December 31, 1995	$19,200	$11,200

Chapter 6

Introduction to Financial Statement Analysis

Chapter Highlights

1. When comparing investment alternatives, the investor's decision is based on the return anticipated from each investment and the risk associated with that return. Most financial statement analysis, therefore, is directed at some aspect of a firm's profitability or its risk.

2. Ratios are useful tools in financial statement analysis because they conveniently summarize data in a form that is more easily understood, interpreted, and compared. Ratios should be used carefully. Once calculated, the ratio must be compared with some criterion or standard. Several possible criteria might be used: (a) the planned ratio for the period being analyzed; (b) the value of the ratio during the preceding period for the same firm; (c) the value of the ratio for a similar firm in the same industry; or (d) the average ratio for other firms in the same industry.

3. Three measures of profitability are (a) rate of return on assets; (b) rate of return on common shareholders' equity; and (c) earnings per common share.

4. The rate of return on assets is a measure of a firm's performance in using assets to generate earnings independent of the financing of those assets. The rate of return on assets relates the results of operating performance to the investments of a firm without regard to how the firm financed the acquisition of those investments. The rate of return is computed as follows:

$$\frac{\text{Net Income} + \text{Interest Expense (Net of Tax Savings)}}{\text{Average Total Assets}}.$$

5. The rate of return on assets is dependent upon a firm's profit margin ratio and total asset turnover ratio. The relationship between the three ratios can be expressed as follows:

$$\text{Rate of Return on Assets} = \frac{\text{Profit Margin}}{\text{Ratio}} \times \frac{\text{Total Assets}}{\text{Turnover}}.$$

Therefore, an improvement in the rate of return on assets can be accomplished by increasing the profit margin ratio, the rate of assets turnover, or both.

6. The profit margin ratio, the percentage of net income plus interest expense (net of tax savings) to sales, is a measure of a firm's ability to control the level of costs, or expenses, relative to sales. By controlling

costs, a firm will be able to increase the profits from a given amount of sales and improve its profit margin ratio.

7. To identify the reasons for a change in the profit margin ratio, changes in a firm's expenses must be examined. Any important expense can be watched by management by comparing the expense with sales in an effort to note the trend of the expense and to take prompt action to control the expense if it appears to be getting out of line.

8. The total assets turnover, the ratio of sales to average total assets during the period, provides a measure of the sales generated for each dollar invested in assets. Changes in the total assets turnover ratio can be analyzed by computing an accounts receivable turnover, an inventory turnover, and a plant asset turnover.

9. The accounts receivable turnover, which is computed by dividing net sales on account by average accounts receivable, gives an indication of how soon accounts receivable will be converted into cash. The average number of days that accounts receivable are outstanding can be computed by dividing 365 days by the accounts receivable turnover. The average number of days can be compared with the firm's credit sale terms to determine if any corrective action is needed in the firm's credit and collection activity.

10. The inventory turnover indicates how frequently firms sell inventory items. It is computed by dividing cost of goods sold by average inventory. The average number of days that merchandise is held can be computed by dividing 365 days by the inventory turnover.

11. The plant asset turnover, which is computed by dividing sales by average plant assets during the year, is a measure of the relationship between sales and the investment in plant assets.

12. The rate of return on assets must be allocated between the various providers of capital: creditors, preferred shareholders, and common shareholders. The common shareholders have a residual claim on all earnings after creditors and preferred shareholders have received amounts contractually owed them.

13. The rate of return on common shareholders' equity measures a firm's performance in generating earnings that are assignable to the common shareholders' equity. The ratio is computed as follows:

$$\frac{\text{Net Income - Dividends on Preferred Stock}}{\text{Average Common Shareholders' Equity}}.$$

This measure of profitability assesses a firm's performance in using assets to generate earnings and explicitly considers the financing of those assets. The rate of return on common shareholders' equity will exceed the rate of return on assets if the rate of return on assets exceeds the after-tax cost of debt capital.

14. Financing with debt and preferred stock to increase the return to the residual common shareholders' equity is referred to as financial leverage. The common shareholders benefit from leverage when capital contributed by creditors and preferred shareholders earns a greater rate of return than the payments made to creditors and preferred shareholders.

15. In financial leverage, the common shareholders take extra risk (because the firm incurred debt obligations with fixed payments dates) for a potentially higher return. As more debt is added to the capital structure, the risk of default or insolvency increases and lenders will require a higher return to compensate for this additional risk. A point will be reached where leverage can no longer increase the potential rate of return to common shareholders' equity because the cost of the debt will exceed the rate of return that can be earned on assets.

16. The rate of return on common shareholders' equity can be disaggregated as follows:

$$
\begin{array}{c}
\text{Rate of Return} \\
\text{on Common} \\
\text{Shareholders'} \\
\text{Equity}
\end{array}
=
\begin{array}{c}
\text{Profit Margin} \\
\text{Ratio (after} \\
\text{Interest Expense} \\
\text{\& Preferred} \\
\text{Dividends)}
\end{array}
\times
\begin{array}{c}
\text{Total Assets} \\
\text{Turnover} \\
\text{Ratio}
\end{array}
\times
\begin{array}{c}
\text{Leverage} \\
\text{Ratio}
\end{array}
$$

17. The leverage ratio indicates the extent to which total assets have been provided by common shareholders. The ratio is computed as follows:

$$
\frac{\text{Average Total Assets}}{\text{Average Common Shareholders' Equity}}.
$$

The larger the leverage ratio, the smaller the portion of capital provided by common shareholders and the larger the proportion provided by creditors and preferred shareholders. Therefore, the larger the leverage ratio, the greater the extent of financial leverage.

18. Earnings per share of common stock is computed as follows:

$$
\frac{\text{Net Income - Preferred Stock Dividends}}{\begin{array}{c}\text{Weighted Average Number of Common}\\\text{Shares Outstanding}\end{array}}.
$$

Earnings per share amounts are often compared with the market price of the stock. This is called a price-earnings ratio and is computed as follows:

$$
\frac{\text{Market Price per Share}}{\text{Earnings per Share}}.
$$

19. A dual presentation of primary and fully diluted earnings per share is required when a firm has outstanding securities that, if exchanged for shares of common stock, would decrease earnings per share by 3 percent or more. Primary earnings per share is the amount of earnings attributable to each share of the total of common stock and common stock equivalents. Fully diluted earnings per share is the amount of earnings per share reflecting the maximum dilution that would occur if all options, warrants, and convertible securities outstanding at the end of the accounting period were exchanged for common stock.

20. Common stock equivalents are securities whose principal value arises from their capability of being exchanged for, or converted into, common stock rather than from the securities' own periodic cash yields. Stock options and warrants are always common stock equivalents. Convertible bonds and convertible preferred stock may or may not be common stock equivalents.

21. When assessing risk, the focus is generally on the firm's relative liquidity. Cash and near-cash assets provide a firm with the resources needed to adapt to the various types of risk. Four measures for assessing short-term liquidity risk are (a) current ratio; (b) quick ratio; (c) operating cash flow to current liabilities; and (d) working capital turnover ratios.

22. The current ratio, which is calculated by dividing current assets by current liabilities, is of particular significance to short-term creditors because it indicates the ability of the firm to meet its short-term obligations. The quick ratio, or acid test ratio, is computed by including in the numerator of the fraction only those current assets that could be converted into cash quickly (cash, marketable securities, and receivables).

23. The current ratio and quick ratio are criticized because they are calculated using amounts at a specific point in time. The cash flow from operations to current liabilities ratio, which is calculated by dividing cash flow from operations by average current liabilities, overcomes this deficiency. A ratio of 40 percent or more is common for a healthy firm.

24. The operating cycle of a firm is a sequence of activities in which (a) inventory is purchased on account from suppliers; (b) inventory is sold on account to customers; (c) customers pay amounts due; and (d) suppliers are paid amounts due. The longer the cycle, the longer the time that funds are tied up in receivables and inventories and the less liquid is the firm.

25. The operating cycle of a firm can be evaluated by computing several ratios. The inventory turnover ratio indicates the length of the period between the purchase and sale of inventory during each operating cycle. The accounts receivable turnover ratio indicates the length of the period between the sale of inventory and the collection of cash from customers during each operating cycle. The accounts payable turnover ratio indicates the length of the period between the purchase of inventory on account and the payment of cash to suppliers during each operating cycle. The accounts payable turnover ratio is computed by dividing purchases on account by average accounts payable.

26. Measures of long-term liquidity risk are used in assessing the firm's ability to meet interest and principal payments on long-term debt and similar obligations as they become due. A good indicator of long-term liquidity risk is a firm's ability to generate profits over a period of years. If a firm is profitable, it will either generate sufficient cash from operations or be able to obtain needed capital from creditors and owners. In addition to measures of profitability, three other measures of long-term liquidity risk are debt ratios, the cash flow from operations to total liabilities ratio, and the interest coverage ratio.

27. The long-term debt ratio (which is calculated by dividing total long-term debt by the sum of total long-term debt and total shareholders' equity) and the debt-equity ratio (which is calculated by dividing total liabilities by total equities) are used to measure a firm's long-term liquidity risk. These ratios must be evaluated in relation to the stability of the firm's earnings and cash flows from operations. In general, the more stable the earnings, the higher the debt ratio that is considered acceptable or safe.

28. The debt ratios do not consider the availability of liquid assets to cover various levels of debt. A ratio that overcomes this deficiency is the cash flow from operations to total liabilities ratio. The ratio is calculated as follows:

$$\frac{\text{Cash Flow from Operations}}{\text{Average Total Liabilities}}.$$

A financially healthy company normally has a cash flow from operations to total liabilities ratio of 20 percent or more.

29. Another measure of long-term liquidity risk, the number of times that earnings cover interest charges, is calculated by dividing net income before interest and income taxes by interest charges. The interest coverage ratio is used to indicate the relative protection of bondholders and to assess the probability of a firm's failing to meet required interest payments.

30. Accountants use the term "pro forma financial statements" to refer to financial statements prepared under a particular set of assumptions. The usefulness of the pro forma financial statements depends on the reasonableness of those assumptions.

118

31. The preparation of pro forma financial statements typically begins with the income statement, followed by the balance sheet and then the statement of cash flows. The level of operating activity usually dictates the amount of assets required, which in turn affects the level of financing needed. Amounts for the statement of cash flows flow directly from the income statement and comparative balance sheets.

32. Managers, security analysts, and others analyze financial statements (both historical and pro forma) to form judgements about the market value of a firm. One approach to approximating market value projects the amount of cash flows a firm will generate from operating and investing activities over some number of years in the future and discounts this net amount at an appropriate discount rate to find the present value of these future cash flows.

33. Other approaches to approximating a firm's market value rely on market multiples of certain financial statement items for similar firms in the market. One common valuation approach relates market prices to multiples of earnings. Another valuation approach relates market values to the book values of common shareholders' equity of similar firms.

Questions and Exercises

True/False. **For each of the following statements, place a T or F in the space provided to indicate whether the statement is true or false.**

_____ 1. The leverage ratio indicates the extent to which total assets have been provided by common shareholders.

_____ 2. A point will be reached where financial leverage can no longer increase the potential rate of return to common shareholders' equity.

_____ 3. The quick ratio is a measure of the relationship between sales and the investment in plant assets.

_____ 4. The cash flow from operations to total liabilities ratio is one measure of long-term liquidity risk.

_____ 5. To determine the amount of earnings assignable to the common shareholders, any dividends on preferred stock declared during the period must be deducted from net income.

_____ 6. In some situations, it may be preferable to compute the number of times that earnings cover interest charges by using cash flows rather than earnings in the numerator.

_____ 7. In computing the quick ratio, inventories are usually omitted from the listing of assets that can be converted into cash quickly.

_____ 8. In computing the rate of return on common shareholders' equity, dividends on preferred stock must be added to net income.

_____ 9. If the common stock of the Burrell Company is selling for $50 per share and the earnings per share for the current year is $2, then the price-earnings ratio is 100 to 1.

_____ 10. If the average number of days that an accounts receivable is outstanding is about 46 days, the accounts receivable turnover for the year is about six times.

_____ 11. A dual presentation of primary and fully diluted earnings per share is required when a firm has outstanding securities that, if exchanged for more shares of common stock, would decrease earnings per share by 3 percent or more.

_____ 12. Financial leverage increases the rate of return on common shareholders' equity when the rate of return on assets is less than the after-tax cost of debt.

_____ 13. Rate of return on assets is computed using income before deducting any payment or distributions to the providers of capital.

_____ 14. Primary earnings per share is the amount of earnings per share reflecting the maximum dilution that would occur if all options, warrants, and convertible securities outstanding at the end of the accounting period were exchanged for common stock.

_____ 15. The operating cash flow from operations to average current liabilities is a measure of profitability.

_____ 16. The current ratio is susceptible to "window dressing" by completing certain transactions just before the end of the period.

_____ 17. A person concerned with the long-term liquidity risk of a firm is primarily interested in whether the firm will have sufficient cash available to pay current debt.

_____ 18. In computing the rate of return on assets, the denominator should reflect average total assets during the year.

_____ 19. The rate of return on assets can be disaggregated into two other ratios as follows:

$$\text{Rate of Return on Assets} = \text{Profit Margin Ratio} \times \text{Current Ratio} .$$

_____ 20. The rate of return on assets measures the profitability of a firm before any payments to the suppliers of capital.

_____ 21. Ratios are more meaningful if they are compared to a budgeted standard or an industry standard.

_____ 22. Improving the rate of return on assets can be accomplished by increasing the profit margin ratio, the rate of asset turnover, or both.

_____ 23. If the inventory of a company turns over five times each year, the average number of days that merchandise is held during the year is 73 days.

_____ 24. The long-term debt ratio is calculated by dividing total liabilities by total equities.

_____ 25. The shorter the time that funds are tied up in receivables and inventories, the shorter the operating cycle.

_____ 26. The accounts payable turnover ratio indicates the length of the period between the purchase of inventory on account and the payment of cash to suppliers.

_____ 27. The preparation of pro forma financial statements usually begins with the preparation of a statement of cash flows.

_____ 28. The interest coverage ratio is used to indicate the relative protection of bondholders and to assess the probability of a firm's failing to meet required interest payments.

_____ 29. The accounts payable turnover is computed by dividing cost of goods sold by average accounts payable.

_____ 30. The inventory turnover ratio indicates the length of the period between the sale of inventory and the collection of cash from customers.

Matching. From the list of terms below, select that term which is most closely associated with each of the descriptive phrases or statements that follows and place the letter for that term in the space provided.

a. Accounts Payable Turnover
b. Accounts Receivable Turnover
c. Cross-Section Analysis
d. Current Ratio
e. Debt-Equity Ratio
f. Earnings Per Share
g. Financial Leverage
h. Interest Coverage Ratio
i. Inventory Turnover
j. Liquidity
k. Long-Term Debt Ratio

l. Cash Flow from Operations to Current Liabilities
m. Cash Flow from Operations to Total Liabilities
n. Plant Asset Turnover
o. Pro Forma Financial Statements
p. Profit Margin Ratio (before interest effects)
q. Quick Ratio
r. Rate of Return on Assets
s. Rate of Return on Common Shareholders' Equity
t. Time-Series Analysis
u. Total Assets Turnover

_____ 1. This ratio is a measure of a firm's ability to control the level of costs, or expenses, relative to sales.

_____ 2. This ratio provides a measure of the sales generated for each dollar invested in assets.

_____ 3. This ratio indicates the number of times that the average inventory has been sold during the period.

_____ 4. This ratio measures the firm's performance in generating earnings that are assignable to the common shareholders' equity.

_____ 5. Refers to a firm's financing with debt and preferred stock to increase the return to the common shareholders' equity.

_____ 6. This ratio is computed by dividing net income attributable to common stock by the average number of common shares outstanding during the period.

_____ 7. This ratio is supposed to indicate the ability of the firm to meet its current obligations.

_____ 8. This ratio generally includes cash, marketable securities, and accounts receivable in its numerator.

_____ 9. This ratio is computed by dividing cash flow from operations by average current liabilities.

_____ 10. This ratio considers the availability of liquid assets to cover various levels of debt. For a financially healthy firm, the ratio should be 20 percent or more.

_____ 11. Refers to the "nearness of cash" of a firm's assets.

_____ 12. This analysis involves comparing a given firm's ratios with those of other firms for a particular period.

_____ 13. This ratio indicates the proportion of total capital supplied by creditors.

_____ 14. This ratio is used to indicate the relative protection of bondholders and to assess the probability of a firm's failing to meet required interest payments.

_____ 15. This ratio provides a measure of the sales generated for each dollar invested in plant assets.

_____ 16. This ratio assesses the firm's operating performance independently of financing decisions.

_____ 17. This ratio measures how many times during each period accounts receivable are turned over (or converted to cash).

_____ 18. This ratio indicates the proportion of a firm's long-term capital that is provided by creditors.

_____ 19. Financial statements prepared using a particular set of assumptions.

_____ 20. This ratio indicates the length of the period between the purchase of inventory on account and the payment of cash to suppliers.

_____ 21. This analysis involves comparing the changes in a firm's ratios over a multiple-year period.

Multiple Choice. **Choose the best answer for each of the following questions and enter the identifying letter in the space provided.**

_____ 1. Which of the following is not used to assess short-term liquidity risk?

    a. Accounts Receivable Turnover.
    b. Operating Cash Flow to Current Liabilities Ratio.
    c. Current Ratio.
    d. Quick Ratio.

_____ 2. Which of the following is not a working capital turnover ratio?

    a. Accounts Payable Turnover Ratio.
    b. Inventory Turnover Ratio.
    c. Current Ratio.
    d. Accounts Receivable Turnover Ratio.

_____ 3. The Arcadia Company sells on credit with terms of "net 30 days." If the company's credit policy and collection activity is working efficiently, how many times should the company's accounts receivable turn over in a year?

    a. Approximately 6 times.
    b. Approximately 8 times.
    c. Approximately 10 times.
    d. Approximately 12 times.

_____ 4. Which of the following ratios would not be used in assessing a firm's long-term liquidity risk?

    a. Debt-Equity Ratio.

    b. Long-Term Debt Ratio.

    c. Interest Coverage Ratio.

    d. Current Ratio.

_____ 5. This ratio is a useful measure for assessing a firm's performance in using assets to generate earnings.

    a. Profit Margin Ratio.

    b. Financial Leverage.

    c. Rate of Return on Assets.

    d. Working Capital.

_____ 6. Which of the following is not a component of the rate of return on common shareholders' equity?

    a. Leverage Ratio.

    b. Profit Margin Ratio.

    c. Total Assets Turnover Ratio.

    d. All three of the above ratios are components of the rate of return on common shareholders' equity.

_____ 7. The phenomenon of common shareholders trading extra risk for a potentially higher return is called

    a. Financial Leverage.

    b. Operating Leverage.

    c. Liquidity.

    d. Interest Coverage Ratio.

_____ 8. Assume that the current ratio of the Sarasota Company is 2.5 to 1. What effect would an equal dollar increase in current assets and current liabilities have on the current ratio?

    a. Increase the current ratio.

    b. Decrease the current ratio.

    c. No effect on the current ratio.

    d. Answer cannot be determined from information given.

_____ 9. Which of the following is not a measure of profitability?

    a. Rate of Return on Assets.

    b. Accounts Payable Turnover Ratio.

    c. Rate of Return on Common Shareholders' Equity.

    d. Earnings Per Common Share.

_____ 10. Which of the following transactions would result in an increase in a company's current ratio?

    a. Declaring cash dividend payable next period.

    b. Paying long-term debt.

    c. Paying accounts payable.

    d. Borrowing money on a 6-month note.

_____ 11. A company wants to increase its rate of return on assets from 8 percent to 14 percent. It is believed that the firm's total assets turnover of .667 cannot be easily increased at the present time. What must the profit margin percentage be to achieve the desired 14 percent rate of return on assets?

    a. 7 percent.
    b. 14 percent.
    c. 21 percent.
    d. 28 percent.

_____ 12. Comparisons of a given firm's ratios with those of other firms for a particular period is referred to as

    a. Times-Series Analysis.
    b. Defensive Interval Analysis.
    c. Cross-Section Analysis.
    d. None of the above.

_____ 13. If a company's rate of return on assets is 20 percent and the profit margin percentage is 5 percent, the company's total assets turnover must be which of the following?

    a. 1.
    b. 4.
    c. 5.
    d. 20.

_____ 14. The Rate of Return on Assets can be disaggregated into two other ratios. Which of the following is one of the two ratios?

    a. Plant Asset Turnover Ratio.
    b. Debt-Equity Ratio.
    c. Profit Margin Ratio.
    d. Inventory Turnover Ratio.

_____ 15. In computing the quick ratio, which of the following items is customarily excluded from the numerator?

    a. Cash.
    b. Inventory.
    c. Marketable Securities.
    d. Accounts Receivable.

_____ 16. Assume that the debt-equity ratio of the Chandler Company is .5 to 1. If the company issued a long-term note in the purchase of some land, what effect would this transaction have on the debt-equity ratio?

    a. Decrease debt-equity ratio.
    b. Increase debt-equity ratio.
    c. No effect on the debt-equity ratio.
    d. Answer cannot be determined from information given.

_____ 17. Which of the following ratios uses "Sales" in its numerator?

    a. Total Assets Turnover Ratio.

    b. Profit Margin Ratio.

    c. Plant Asset Turnover Ratio.

    d. Both a and c use "Sales" in their numerators.

_____ 18. Financial leverage can increase the return to common shareholders as long as

    a. The rate of return earned on assets equals the rate paid for the capital used to acquire those assets.

    b. The rate of return earned on assets is less than the rate paid for the capital used to acquire those assets.

    c. The rate of return earned on assets exceeds the rate paid for the capital used to acquire those assets.

    d. The firm has a "good" earnings year.

_____ 19. Which of the following ratios would probably not be used to analyze the total assets turnover ratio?

    a. Plant Asset Turnover.

    b. Accounts Receivable Turnover.

    c. Inventory Turnover.

    d. Long-Term Debt Ratio.

_____ 20. In computing the rate of return on assets, interest expense net of income tax savings is added to net income. Assume that the RBC Company has interest expense of $10 million and net income of $25 million. Assume that the income tax rate is 30 percent. In computing the rate of return on assets, the numerator would be

    a. $28 million.

    b. $32 million.

    c. $35 million.

    d. None of the above.

Exercises

1. The Comparative Balance Sheets for Year 1 and Year 2 and the Year 2 Income Statement for Joanne's Costume Shop are as follows:

Joanne's Costume Shop
Balance Sheet

Assets	12/31 Year 2	12/31 Year 1
Cash	$ 50,000	$ 15,000
Accounts Receivable	100,000	150,000
Inventory	300,000	200,000
Property, Plant, and Equipment	700,000	735,000
Total Assets	$1,150,000	$1,100,000

Liabilities and Shareholders' Equity	12/31 Year 2	12/31 Year 1
Accounts Payable	$ 189,000	$ 250,000
5% Mortgage Payable	400,000	415,000
Common Stock (150,000 shares outstanding)	300,000	300,000
Retained Earnings	261,000	135,000
Total Equities	$1,150,000	$1,100,000

Joanne's Costume Shop
Income Statement
For Year Ended December 31, Year 2

Sales on Account		$900,000
Less Expenses:		
Cost of Sales	$ 500,000	
Salary Expense	165,000	
Depreciation Expense	35,000	
Interest Expense	20,000	
Total Expenses		$720,000
Income before Taxes		$180,000
Income Tax Expense (30% rate)		54,000
Net Income		$126,000

Compute the following ratios for Joanne's Costume Shop for Year 2.

a. Current ratio.

b. Quick ratio (inventory cannot be quickly converted to cash).

c. Debt-equity ratio.

d. Rate of return on assets.

e. Rate of return on common shareholders' equity.

f. Earnings per share of common stock.

g. Profit margin ratio (before interest expense and related income tax effects).

h. Total assets turnover.

i. Interest coverage ratio.

j. Inventory turnover.

k. Average number of days inventory on hand.

l. Accounts receivable turnover.

m. Average collection period for accounts receivable.

n. Long-term debt ratio.

o. Plant asset turnover ratio.

p. Leverage ratio.

q. Accounts payable turnover ratio.

r. Profit margin ratio (after interest expense and preferred dividends).

2.   This exercise is a continuation of Exercise 1, Joanne's Costume Shop.

a. Disaggregate the rate of return on assets into its two components:

Rate of Return on Assets	=	Profit Margin Ratio (before interest expense and related income tax effects)	×	Total Assets Turnover Ratio

——————— = ——————— × ———————

b. Disaggregate the rate of return on common shareholders' equity into its three components:

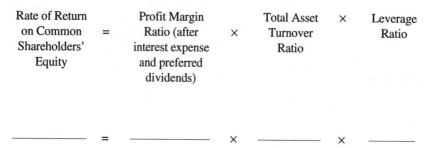

Rate of Return on Common Shareholders' Equity	=	Profit Margin Ratio (after interest expense and preferred dividends)	×	Total Asset Turnover Ratio	×	Leverage Ratio
———————	=	———————	×	———————	×	———————

c. Why is Joanne's rate of return on common shareholders' equity (part b above) greater than its rate of return on assets (part a above)?

3.   This exercise is a continuation of Exercise 1, Joanne's Costume Shop. Given below is information about sales, cost of goods sold, and average inventory for Years 3, 4, and 5:

	Year 3	Year 4	Year 5
Sales (all on credit)	$975,000	$1,100,000	$1,250,000
Cost of Goods Sold	526,500	577,500	625,000
Average Inventory	225,000	230,000	228,000

a. Compute the inventory turnover for each year.

b. Compute the average number of days that inventory is on hand each year.

c. What percentage is cost of goods sold to sales for each year?

d. Evaluate Joanne's management of its inventories over the 3 years.

4. This exercise is a continuation of Exercise 1, Joanne's Costume Shop. Given below is information about sales and average accounts receivable for Years 3, 4, and 5. Joanne's credit terms are net 30 days.

	Year 3	Year 4	Year 5
Sales (all on credit)	$975,000	$1,100,000	$1,250,000
Average Accts. Rec.	150,000	200,000	250,000

a. Compute the accounts receivable turnover for each year.

b. Compute the average collection period for accounts receivable for each year.

c. Evaluate Joanne's management of its accounts receivable over the 3-year period.

5.   This exercise is a continuation of Exercise 1, Joanne's Costume Shop. Given below is information about cost of goods sold, beginning and ending inventories, and average accounts payable for Years 3, 4, and 5:

	Year 3	Year 4	Year 5
Cost of Goods Sold	$526,500	$577,500	$625,000
Beginning Inventory	300,000	150,000	310,000
Ending Inventory	150,000	310,000	146,000
Average Accounts Payable	63,000	134,000	90,000

All of Joanne's purchases are made on credit terms of "net 45 days."

a. Compute the accounts payable turnover for each year.

b. Evaluate Joanne's management of its accounts payable over the 3-year period.

6. Robert Company's balance sheet indicates that the company has $2 million of 7 percent debt and total shareholders' equity of $1 million.

   Jeffrey Company's balance sheet indicates that the company has no debt and total shareholders' equity of $3 million.

   Assume that both companies are identical in all respects except for the difference outlined above. If both companies report income before interest and taxes of $600,000 and the tax rate is 30 percent.

   a. Compute the rate of return on assets for both companies.

   b. Compute the rate of return on common shareholders' equity.

   c. Explain any difference in the computed ratios for the two companies.

Answers to Questions and Exercises

True/False

1.	T	8.	F	15.	F	22.	T	29.	F
2.	T	9.	F	16.	T	23.	T	30.	F
3.	F	10.	F	17.	F	24.	F		
4.	T	11.	T	18.	T	25.	T		
5.	T	12.	F	19.	F	26.	T		
6.	T	13.	T	20.	T	27.	F		
7.	T	14.	F	21.	T	28.	T		

Matching

1.	p	6.	f	11.	j	16.	r	21.	t
2.	u	7.	d	12.	c	17.	b		
3.	i	8.	q	13.	e	18.	k		
4.	s	9.	l	14.	h	19.	o		
5.	g	10.	m	15.	n	20.	a		

Multiple Choice

1.	a	6.	d	11.	c	16.	b		
2.	c	7.	a	12.	c	17.	d		
3.	d	8.	b	13.	b	18.	c		
4.	d	9.	b	14.	c	19.	d		
5.	c	10.	c	15.	b	20.	b		

Exercises

1.   a.   Current Ratio

$$= \frac{\text{Current Assets}}{\text{Current Liabilities}}$$

$$= \frac{\$450,000}{\$189,000} = 2.38{:}1$$

b. Quick Ratio

$$= \frac{\text{Cash} + \text{Receivables} + \text{Marketable Securities}}{\text{Current Liabilities}}$$

$$= \frac{\$50,000 + \$100,000}{\$189,000} = .794{:}1$$

c. Debt-Equity Ratio

$$= \frac{\text{Total Liabilities}}{\text{Total Liabilities} + \text{Shareholders' Equity}}$$

$$= \frac{\$\ 589,000}{\$1,150,000} = .512$$

d. Rate of Return on Assets

$$= \frac{\text{Net Income} + \text{Interest Expense (Net of Tax Savings)}}{\text{Average Total Assets}}$$

$$= \frac{\$126,000 \quad + \quad \$14,000}{1/2\ (\$1,150,000 \quad + \quad \$1,1000,000)} = .124$$

e. Rate of Return on Common Shareholders' Equity

$$= \frac{\text{Net Income} - \text{Dividends on Preferred Stock}}{\text{Average Common Shareholders' Equity During Period}}$$

$$= \frac{\$126,000}{1/2\ (\$561,000 + \$435,000)} = .253$$

f. Earnings per Share of Common Stock

$$= \frac{\text{Net Income} - \text{Preferred Stock Dividends}}{\text{Weighted Average Number of Common Shares Outstanding During Period}}$$

$$= \frac{\$126,000}{150,000} = \$.84$$

g. Profit Margin Ratio (before interest expense and related income tax effects)

$$= \frac{\text{Net Income} + \text{Interest Expense (Net of Tax Savings)}}{\text{Sales}}$$

$$= \frac{\$126,000 + \$14,000}{\$900,000} = .156$$

h. Total Assets Turnover

$$= \frac{\text{Sales}}{\text{Average Total Assets During Period}}$$

$$= \frac{\$900,000}{1/2\,(\$1,150,000 + \$1,100,000)} = .8$$

i. Interest Coverage Ratio

$$= \frac{\text{Net Income before Interest Income Taxes}}{\text{Interest Expense}}$$

$$= \frac{\$200,000}{\$\ 20,000} = 10 \text{ times}$$

j. Inventory Turnover

$$= \frac{\text{Cost of Goods Sold}}{\text{Average Inventory During Period}}$$

$$= \frac{\$500,000}{1/2\,(\$300,000 + \$200,000)} = 2$$

k. Average Number of Days Inventory on Hand

$$= \frac{365}{\text{Inventory Turnover}}$$

$$= \frac{365}{2} = 182.5$$

l. Accounts Receivable Turnover

$$= \frac{\text{Net Sales on Account}}{\text{Average Accounts Receivable During Period}}$$

$$= \frac{\$900,000}{1/2\ (\$100,000 + \$150,000)} = 7.2$$

m. Average Collection Period for Accounts Receivable

$$= \frac{365}{\text{Accounts Receivable Turnover}}$$

$$= \frac{365}{7.2} = 50.7 \text{ days}$$

n. Long-Term Debt Ratio

$$= \frac{\text{Total Long-Term Debts}}{\text{Total Long-Term Debt Plus Shareholders' Equity}}$$

$$= \frac{\$400,000}{\$400,000 + \$561,000} = .416$$

o. Plant Asset Turnover Ratio

$$= \frac{\text{Sales}}{\text{Average Plant Assets During Period}}$$

$$= \frac{\$900,000}{1/2\ (\$700,000 + \$735,000)} = 1.25$$

p. Leverage Ratio

$$= \frac{\text{Average Total Assets During Period}}{\text{Average Common Shareholders' Equity During Period}}$$

$$= \frac{1/2\ (\$1,150,000 + \$1,100,000)}{1/2\ (\$\ \ 561,000 + \$\ \ 435,000)} = 2.26$$

q. Accounts Payable Turnover Ratio

$$= \frac{\text{Purchases*}}{\text{Average Accounts Payable}}$$

$$= \frac{\$600,000}{1/2\ (\$189,000 + \$250,000)} = 2.73$$

*Purchases = Cost of Goods Sold + Ending Inventory – Beginning Inventory
= $500,000 + $300,000 – $200,000
= $600,000

r. Profit Margin Ratio (after interest expense and preferred dividends)

$$= \frac{\text{Net Income} - \text{Preferred Stock Dividends}}{\text{Sales}}$$

$$= \frac{\$126,000}{\$900,000} = .14$$

2. a.

Rate of Return on Assets	=	Profit Margin Ratio (before interest expense and related income tax effects)	×	Total Asset Turnover Ratio
.124	=	.156	×	.8

b.

Rate of Return on Common Shareholders' Equity	=	Profit Margin Ratio (after interest expense and preferred dividends)	×	Total Asset Turnover Ratio	×	Leverage Ratio
.253	=	.14	×	.8	×	2.26

c. The rate of return on common shareholders' equity is greater than the rate of return on assets because the company is using financial leverage to increase the return to its common shareholders.

140

3. a.

$$\text{Inventory Turnover} = \frac{\text{Cost of Goods Sold}}{\text{Average Inventory During Period}}$$

Year 3: Inventory Turnover $= \dfrac{\$526,500}{\$225,000} = 2.34$

Year 4: Inventory Turnover $= \dfrac{\$577,500}{\$230,000} = 2.51$

Year 5: Inventory Turnover $= \dfrac{\$625,000}{\$228,000} = 2.74$

b.

$$\text{Av. Number of Days Inventory on Hand} = \frac{365}{\text{Inventory Turnover}}$$

Year 3: Av. Number of Days Invty. on Hand $= \dfrac{365}{2.34} = 156$

Year 4: Av. Number of Days Invty. on Hand $= \dfrac{365}{2.51} = 145$

Year 5: Av. Number of Days Invty. on Hand $= \dfrac{365}{2.74} = 133$

c.

$$\text{Cost of Goods Sold Percentage} = \frac{\text{Cost of Goods Sold}}{\text{Sales}}$$

Year 3: Cost of Goods Sold Percentage $= \dfrac{\$526,500}{\$975,000} = 54\%$

Year 4: Cost of Goods Sold Percentage $= \dfrac{\$577,500}{\$1,100,000} = 52.5\%$

Year 5: Cost of Goods Sold Percentage $= \dfrac{\$625,000}{\$1,250,000} = 50\%$

d. Joanne has made steady progress in managing its inventories over the 3-year period. Inventory turnover has increased each year; the number of days that inventory is on hand has decreased each year; and the cost of goods sold percentage has decreased each year, which means that the gross profit margin percentage has increased each year.

4.   a. $\text{Accounts Receivable Turnover} = \dfrac{\text{Net Sales on Account}}{\text{Average Accounts Receivable}}$

Year 3: Accounts Receivable Turnover $= \dfrac{\$975,000}{\$150,000} = 6.5$

Year 4: Accounts Receivable Turnover $= \dfrac{\$1,000,000}{\$200,000} = 5.5$

Year 5: Accounts Receivable Turnover $= \dfrac{\$1,250,000}{\$250,000} = 5$

b. $\text{Av. Collection Period for Accts. Rec.} = \dfrac{365}{\text{Accts. Rec. Turnover}}$

Year 3: Collection Period for Accts. Rec. $= \dfrac{365}{6.5} = 56 \text{ days}$

Year 4: Collection Period for Accts. Rec. $= \dfrac{365}{5.5} = 66 \text{ days}$

Year 5: Collection Period for Accts. Rec. $= \dfrac{365}{5} = 73 \text{ days}$

c.   Joanne has experienced steady erosion in its ability to collect its accounts receivable on a timely basis. Joanne should be able to collect its accounts in 30 days since that is the credit policy. The buildup in accounts receivable is occurring because accounts are not being collected on a timely basis. As a result, the turnover of accounts receivable is decreasing each year.

5.   a.   Account Payable Turnover $= \dfrac{\text{Purchases*}}{\text{Average Accounts Payable}}$

*Purchases   =   Cost of Goods Sold
        +   Ending Inventory
        −   Beginning Inventory

Year 3: Accounts Payable Turnover $= \dfrac{\$376,500}{\$\,63,000} = 5.98$

Year 4: Accounts Payable Turnover $= \dfrac{\$737,500}{\$134,000} = 5.50$

Year 5: Accounts Payable Turnover $= \dfrac{\$461,000}{\$90,000} = 5.12$

   b.   Since all purchases are made on credit terms of "net 45 days," the accounts payable turnover should be about 8.11 (365 days/45 days). For the 3 years, Joanne is taking longer to pay for the purchases than the credit terms offered. The average payment period (in days) is as follows:

Year 3: 61 days (365/5.98)
Year 4: 66 days (365/5.50)
Year 5: 71 days (365/5.12)

6. a.

Computation of Net Income for the following:	Robert	Jeffrey
Income before Interest and Taxes	$600,000	$600,000
Interest Expense	140,000	-0-
Income before Taxes	$460,000	$600,000
Tax Expense	138,000	180,000
Net Income	$322,000	$420,000

$$\text{Rate of return on assets} \;=\; \frac{\text{Net Income + Interest Expense (Net of Tax Savings)}}{\text{Average Total Assets}}$$

Robert: $\dfrac{\$322,000 + \$98,000}{\$3,000,000} = .140$

Jeffrey: $\dfrac{\$420,000}{\$3,000,000} = .140$

b.

$$\text{Rate of return on common shareholders' equity} \;=\; \frac{\text{Net Income} - \text{Preferred stock dividends}}{\text{Average shareholders' equity}}$$

Robert: $\dfrac{\$322,000}{\$1,000,000} = .322$

Jeffrey: $\dfrac{\$420,000}{\$3,000,000} = .140$

c. The rate of return on assets is 14 percent for both companies. Robert is using financial leverage to increase the return to its common shareholders. Jeffrey has financed its assets through common shareholders' equity and is not using any financial leverage. Robert's return to common shareholders' equity is 32.2 percent, which is greater than the company's rate of return on assets of 14 percent.

Leverage increased the rate of return to shareholders because the capital provided by long-term creditors earned 14 percent but required an after-tax interest payment of only 4.9 percent: (.07) × (1–.30 tax rate). The additional 9.1 percent (.14 – .049) return on assets financed by creditors increased the return to common shareholders:

Excess return of 9.1 percent on assets financed by creditors:

$(.091) \times (\$2,000,000)$	$182,000

Return of 14 percent on assets financed by common shareholders:

$(.14 \times \$1,000,000)$	$140,000
Total return to common shareholders	$322,000

Rate of return on common shareholders' equity

($322,000/$1,000,000)	32.2%

Chapter 7

The Liquid Assets:
Cash, Marketable Securities, and Receivables

Chapter Highlights

1. Cash is the most liquid asset. It is also the most vulnerable to loss because of its susceptibility to theft or embezzlement.

2. To be included in "cash" on the balance sheet, items should be freely available for exchange. Typically included in this category are coins, currency, travelers' checks, undeposited checks, and cash in the bank.

3. Compensating balances are frequently excluded from cash. A compensating balance usually takes the form of a minimum balance that must be maintained in connection with a borrowing agreement with a bank. The SEC requires that legally restricted deposits held as compensating balances against short-term borrowing arrangements be classified as a current asset, but not as "cash." Compensating balances held against long-term borrowing arrangements should be classified preferably as investments.

4. The management of cash involves two principal considerations. First, management must establish a system of internal control to ensure that cash is properly safeguarded from theft or embezzlement. Second, management wants to regulate cash amounts to balance the conflicting goals of having enough cash to conduct business effectively while not losing the earnings that invested cash can generate. One effective tool in cash management is the preparation of weekly or monthly budgets of cash receipts and disbursements.

5. The business may invest some of its excess cash in income-yielding securities such as bonds or stocks. These investments are called marketable securities as long as they can be readily converted into cash and management intends to do so when cash is needed. Marketable securities are classified as current assets on the balance sheet and are initially recorded at acquisition cost, which includes the purchase price, plus any commissions, taxes, and other costs incurred.

6. Generally accepted accounting principles require firms to classify securities into three categories: (a) debt securities for which a firm has a positive intent and ability to hold to maturity; (b) debt and equity securities held as trading securities; and (c) debt and equity securities held as securities available for sale.

7. Debt securities for which a firm has a positive intent and ability to hold to maturity appear in the balance sheet at amortized acquisition cost. The acquisition cost of debt securities may differ from their maturity value. The difference between acquisition cost and maturity value is amortized over the life of the debt security as an adjustment to interest revenue.

8. Trading securities are reported on the balance sheet at market value because (a) active securities markets provide objective measures of market values, and (b) market values provide financial statement users with the most relevant information for assessing the success of a firm's trading activities over time.

9. Decreases in the market value of trading securities are reported as "Unrealized Holding Losses" and increases are reported as "Unrealized Holding Gains" on the income statement.

10. Debt and equity securities held as securities available for sale trade in active securities markets and have easily measurable market values. Securities which a firm intends to sell within one year appear in Marketable Securities in the current assets section of the balance sheet.

11. Securities available for sale are reported on the balance sheet at market value. Any unrealized holding gain or holding loss each period does not affect income immediately but instead increases or decreases a separate shareholders' equity account. Holding gains and losses on securities available for sale affect net income only when the securities are sold.

12. When securities are transferred from one of the three categories to another one, the firm transfers the security at its market value at the time of the transfer and recognizes a realized gain or loss.

13. The third liquid asset considered in Chapter Seven is accounts receivable. Accounts receivable result from the sale of goods or services on account. Accounts receivable are initially recorded at the amount owed by customers. The amount is reduced for estimated uncollectible accounts, sales discounts, and sales returns and allowances. The reporting objective is to state accounts receivable at the amount expected to be collected in cash.

14. Charges against income for expected uncollectible accounts, sales discounts, and sales returns and allowances are preferably made in the period when the sales occur.

15. When credit is extended there will be some customers whose accounts will never be collected. The principal accounting issue related to uncollectible accounts concerns when firms should recognize the loss from uncollectibles.

16. The direct write-off method recognizes losses from uncollectible accounts in the period when a firm decides that specific customers' accounts are uncollectible.

17. The direct write-off method has three shortcomings: (a) it does not usually recognize the loss from uncollectible accounts in the period in which the firm recognizes revenue; (b) it provides firms with an opportunity to manipulate earnings each period by deciding when particular customers's accounts are uncollectible; and (c) the amount of accounts receivable on the balance sheet under the direct write-off method does not reflect the amount a firm expects to collect in cash.

18. Generally accepted accounting principles do not allow the direct write-off method for financial reporting when losses from uncollectible accounts are significant in amount, occur frequently, and are reasonably predictable. The direct write-off method is required for income tax reporting.

19. When the amount of uncollectibles can be estimated with reasonable precision, GAAP requires that the allowance method be used. The allowance method involves (a) estimating the amount of uncollectibles that will occur in connection with the sales of each period and (b) making an adjusting entry that reduces the reported income on the income statement and reduces the Accounts Receivable on the balance sheet for the net amount of accounts expected to be uncollectible. The adjusting entry involves a debit to Bad Debts Expense to reduce income and a credit to Allowance for Uncollectible Accounts, a contra account to Accounts Receivable.

20. Views differ as to the type of account that "Bad Debts Expense" is—expense or revenue contra. Arguments for treating it as a revenue contra may be persuasive, but treatment as an expense is more widely used in practice.

21. When a particular account is judged uncollectible, it is written off by debiting Allowance for Uncollectible Accounts and crediting Accounts Receivable. Writing off the specific account does not affect net assets nor income. The reduction in net assets and the affect on income took place when the firm estimated the amount of eventual uncollectibles and recorded Bad Debts Expense and credited the Allowance for Uncollectible Accounts.

22. The allowance method for uncollectible accounts (a) provides a better matching of revenues and expenses in the period of sale, (b) does not provide management an opportunity to manipulate earnings through the timing of write-offs, and (c) results in reporting accounts receivable at the amount the firm expects to collect in cash in future periods.

23. There are two basic approaches for calculating the amount of the adjustment under the allowance method. The easiest method in most cases is to apply an appropriate percentage to total sales on account for the period. Another method, called aging the accounts, involves the analysis of customers' accounts classified by the length of time the accounts have been outstanding. The rationale is that the longer an account has been outstanding, the greater the probability that it will never be collected. By applying judgment to the aging analysis, an estimate is made of the approximate balance needed in the allowance for uncollectible accounts at year-end.

24. When the percentage-of-sales method is used, the periodic provision for uncollectible accounts is merely added to the existing balance in the Allowance account. When the aging method is used, the balance in the Allowance account is adjusted to reflect the desired ending balance.

25. Often, a seller of merchandise offers a reduction from the invoice price for prompt payment, called a sales discount or cash discount. The amount of sales discounts appears as an adjustment in measuring net sales revenue.

26. When a customer returns merchandise, the sale has in effect been canceled and an entry that reverses the recording of the sale is appropriate. The account, Sales Returns, is treated as a sales contra account on the income statement.

27. A sales allowance is a reduction in price granted to a customer, usually after the goods have been purchased and found to be unsatisfactory or damaged. The effect of the allowance is to reduce sales revenue. It may be desirable to accumulate the amount of such an adjustment in a Sales Allowances account.

28. In some cases, a firm may find itself temporarily short of cash and unable to obtain financing from its usual sources. In such cases accounts receivable may be assigned, pledged, or factored.

29. Accounts are assigned to a bank or finance company in order to obtain a loan. The borrowing company usually maintains physical control of the receivables, collects customers' remittances, and forwards the proceeds to the lending institution to liquidate the loan.

30. Accounts may be pledged as collateral for a loan. If the borrower fails to repay the loan when due, the lending agency has the power to sell the accounts receivable in order to obtain payment.

31. Accounts receivable may be factored, which is in effect a sale of the receivables to a bank or finance company.

32. A promissory note is a written contract in which one person (maker) promises to pay another person (payee) a definite sum of money, either on demand or at a definite point in time. The holder of the note has a liquid asset called a note receivable.

33. Interest is the price paid for the use of borrowed funds. For the holder of a note receivable it is a source of revenue. The amount of interest is usually based upon a percentage rate stated on an annual basis. The general formula for the computation of simple interest is

$$\text{Interest} = \text{Base (Principal or Face)} \times \text{Interest Rate} \times \text{Elapsed Time.}$$

34. An interest-bearing note includes explicit interest at a stated rate, which is generally paid at maturity in addition to the face amount of the note. If the accounting period ends prior to maturity, an adjusting entry is needed to record the interest that has been earned but that will not be collected until the note matures.

35. A note may be transferred to another party, thereby providing the original holder of the note with cash proceeds prior to maturity. The transfer may be made with or without recourse. If the transfer is made without recourse, it is tantamount to a sale because the original holder (transferor) has no further liability even if the maker fails to pay at maturity. More commonly, however, the transfer is made with recourse, which places a potential or "contingent" liability on the transferor of the note if the maker fails to pay at maturity. Contingent liabilities are disclosed in footnotes to the balance sheet.

36. The statement of cash flows explains the change in cash and cash equivalents during a period. Cash equivalents include marketable debt securities that had a maturity date of 3 months or less at the time the firm acquired them. Changes in this type of marketable security appear at the bottom of the statement of cash flows as a component of the change in cash and cash equivalents. The statement of cash flows classifies acquisitions and dispositions of other marketable securities as investing transactions. Transactions changing accounts receivable are operating activities. An increase in accounts receivable is subtracted from (and a decrease in accounts receivable is added to) net income to compute cash flows from operations.

Questions and Exercises

True/False. For each of the following statements, place a T or F in the space provided to indicate whether the statement is true or false.

_____   1. When securities are transferred from one category to another one, the firm transfers the security at it market value at the time of the transfer and recognizes a realized gain or loss.

_____   2. Liquid assets are generally stated at their cash or cash equivalent value on the balance sheet.

_____   3. To be included in "cash" on the balance sheet, items should be freely available for exchange.

_____   4. Debt securities, which a firm will hold to maturity, will appear on the firm's balance sheet at market value.

_____   5. Simple interest on a note is calculated by multiplying the principal amount of the note by the stated interest rate and this amount by the period of time for which the note is to be outstanding.

_____ 6. When the market value of an investment in trading securities is less than its cost, the decrease is reported as "Unrealized Holding Losses" on the firm's income statement.

_____ 7. When the market value of an investment in securities available for sale is less than its cost, the holding loss is reported in a shareholders' equity account.

_____ 8. Holding gains and losses on securities available for sale affect net income only when the securities are sold.

_____ 9. A compensating balance is usually a minimum balance that must be maintained in connection with a borrowing arrangement.

_____ 10. The appearance of the Allowance for Uncollectible Accounts on the balance sheet indicates the use of the direct write-off method.

_____ 11. The method of accounting for uncollectible accounts that recognizes a loss when a customer's account has clearly been demonstrated to be uncollectible is the direct write-off method.

_____ 12. One method of obtaining cash from accounts receivable is to pledge the accounts, which is equivalent to a sale.

_____ 13. Debt and equity securities, which a firm intends to sell within one year, are reported as current assets on the balance sheet.

_____ 14. When the market value of an investment in securities available for sale is more than cost, the increase is reported as "Unrealized Holding Gains" on the firm's income statement.

_____ 15. Under the direct write-off method, the amount of accounts receivable on the balance sheet reflects the amount the firm expects to collect in cash.

_____ 16. The direct write-off method provides a better matching of revenues and expenses in the period of sale than the allowance method for uncollectible accounts.

_____ 17. A cash discount that is offered as an incentive for prompt payment is actually a form of interest expense to the buyer.

_____ 18. Compensating balances required by a bank are always included in the "cash" classification on the balance sheet.

_____ 19. Under the allowance method for uncollectible accounts, writing off a specific account decreases net assets and decreases net income.

_____ 20. For all firms the optimal amount of bad debts is zero.

_____ 21. The allowance method for uncollectible accounts results in reporting accounts receivable at the amount the firm expects to collect in cash in future periods.

_____ 22. The definition of cash excludes such items as demand deposits and savings accounts because these items are not physically in the firm's possession.

_____ 23. Cash balances should be managed in such a way that having too little cash is to be avoided but having too much cash is of no significant concern.

_____ 24. The principal accounting issue related to uncollectible accounts concerns when firms should recognize the loss from uncollectibles.

_____ 25. The allowance method recognizes losses from uncollectible accounts in the period when a firm decides that specific customers' accounts are uncollectible.

_____ 26. When the aging method is used to estimate uncollectible accounts, the balance in the Allowance for Uncollectible Accounts is adjusted to bring the account balance to a desired ending balance.

_____ 27. A firm has a contingent liability whenever it transfers a note receivable to another party, with recourse.

_____ 28. The computation of bad debt expense using the percentage-of-sales method involves multiplying the bad debt percentage times the credit sales for the period.

_____ 29. The realized gain or loss on the sale of "securities available for sale" is the difference between the sales price and the original cost of the security.

_____ 30. Under the allowance method, when a particular account is judged uncollectible, it is written off by debiting Bad Debts Expense and crediting Accounts Receivable.

Matching. From the following list of terms, select that term which is most closely associated with each of the descriptive phrases or statements that follows and place the letter for that term in the space provided.

a.	Accounts Receivable	k.	Pledging of Accounts Receivable
b.	Allowance for Uncollectible Accounts	l.	Sales Returns & Allowances
c.	Allowance Method	m.	Securities Available for Sale
d.	Bad Debts Expense	n.	Simple Interest Formula
e.	Cash	o.	Time Deposit
f.	Compensating Balance	p.	Trading Securities
g.	Debt Securities	q.	Transfer with Recourse
h.	Direct Write-Off Method	r.	Unrealized Holding Gains
i.	Factor	s.	Unrealized Holding Losses
j.	Notes Receivable		

_____ 1. A trade receivable.

_____ 2. A contra to Accounts Receivable.

_____ 3. A firm sells its accounts receivable to a bank or finance company to obtain cash.

_____ 4. The preferable method of accounting for uncollectibles.

_____ 5. Decreases in the market value of trading securities.

_____ 6. The most liquid asset.

_____ 7. A promise in writing for the receipt of a definite sum of money at some future point in time.

_____ 8. A method in which uncollectible accounts are charged to expense when they are clearly demonstrated to be uncollectible.

_____ 9. Transfer of a note that places a contingent liability on the transferor.

_____ 10. If the borrower does not repay a note when due, the lending institution can sell the accounts receivable maintained as collateral for the loan.

_____ 11. Principal x Rate x Time.

_____ 12. Treated as a contra to sales revenue.

_____ 13. Usually classified as cash even though not always immediately available for withdrawal from a bank.

_____ 14. Increases in the market value of trading securities.

_____ 15. A negative consequence of extending credit.

_____ 16. Minimum checking account balance that must be maintained in connection with a borrowing arrangement from a bank.

_____ 17. These securities appear in the balance sheet at amortized acquisition cost.

_____ 18. Increases and decreases in the market value of these securities are reported as unrealized holding gains and losses on the income statement.

_____ 19. Increases and decreases in the market value of these securities do not affect income until the securities are sold.

Multiple Choice. **Choose the best answer for each of the following questions and enter the identifying letter in the space provided.**

_____ 1. On March 3, Year 1, Bartok purchased shares of Perz Company for $220,000. At the end of the year the market value of these securities was $235,000. Bartok actively trades securities with the objective of generating profits from short-term differences in market prices. Which of the following statements is true?

   a. On its December 31, Year 1, balance sheet, Bartok will report the Perz Company stock at its market value of $235,000.
   b. The $15,000 increase in the market value of the Perz Company stock will be reported in Bartok's Year 1 income statement.
   c. Bartok's entry to record the increase in the market value of the Perz Company stock will include a $15,000 credit to Unrealized Holding Gains on Trading Securities.
   d. All of the above statements are true.

_____ 2. Refer to Question 1 above. Assume that Bartok sold the Perz Company stock for $245,000 in Year 2. What would Bartok report on its Year 2 income statement?

   a. An unrealized holding gain on trading securities of $25,000.
   b. A realized gain on the sale of trading securities of $25,000.
   c. An unrealized holding gain on trading securities of $10,000.
   d. A realized gain on the sale of trading securities of $10,000.

_____ 3. The proper handling in the financial statements of the account, Allowance for Uncollectible Accounts, is

    a. A revenue contra account.
    b. A selling expense.
    c. A contra to Accounts Receivable.
    d. A current liability.

_____ 4. A 4-month, 6 percent, $15,000 note is received by the Nokomis Co. during Year 1. How much interest will Nokomis earn if it holds the note to maturity?

    a. $300.
    b. $225.
    c. $-0-.
    d. $900.

_____ 5. Nordmark Co. acquired marketable securities in Year 1 at a cost of $20,000. The securities can be readily converted into cash and Nordmark intends to convert the securities into cash when it needs cash. How would Nordmark report this investment on its Year 1 balance sheet?

    a. As a current asset, Marketable Securities.
    b. As a current asset, Investment in Securities.
    c. As a noncurrent asset, Marketable Securities.
    d. As a noncurrent asset, Investment in Securities.

_____ 6. Jenzac Company purchased securities at a cost of $110,000 on April 16. Additionally the company paid a 5-percent commission ($5,500) on the purchase, a 6-percent tax ($6,600), and a transfer fee of $1,500. At what amount should the company record the acquisition cost of the securities?

    a. $110,000.
    b. $123,600.
    c. $122,100.
    d. $117,000.

_____ 7. Which of the accounts below would not be treated as a reduction in sales revenue on the income statement?

    a. Sales Discounts Taken.
    b. Sales Allowances.
    c. Sales Returns.
    d. Bad Debts Expense.

_____ 8. Kristov Company purchased some debt securities in Year 2 with the intent of selling the securities when the company needs the cash in its operations. Under generally accepted accounting principles, this investment would fall under which of the following categories?

    a. Debt securities, which the firm intends to hold to maturity.
    b. Debt and equity securities held as trading securities.
    c. Debt and equity securities held as securities available for sale.
    d. None of the above.

_____ 9. How should debt securities, which a firm intends to hold to maturity, be reported on the balance sheet?

    a. At acquisition cost.
    b. At market value.
    c. At amortized acquisition cost.
    d. None of the above.

_____ 10. The Red River Valley Bank actively trades in debt securities with the intent of earning profits from short-term differences in market prices. How should the bank report the debt securities on its balance sheet?

    a. At acquisition cost.
    b. At market value.
    c. At amortized acquisition cost.
    d. None of the above.

_____ 11. Wallenda Co. had $450,000 of sales during Year 1, $200,000 of which were on account. The balances in its Accounts Receivable and its Allowance for Uncollectible Accounts on December 31, Year 1, were $60,000 and $8,000, respectively. Past experience indicates that 5 percent of all credit sales will not be collected. What is the correct amount for Wallenda to debit to Bad Debts Expense?

    a. $30,000.
    b. $10,000.
    c. $ 5,000.
    d. $20,000.

_____ 12. Refer to the question above, but assume that an aging of accounts indicated that $15,000 of the receivable balance would not be collected. What is the correct amount for Wallenda to debit to Bad Debts Expense?

    a. $23,000.
    b. $10,000.
    c. $15,000.
    d. $ 7,000.

_____ 13. Walker Co. acquired common stock of the Pike Co. to develop a long-term relationship with Pike, which is a major supplier of the raw material used to manufacture Walker's product. How would Walker report these securities on its balance sheet?

    a. At acquisition cost and classified as a current asset, Marketable Securities.
    b. At acquisition cost and classified as a noncurrent asset, Investments in Securities.
    c. At market value and classified as a current asset, Marketable Securities.
    d. At market value and classified as a noncurrent asset, Investment in Securities.

    155

_____ 14. Herriott Co. accepted a 10 percent, $50,000 note from a customer on August 1, Year 1, due on February 1, Year 2. If the accounting year ends on December 31, how much interest revenue is recorded when the note is collected?

    a. $5,000.

    b. $2,500.

    c. $ 417.

    d. $ 835.

_____ 15. Of the numerous ways of turning receivables into cash, which one below is the same as an out-right sale?

    a. Assignment of receivables.

    b. Factoring of receivables.

    c. Pledging of receivables.

    d. Collection of receivables.

The following information relates to Questions 16–20. Hammond Company has three securities in its portfolio of securities available for sale:

Security	Cost	Market Value 12/31, Year 1	Market Value 12/31, Year 2
Beatty	$60,000	$72,000	$77,000
Cole	$90,000	$93,000	—
Sells	$45,000	$41,000	$39,000

The Cole stock was sold in Year 2 for $98,000.

_____ 16. Which of the following statements is true?

    a. On its 12/31, Year 1, balance sheet, Hammond would report the Beatty stock at its cost of $60,000.

    b. On its income statement for the year ending 12/31, Year 1, Hammond would report an un-realized holding gain on the Beatty stock of $12,000.

    c. On its 12/31, Year 1, balance sheet, Hammond would report an unrealized holding gain on the Beatty stock of $12,000 in a shareholders' equity account.

    d. Statements a and b are true.

_____ 17. Which of the following statements is true?

    a. On its 12/31, Year 2, balance sheet, Hammond would report the Beatty stock at its market value of $77,000.

    b. On its income statement for the year ending 12/31, Year 2, Hammond would report an unreal-ized holding gain on the Beatty stock of $5,000.

    c. On its 12/31, Year 2, balance sheet, Hammond would report an unrealized holding gain on the Beatty stock of $17,000 in a shareholders' equity account.

    d. Statements a and c are true.

_____ 18. What would Hammond report on its income statement for the year ending 12/31, Year 2, relative to the sale of the Cole stock in Year 2?

    a. A realized gain of $5,000.
    b. A realized gain of $5,000 and an unrealized gain of $3,000.
    c. A realized gain of $8,000.
    d. An unrealized gain of $8,000.

_____ 19. Which of the following statements is true?

    a. On its 12/31, Year 1, balance sheet, Hammond would report the Sells stock at its cost of $45,000.
    b. On its income statement for the year ending 12/31, Year 1, Hammond would report an unrealized holding loss of $4,000.
    c. On its income statement for the year ending 12/31, Year 2, Hammond would report an unrealized holding loss of $2,000.
    d. None of the above statements is true.

_____ 20. Assume that on 12/31, Year 2, Hammond reclassifies the Sells stock to a "trading security" status. What would Hammond report on its income statement for the year ending 12/31, Year 2, relative to the reclassification?

    a. An unrealized loss of $2,000.
    b. A realized loss of $2,000.
    c. An unrealized loss of $6,000.
    d. A realized loss of $6,000.

_____ 21. Which of the following events reduces total assets?

    a. A customer returns merchandise for credit.
    b. The write-off of uncollectible accounts under the allowance method.
    c. The collection of an account receivable.
    d. The reclassification of a security when the cost of the security is less than its market value.

_____ 22. Which of the following is not classified as cash and shown among current assets?

    a. Cash on hand.
    b. Certificates of deposit.
    c. Demand deposit.
    d. Bond sinking fund.

The following information relates to Questions 23–25. Kelly Co. reported Accounts Receivable of $50,000 and an Allowance for Uncollectible Accounts of $5,000 on its 12/31, Year 1, Balance Sheet. During Year 2, credit sales totaled $1,500,000; collections on account totaled $1,400,000; and write-offs totaled $8,000. After aging its Accounts Receivable, Kelly estimated that 10 percent of its Accounts Receivable at 12/31, Year 2, will be uncollectible.

_____ 23. What is the balance in Accounts Receivable on 12/31, Year 2?

    a. $137,000.
    b. $139,000.
    c. $142,000.
    d. $145,000.

_____ 24. What amount would Kelly report as Bad Debts Expense in its Year 2 Income Statement?

    a. $14,200.
    b. $15,000.
    c. $18,000.
    d. $17,200.

_____ 25. Assume that Kelly estimates its bad debts to be 2 percent of credit sales. What balance would Kelly report in Allowance for Uncollectible Accounts on its 12/31, Year 2, balance sheet?

    a. $22,000.
    b. $27,000.
    c. $30,000.
    d. $35,000.

The following information relates to Questions 26–29. On September 1, Year 1, Carson received a 15 percent, $75,000, 6-month note from Barnes. On November 1, Carson transferred the note with recourse to the Hugo Bank in return for a cash payment of $76,500.

_____ 26. If the bank holds the note to its maturity, how much cash will the bank collect from Barnes, the maker of the note?

    a. $75,000.
    b. $80,625.
    c. $78,750.
    d. None of the above.

_____ 27. How much interest revenue will the bank earn for the time it holds the note?

    a. $5,625.
    b. $4,125.
    c. $3,750.
    d. None of the above.

_____ 28. How much interest revenue did Carson earn during the period it held the note?

    a. $3,750.

    b. $1,875.

    c. $1,500.

    d. None of the above.

_____ 29. On November 1 when Carson transferred the note with recourse to the Hugo Bank, Carson would report a finance expense of

    a. $4,125.

    b. $1,875.

    c. $1,500.

    d. $ 375.

_____ 30. Allen Hill Co. received a 6-month, 8 percent, $12,000 note on September 1, Year 1. Allen Hill Co. closes its books on 12/31. When the note is collected on March 1, Year 2, how much interest revenue will be recorded as earned?

    a. $480.

    b. $320.

    c. $240.

    d. $160.

_____ 31. Brian's Magic Shop had credit sales of $2,500,000 during Year 1. At 12/31, Year 1, the balance in Accounts Receivable was $75,000. The company estimates bad debts to equal 1 percent of credit sales. What effect will the company's 12/31 adjusting entry have on the company's income statement and balance sheet?

    a. Decrease income by $25,000; no effect on balance sheet.

    b. Decrease income by $25,000; decrease assets by $25,000.

    c. No effect on either income statement or balance sheet.

    d. None of the above.

_____ 32. Refer to the previous question. During Year 2, a customer's account for $1,500 was written off as uncollectible. What effect will the write-off have on the company's Year 2 income statement and balance sheet?

    a. No effect on income; decrease assets by $1,500.

    b. Decrease income by $1,500; decrease assets by $1,500.

    c. No effect on either income statement or balance sheet.

    d. None of the above.

_____ 33. When a firm uses its accounts receivable as collateral for a loan, this transaction is known as a(an)

    a. Factoring of accounts receivable

    b. Assignment of accounts receivable.

    c. Pledging of accounts receivable.

    d. Sale of accounts receivable.

Exercises

1. The balances in selected accounts for Dubsky Co. on May 1, Year 1, are as follows:

Accounts Receivable	$150,000
Allowance for Uncollectible Accounts	(80,000)

    a. A 20-day, 10 percent note from Winn Co. was received in early May for its $9,500 overdue account. Payment of the note plus interest was received during the month when due.

    b. Gross sales on account for the month of May were $1,400,000. Cash sales were $300,000.

    c. Customers received credit for $5,000 of merchandise purchased on account and returned during May.

    d. Customers' accounts totaling $850,000 were collected.

    e. Accounts receivable of $90,000 were written off as uncollectible during the month.

    f. At month-end, an aging of the accounts indicated that $30,000 would be uncollectible.

    Record in journal form the May transactions.

2.   The Lundsford Company reported sales of $1,000,000 in Year 1 (of which $400,000 were for cash). It had the following balances at year end:

Accounts Receivable	$250,000
Allowance for Uncollectible Accounts	(50,000)

The accounts written off as uncollectible during Year 1 totaled $45,000. Calculate the Bad Debts Expense for each method below.

a. The direct write-off method.

b. The percentage-of-credit-sales method, where experience indicates a 5 percent rate is appropriate.

c. The aging method, where an evaluation of accounts indicates that $100,000 will not be collected.

d. Same as c above except assume that the Allowance for Uncollectible Accounts has a <u>debit</u> balance of $50,000 instead of a <u>credit</u> balance.

3. On November 1, Year 1, Gastone Co. received a 6-month, 12-percent, $100,000 note from Vic Traders, Inc., to apply on its open accounts receivable. On December 1, Gastone transferred the note, with recourse, to the Lake State Bank in return for a payment of $100,350. On May 1, Year 2, the bank notified Gastone that Vic Traders had paid the note when it matured.

Record Gastone's journal entries for November 1, December 1, and May 1 relating to this note.

4.   Tihany Co. purchased 50,000 shares of Vargas Co. stock on January 17, Year 1, at $12 per share. At year end December 31, Year 1, the market value for the Vargas Co. shares was $14 per share. On February 17, Year 2, a $.10 per share dividend was received on the Vargas Co. stock. On July 11, Year 2, 20,000 shares of Vargas Co. stock were sold for $13 per share. At the end of Year 2, the market value for the Vargas Co. stock was $17 per share.

   a. Use proper journal form to record all original entries and year-end adjusting entries for Tihany Co. that would be needed for Year 1 and Year 2. Assume that Tihany Co. actively trades securities with the objective of generating profits from short-term differences in market prices.

   b. What would Tihany Co. report on its income statements for Year 1 and Year 2 relating to its investment in marketable securities?

5.   Refer to Exercise 4. Now assume that Tihany Co. acquired these securities for an operating purpose instead of for their short-term profit potential.

   a. Record in proper journal form all original entries and year-end adjusting entries that would be needed for Year 1 and Year 2.

   b. What would Tihany Co. report on its income statements for Year 1 and Year 2 relating to its investment in marketable securities?

6.   On 12/31, Year 1, Estes Company reported the following on its balance sheet:

<u>Current Assets</u>

Accounts Receivable	$50,000	
Less: Allowance for Uncollectible Accounts	2,000	$48,000

On 12/31, Year 2, the company reported Accounts Receivable of $85,000 and an Allowance account balance of $4,250 (which was based on an aging of accounts receivable). During Year 2, credit sales totaled $571,000 and write-offs of uncollectible accounts totaled $6,000.

a. How much cash did Estes collect from its credit customers during Year 2?

b. What did the company report as its "Bad Debts Expense" on its Year 2 income statement?

Answers to Questions and Exercises

True/False

1.	T	7.	T	13.	T	19.	F	25.	F
2.	T	8.	T	14.	F	20.	F	26.	T
3.	T	9.	T	15.	F	21.	T	27.	T
4.	F	10.	F	16.	F	22.	F	28.	T
5.	T	11.	T	17.	T	23.	F	29.	T
6.	T	12.	F	18.	F	24.	T	30.	F

Matching

1.	a	5.	s	9.	q	13.	o	17.	g
2.	b	6.	e	10.	k	14.	r	18.	p
3.	i	7.	j	11.	n	15.	d	19.	m
4.	c	8.	h	12.	l	16.	f		

Multiple Choice

1.	d	8.	c	15.	b	22.	d	29.	d
2.	d	9.	c	16.	c	23.	c	30.	d
3.	c	10.	b	17.	d	24.	d	31.	b
4.	a	11.	b	18.	c	25.	b	32.	c
5.	a	12.	d	19.	d	26.	b	33.	c
6.	b	13.	d	20.	d	27.	b		
7.	d	14.	c	21.	a	28.	b		

Exercises

			Dr.	Cr.
1.	a.	Notes Receivable, Winn Co.	9,500	
		Accounts Receivable		9,500
		Receipt of 10-percent, 20-day note in exchange for overdue account.		
		Cash	9,552	
		Notes Receivable, Winn Co.		9,500
		Interest Revenue		52
		Collection of Winn Co. note plus 20 days of interest.		
	b.	Accounts Receivable	1,400,000	
		Cash	300,000	
		Sales Revenue		1,700,000
		Sales for May.		
	c.	Sales Returns and Allowances	5,000	
		Accounts Receivable		5,000
		Sales returns for May		
	d.	Cash	850,000	
		Accounts Receivable		850,000
		Collections on account during May.		
	e.	Allowance for Uncollectible Accounts	90,000	
		Accounts Receivable		90,000
		To write-off uncollectible accounts.		
	f.	Bad Debts Expense	40,000	
		Allowance for Uncollectible Accounts		40,000
		To increase allowance to $30,000 as determined by aging process.		

Allowance, May 1, Year 1	$80,000
Write-offs during May	90,000
Balance prior to adjustment	($10,000)
Required balance, per aging of accounts	30,000
Increase in Allowance	$40,000

2.

    a. $45,000

    b. .05 × $600,000 = $30,000

    c. Total uncollectible $100,000

        Credit in Allowance Account   50,000

                                        $ 50,000

    d. Total uncollectible $100,000

        Debit in Allowance Account   50,000

                                        $150,000

3.

		Dr.	Cr.
11/1, Year 1:	Notes Receivable	100,000	
	Accounts Receivable		100,000
	Receipt of note on open accounts receivable.		
12/1, Year 1:	Interest Receivable	1,000	
	Interest Revenue		1,000
	To accrue interest for one month.		
12/1, Year 1:	Cash	100,350	
	Financial Expense	650	
	Notes Receivable		100,000
	Interest Receivable		1,000
	To record transfer of note to Lake State Bank in return for a payment of $100,350.		
5/1, Year 2:	Gastone would make no formal entry. The company would prepare a memorandum for the records to indicate that the note was collected by the bank at maturity.		

4.

		Dr	Cr.

a.   1/17, Year 1: Marketable Securities   600,000
                      Cash   600,000
                      Purchase of 50,000 shares of Vargas Co.
                      stock for $12 per share

       12/31, Year 1: Marketable Securities   100,000
                            Unrealized Holding Gain on Trading Securities   100,000
                      To revalue trading securities to market value and
                      recognize an unrealized holding gain of $100,000
                      (50,000 × $2 = $100,000)

       2/17, Year 2: Cash   5,000
                            Dividend Income   5,000
                      Receipt of $.10 per share dividend on Vargas Co. stock.

       7/11, Year 2: Cash   260,000
                      Realized Loss on Sale of Trading Securities   20,000
                          Marketable Securities   280,000
                      Sold 20,000 shares of Vargas Co. stock for $13 per share.

       12/31, Year 2: Marketable Securities   90,000
                            Unrealized Holding Gain on Trading Securities   90,000
                      To revalue trading securities to market value and
                      recognize an unrealized holding gain of $90,000
                      (30,000 × $3 = $90,000).

b.   Year 1 income statement:
       Unrealized Holding Gain on Trading Securities, $100,000

     Year 2 income statement:

Dividend Income	$ 5,000
Realized Loss on Sale of Trading Securities	20,000
Unrealized Holding Gain on Trading Securities	90,000

     169

5.

		Dr.	Cr.
a.	1/17, Year 1: Marketable Securities	600,000	
	Cash		600,000
	Purchase of 50,000 shares of Vargas Co. stock for $12 per share		

12/31, Year 1: Marketable Securities — 100,000 Dr.
Unrealized Holding Gain on Securities Available for Sale — 100,000 Cr.
To revalue Vargas Co. stock to market value
(50,000 × $2 = $100,000)

2/17, Year 2: Cash — 5,000 Dr.
Dividend Income — 5,000 Cr.
Receipt of $.10 per share dividend on Vargas Co. stock.

7/11, Year 2: Cash — 260,000 Dr.
Unrealized Holding on Sale of Securities Available for Sale — 40,000 Dr.
Realized Gain on Sale of Securities Available for Sale — 20,000 Cr.
Marketable Securities — 280,000 Cr.
Sold 20,000 shares of Vargas Co. stock for $13 per share.

12/31, Year 2: Marketable Securities — 90,000 Dr.
Unrealized Holding Gain on Securities Available for Sale — 90,000 Cr.
To revalue Vargas Co. stock to market value
(30,000 × $3 = $90,000).

b. Year 1 income statement:

Nothing would be reported on Tihany's Year 1 income statement relating to the investment in marketable securities. The Unrealized Holding Gain on Securities Available for Sale account is reported in the balance sheet as a shareholders' equity item.

Year 2 income statement:

Dividend Income	$ 5,000
Realized Gain on Sale of Securities Available for Sale	20,000

6. a. Beginning balance, Accounts Receivable $ 50,000

      Credit Sales   571,000

      Total Accounts Receivable $621,000

      Less: Write-offs of uncollectible accounts   (6,000)

              Ending Balance, Accounts Receivable   (85,000)

      Cash collected from customers during Year 2 $530,000

   b. Ending balance, Allowance for Uncollectible Accounts $ 4,250

      Write-offs of uncollectible accounts   6,000

      Total $ 10,250

      Less: Beginning balance, Allowance for Uncollectible

              Accounts   2,000

      Year 2 Bad Debts Expense $ 8,250

Chapter 8

Inventories: The Source of Operating Profits

Chapter Highlights

1. The term "inventory" means a stock of goods or other items a firm owns and holds for sale or for processing as part of a firm's ordinary business operations. Merchandise or merchandise inventory refers to goods held by a retail or wholesale business. Finished goods denotes goods held for sale by a manufacturing company. The inventories of manufacturing firms also include work in process (partially completed products) and raw materials (materials which will become part of goods produced).

2. To inventory a stock of goods means to prepare a list of the items on hand at some specified date, to assign a unit price to each item, and to calculate the total cost of the inventory.

3. Accounting for inventories includes the process of determining the proper assignment of expenses to various accounting periods. Accounting must allocate the total cost of goods available for sale or use during a period between the current period's usage (cost of goods sold, an expense) and the amounts carried forward to future periods (the end of period inventory, an asset).

4. The following equation aids the understanding of the accounting for inventory. Beginning Inventory + Additions – Withdrawals = Ending Inventory. Slightly different terminology applied to the same equation is Beginning Inventory + Net Purchases – Cost of Goods Sold = Ending Inventory. Rearranging these terms produces the equation: Beginning Inventory + Net Purchases – Ending Inventory = Cost of Goods Sold. The valuation for ending inventory will appear on the balance sheet as the asset, merchandise inventory; the amount of cost of goods sold will appear on the income statement as an expense of producing sales revenue.

5. Some problems of inventory accounting are (a) the costs to be included in acquisition costs, (b) the valuation basis for items in inventory, (c) the frequency of computing inventory periodically or perpetually, and (d) the choice of cost flow assumptions used to trace the movement of costs into and out of inventory.

6. The amount on a balance sheet for inventory includes all costs incurred to acquire goods and prepare them for sale. For a merchandising firm, such costs include purchasing, transportation, receiving, unpacking, inspecting, and shelving costs. Because many of these costs are relatively small and because of the difficulty in assigning a definite dollar amount to specific purchases, the tendency is to treat these costs as operating expenses, although logically they are part of the total cost of merchandise available for sale.

7. For manufacturing firms, a procedure for including all production costs in the cost of the product is referred to as absorption costing. An alternative procedure, variable costing (direct costing), classifies production costs into two elements: variable manufacturing costs (those costs that tend to vary with output) and fixed manufacturing costs (those costs that tend to be relatively unaffected in the short run by the number of units produced). In variable costing (direct costing), only the variable manufacturing costs become product costs, while the fixed manufacturing costs are recognized as expenses in the period incurred.

8. Under absorption costing, unit costs of identical units of product can vary depending upon the volume of production during the period when the units are produced. The unit costs will vary because the fixed manufacturing costs are being absorbed by a different number of units produced in each period. For example, in a period of low production, each unit of product will absorb a greater amount of fixed costs; while in periods of high production, each unit will absorb a smaller amount of fixed cost. Therefore, under absorption costing, volume of production becomes a primary determinant of income, while under direct costing, production volume does not affect net income determination. Direct costing is used internally for management decisions, but currently is not allowed for published financial reports nor income tax reporting.

9. The procedure for recording purchases of merchandise, raw materials, and supplies varies from one business to another. Accountants usually recognize purchases only after a firm receives the invoice and inspects the goods. Adjustments may be made at the end of the accounting period to reflect any legal formalities dealing with passage of title.

10. The invoice price of merchandise seldom measures the total acquisition cost. A firm records adjustments for costs such as handling and transporting the goods, and for deductions of cash discounts, goods returned, and other allowances, in adjunct and contra accounts in order to provide a complete analysis of the cost of purchases. An adjunct account accumulates additions to another account. A contra account accumulates subtractions from another account.

11. The largest adjustment to the invoice price of merchandise is likely to be that for purchase discounts. Purchase discounts become a reduction in the purchase price. Often the implied interest rate for sales contracts with purchase discounts is extremely high. Purchasers find it advantageous to take the discount using money borrowed at a lower rate.

12. Five bases of inventory valuation (rules for assigning cost to physical units) used for one purpose or another are (a) acquisition cost, (b) current cost measured by replacement cost, (c) current cost measured by net realizable value, (d) lower-of-(acquisition) cost-or-market, and (e) standard cost.

13. When the acquisition cost (historical cost) basis is used, units in inventory are carried at their historical cost until sold. Any changes in the value of inventory items occurring between the time of acquisition and the time of sale do not appear in the financial statements.

14. Two current value bases are replacement cost, a current entry value, and net realizable value, a current exit value. Stating inventories at current cost requires firms to recognize gains and losses from changes in prices during the holding period that elapses between acquisition date and sale date. Whereas an acquisition cost basis for inventory shows objective, verifiable information that may be outdated, a current value basis shows current information that can be more useful but the amount shown may be more difficult to obtain and to audit.

174

15. The replacement cost of an inventory item at a given time is the amount the firm would have to pay to acquire the item at that time.

16. All items of inventory are not in a form ready for sale (there may be partially complete inventory in a manufacturing firm, for example) and a sales commission and other selling costs may often be incurred in ordinary sales transactions. Therefore, net realizable value is defined as the estimated selling price of the inventory less any estimated costs to make the item ready for sale and to sell it.

17. The lower-of-cost-or-market valuation basis is the lesser of the two amounts; acquisition cost or "market value." Market value is generally replacement cost but no more than net realizable value nor less than the net realizable value reduced by a "normal profit margin" on sales of items of this type.

18. The lower-of-cost-or-market basis for inventory valuation is a conservative policy because (a) accounting recognizes losses from decreases in market value before the firm sells goods, but does not record gains from increases in market value before a sale takes place, and (b) inventory figures on the balance sheet are never greater, but may be less, than acquisition costs. In other words, unrealized holding losses are recognized in the financial statement, whereas unrealized holding gains are not recognized.

19. Manufacturing firms frequently use standard cost systems for internal performance measurement and control. Standard cost is a predetermined estimate of what each item of manufactured inventory should cost, based on past experience and planned production methods.

20. Generally accepted accounting principles for inventory valuation and measurement of cost of goods sold require a combination of three valuation bases: acquisition cost, replacement cost, and net realizable value. Accounting generally uses historical cost basis but when "market value" is significantly less than acquisition cost, generally accepted accounting principles require the use of lower-of-cost-or-market.

21. Two principal approaches to calculating the physical quantity and dollar amount of an inventory are the periodic inventory system and the perpetual inventory system.

22. When a firm uses the periodic inventory system, it makes no entry as withdrawals take place (cost of goods sold or used). At the end of the accounting period, the firm takes a physical count of the units of inventory and multiplies by the cost per unit. The firm then uses this inventory value in the inventory equation (see Chapter Highlight 4) to determine the cost of goods sold.

23. A periodic inventory system generates no separate information to aid in controlling the amount of inventory shrinkage (the general name for losses such as breakage, theft, evaporation, and waste).

24. To count every item in inventory is generally expensive. Firms try to do it as seldom as possible, consistent with requirements of GAAP and proper inventory control. Firms use estimates to determine ending inventory and cost of goods sold for interim (monthly or quarterly) statements. Gross margin methods and retail methods provide reasonably good estimates. The foundation of these estimating methods is the fact that most businesses mark up the cost of similar kinds of merchandise by a relatively constant percentage in obtaining selling prices.

25. A perpetual (or continuous) inventory system calculates and records the cost of withdrawals at the time the items are withdrawn from the inventory. By inserting the value of the withdrawal into the inventory equation the remaining inventory may be determined after each withdrawal. Even under a perpetual inventory system, a physical count of items on hand must be made from time to time in order to check

the accuracy of the book figures and to gauge the loss from shrinkage. While all items in the inventory should be counted at least once a year, many firms stagger the count by scheduling the count of particular items when the stock on hand is near its low point for the year.

26. The perpetual system, which is usually more costly to administer than the periodic system, is justified when being "out of stock" may lead to costly consequences such as customer dissatisfaction or the need to shut down production. The periodic inventory system can cost less to administer than the perpetual inventory system, but it provides no data on inventory shortages. The periodic inventory system is likely to be cost-effective when being out of stock is not extremely costly, when there is a large volume of items with a small value per unit, or when items are hard to steal or pilfer.

27. An inventory valuation problem arises because of two unknowns in the inventory equation. The values of beginning inventory and purchases are known; the values of cost of goods sold and ending inventory are not known. The valuation of the ending inventory may be based on the most recent costs, the oldest costs, the average costs, or some other choice. Alternatively, a company may determine cost of goods sold using one of these sets of costs and then determine the valuation of the ending inventory, for once the amount of one unknown is assigned, then the equation automatically determines the amount of the other. The relation between the two unknowns in the inventory equation, cost of goods sold and closing inventory, is such that the higher the value assigned to one of them, the lower must be the value assigned to the other. There is no historical cost-based accounting method for valuing both inventories and cost of goods sold that allows the accountant to show recent costs on both the income statement and the balance sheet during a period of changing prices.

28. If the cost of items sold cannot be specifically identified, some assumption must be made as to the flow of cost in order to estimate the acquisition costs applicable to the units remaining in the inventory and to the unit sold. Three principal cost flow assumptions used for this purpose are first-in, first-out; last-in, first-out; and weighted-average.

29. The first-in, first-out cost flow assumption (FIFO) assigns the costs of the earliest units acquired to the withdrawals and the cost of the most recent acquisitions to the ending inventory.

30. The last-in, first-out cost flow assumption (LIFO) assigns the costs of the most recent acquisitions to the withdrawals and the costs of the earliest units acquired to the ending inventory.

31. The weighted-average method assigns costs to both inventory and withdrawals based upon a weighted average of all merchandise available for sale during the period.

32. FIFO conforms to most actual physical inventory flows, especially in the case of items which either deteriorate or become obsolete. FIFO leads to the highest reported net income of the three methods when prices are rising and the smallest when prices are falling. LIFO, on the other hand, produces a balance sheet valuation of inventory far removed from current cost and a cost-of-goods-sold figure close to current costs. During periods of rising prices LIFO produces a lower net income than FIFO. In recent years, LIFO has been a popular method used to reduce current income taxes. The weighted-average cost flow method falls between FIFO and LIFO in its effects on both the balance sheet and the income statement.

33. In only one major area in accounting, the use of LIFO flow assumption for tax purposes, does the Internal Revenue Service require firms to apply that flow assumption for the determination of income for financial reports to shareholders.

34. If under LIFO, in any year purchases exceed sales, the quantity of units in inventory increases. This increase is called a LIFO inventory layer.

176

35. If under LIFO, a firm must reduce end-of-period physical inventory quantities below what they were at the beginning of the period, then cost of goods sold will include the current period's purchases plus a portion of the older and lower costs in the beginning inventory. Such a firm will have larger reported income and income taxes in that period than if the firm had been able to maintain its ending inventory at beginning-of-period levels.

36. Managers of LIFO inventories are often faced with difficult decisions relative to the use of this inventory method. Managers must weigh the purchase decisions at year-end based on good (costwise) purchases as opposed to decisions to affect the right tax consequences. LIFO gives management the opportunity to manipulate income.

37. During periods of substantial price change, the choice of cost flow assumption for most companies affects financial statement more than any other choice between generally accepted financial accounting principles.

38. The conventionally reported gross margin (sales minus cost of goods sold) consists of (a) an operating margin and (b) a realized holding gain (or loss). In addition, there is usually an unrealized holding gain that is not currently included in income.

39. The operating margin denotes the difference between the selling price of an item and its replacement cost at the time of sale.

40. A holding gain (or loss) is the difference between the current replacement cost of an item and its acquisition cost.

41. The unrealized holding gain is the difference between the current replacement cost of the ending inventory and its acquisition cost.

42. The realized holding gain is the difference between cost of goods sold based on replacement cost and costs of goods sold based on acquisition cost.

43. The principal reason why net income is higher during periods of rising prices under FIFO than LIFO is that under FIFO the realized holding gain is larger since the earlier purchases at lower costs are charged to cost of goods sold.

44. The unrealized holding gain under LIFO is larger than under FIFO since earlier purchases with lower costs are assumed to remain in ending inventory under LIFO.

45. The sum of the operating margin plus all holding gains (both realized and unrealized) is the same under FIFO and LIFO. Most of the holding gain under FIFO is recognized in determining net income each period, whereas most of the holding gain under LIFO is not currently recognized in the income statement.

46. Internationally, all major industrialized countries require lower-of-cost-or-market method in the valuation of inventories. Few countries except in the United States and Japan allow LIFO as an acceptable cost flow assumption.

47. All transactions involving inventory affect the operations section of the statement of cash flows.

Questions and Exercises

True/False. **For each of the following statements, place a T or F in the space provided to indicate whether the statement is true or false.**

_____ 1. FIFO, LIFO, and weighted-average cost flow assumptions relate to costs associated with withdrawals from inventory. As a result, income reports vary but balance sheet valuations reflect little difference.

_____ 2. LIFO cost flow assumption assigns the cost of the latest units acquired to the withdrawals and the costs of the oldest units to the ending inventory.

_____ 3. Net income under FIFO is usually smaller than under LIFO when prices are rising.

_____ 4. Under absorption costing, fixed cost per unit remains the same regardless of changes in production volume.

_____ 5. Variable costs in total change with production volume.

_____ 6. Under direct costing, all variable production costs are expensed when incurred, while under absorption costing, both variable and fixed are expensed.

_____ 7. Direct costing and absorption costing are both used for published reports, but direct costing is utilized more for short-run decision making.

_____ 8. Under absorption costing, net income may increase due to production increases while sales remain the same.

_____ 9. The last-in, first-out cost flow method for tax purposes requires that the businesses carry a certain amount of reserve stock units on hand and that current operations and sales cannot dip into the reserve.

_____ 10. Reductions in inventory appear in the operating section of the statement of cash flows as an addition to net income in deriving cash flow from operations.

_____ 11. LIFO gives managers the opportunity to manipulate income.

_____ 12. Companies who use a periodic inventory system must physically count the inventory on their balance sheet date.

_____ 13. A LIFO inventory layer is created when in any year purchases exceed sales therefore increasing inventory.

_____ 14. One major difference between the perpetual and periodic inventory systems is that withdrawals are recorded when assets are withdrawn under the perpetual system, while they are recorded only at the end of the period under the periodic system.

_____ 15. A physical inventory count is not needed under a perpetual inventory system because a continuous record is kept of items in stock.

_____ 16. To inventory a stock of goods means to prepare a list of the items on hand at some specified date, to assign a unit price to each item, and to calculate the total cost of the inventory.

_____ 17. The term inventory, as used in accounting, means a list of assets—in both the current and noncurrent categories.

_____ 18. In most cases the total acquisition costs of inventory purchases may be measured accurately by the invoice price of the merchandise.

_____ 19. During periods of rising prices, the unrealized holding gain recognized on the income statement using FIFO is greater than the amount recognized under LIFO.

_____ 20. A conventionally reported gross margin on sales consists of a (1) realized holding gain and (2) an unrealized holding gain.

_____ 21. FIFO has the advantage of reporting up-to-date costs for cost of goods sold on the income statement and inventory on the balance sheet.

_____ 22. The term cost (for merchandise) may include invoice price plus cost of transportation, as well as costs of purchasing, receiving, handling, and storage.

_____ 23. The lower-of-cost-or-market basis refers to valuations using a comparison of acquisition cost and replacement cost.

_____ 24. Standard-cost systems employ catalog list prices to value inventory since control of acquisition cost is impossible.

_____ 25. Agricultural products in inventory are often valued at net realizable value, which is defined as selling price less cost of disposal.

_____ 26. The first-in, first-out cost flow assumption assigns the costs of the most recent acquisitions to the inventory and the costs of the earliest units acquired to the withdrawals.

_____ 27. Most industrialized countries require lower-of-cost-or-market basis for inventory valuation.

_____ 28. Most industrialized countries allow LIFO as an acceptable cost flow assumption.

Matching. From the list of terms below, select that term which is most closely associated with each of the descriptive phrases or statements that follows and place the letter for that term in the space provided.

a.	Absorption Costing	m.	Purchases
b.	Acquisition Cost Basis	n.	Purchase Discounts
c.	Cost of Goods Sold	o.	Raw Materials
d.	FIFO	p.	Realized Holding Gain
e.	Finished Goods	q.	Replacement Cost
f.	Inventory	r.	Shrinkage
g.	LIFO	s.	Specific Identification
h.	Lower-of-Cost-or-Market	t.	Standard Cost
i.	Net Realizable Value	u.	Unrealized Holding Gain
j.	Operating Margin	v.	Variable (Direct) Costing
k.	Periodic Inventory System	w.	Weighted-Average Method
l.	Perpetual Inventory System	x.	Work in Process

_____ 1. Materials being stored that will become a part of the goods to be produced.

_____ 2. Procedure by which a manufacturing firm includes all production costs in work in process.

_____ 3. "Losses" from inventory due to theft, evaporation, and waste.

_____ 4. Procedure whereby a manufacturing firm charges fixed production cost to the period rather than as a cost of the product.

_____ 5. A stock of goods owned by a firm and held for sale to customers.

_____ 6. The amount a firm would have to pay to acquire a replacement for an inventory item at that particular time.

_____ 7. The difference between the current replacement cost of the ending inventory and its acquisition cost.

_____ 8. The difference between the selling price of an item and its replacement cost at the time of sale.

_____ 9. The difference between cost of goods sold based on replacement cost and cost of goods sold based on acquisition cost.

_____ 10. Contra account title used to record discounts for early payments for merchandise.

_____ 11. Inventory cost flow assumption which is physically appropriate for liquid or other types of products for which distinguishing different lots is difficult.

_____ 12. Valuation basis which departs from cost when the utility of the goods is no longer as great as their cost.

_____ 13. This cost flow assumption has a parallel description for ending inventory referred to as first-in, still-here, or FISH.

_____ 14. The portion of merchandise available for sale or use that is allocated to the current period's usage.

_____ 15. Partially completed products in the factory.

_____ 16. Selling price less costs of marketing.

_____ 17. Account title and term designating acquisition of merchandise during the accounting period.

_____ 18. Cost flow assumption that assigns the costs of the earliest units acquired to the withdrawals and the costs of the most recent acquisitions to the ending inventory.

_____ 19. Assignment of cost where a firm can physically match individual units sold with a specific purchase.

_____ 20. Under this system, no entry is made for withdrawals from inventory until the end of the period.

_____ 21. A predetermined estimate of what each item of manufactured inventory should cost based on past cost and planned production methods.

_____ 22. Its use entails carrying units in inventory at their acquisition costs until sold.

_____ 23. This inventory system is designed so that the cost of withdrawals is recorded at the time assets are withdrawn from inventory.

_____ 24. Goods held for sale by a manufacturing concern.

Multiple Choice. Choose the best answer for each of the following questions and enter the identifying letter in the space provided.

_____ 1. Characteristics of the use of LIFO include all the following except

    a. Produces higher balance sheet valuation of inventory than FIFO during periods of rising prices.
    b. Produces lower net income than FIFO during periods of rising prices.
    c. Allows managers to manipulate net income.
    d. All of the above are characteristics.

_____ 2. Under this cost flow assumption, the income statement reports out-of-date cost of goods sold.

    a. FIFO method.
    b. LIFO method.
    c. Weighted-average method.
    d. Replacement cost method.

_____ 3. In the statement of cash flows, reductions in inventory

    a. Are treated differently than other reductions in current assets.
    b. Appear as an addition to net income in deriving cash flow from operations.
    c. Appear in the financing section.
    d. Appear in the investing section.

_____ 4. The inventories of a manufacturing company include

    a. Finished goods.
    b. Raw materials.
    c. Work in process.
    d. All of the above.

_____ 5. The differences between the current replacement cost of the ending inventory and its acquisition cost is the

    a. Operating margin.
    b. Realized holding gain.
    c. Unrealized holding gain.
    d. Gross margin.

_____ 6. Conventionally, accountants refer to the difference between sales and cost of goods sold as the

    a. Operating margin.
    b. Realized holding gain.
    c. Unrealized holding gain.
    d. Gross Margin.

_____ 7. The difference between cost of goods sold based on replacement cost and cost of goods sold based on acquisition cost is the

    a. Operating margin.
    b. Realized holding gain.
    c. Unrealized holding gain.
    d. Gross margin.

_____ 8. During periods of rising prices, this cost flow assumption produces the highest reported net income:

    a. FIFO method.
    b. LIFO method.
    c. Weighted-average method.
    d. All produce the same net income.

_____ 9. In an international perspective the following statements are accurate except

    a. Firms in most countries use FIFO and weighted average cost flow assumptions.
    b. All major developed countries require the lower-of-cost-or-market method.
    c. Few countries, except the United States and Japan, allow LIFO.
    d. All the statements are accurate.

_____ 10. Variable costing (direct costing) is acceptable for use in determining inventory cost

    a. By the Financial Accounting Standards Board.
    b. By the Internal Revenue Service.
    c. By either a or b above.
    d. By neither a or b above.

_____ 11. Which equation correctly applies to the determination of cost of goods sold?

    a. Beginning Inventory - Purchases + Ending Inventory = Cost of Goods Sold.
    b. Beginning Inventory + Purchases - Ending Inventory = Cost of Goods Sold.
    c. Beginning Inventory + Purchases + Ending Inventory = Cost of Goods Sold.
    d. None of the above.

_____ 12. Under a perpetual inventory system

    a. No entry is made as withdrawals take place.

    b. The cost to administer is usually less than under the periodic method.

    c. A physical count of items on hand should be made from time to time.

    d. Items in inventory are usually hard to steal or pilfer.

_____ 13. Which of the following is not acceptable for determination of inventory cost?

    a. FIFO method.

    b. LIFO method.

    c. Specific identification method.

    d. All of the above are acceptable.

_____ 14. Characteristics of the use of current value bases to determine inventory values and cost of goods sold include all of the following except

    a. Current value basis shows current information that can be more useful.

    b. The information is generally easier to obtain.

    c. The information may be more difficult to audit.

    d. None of the above.

_____ 15. The estimated selling price of the inventory less any estimated costs to make the item ready for sale and to sell it is the

    a. Replacement cost.

    b. Standard cost.

    c. Net realizable value.

    d. Market selling value.

_____ 16. The amount the firm would have to pay to acquire a replacement for an inventory item at that particular time is the

    a. Replacement cost.

    b. Net realizable value.

    c. Standard cost.

    d. Market selling value.

_____ 17. When applying the lower-of-cost-or-market valuation method each of the following is a factor except

    a. Replacement cost.

    b. Net realizable value.

    c. Standard cost.

    d. Acquisition cost.

_____ 18. A predetermined estimate of what each item of manufactured inventory should cost, based on past experience and planned production methods, is the

    a. Replacement cost.
    b. Net realizable value.
    c. Standard cost.
    d. Acquisition cost.

_____ 19. What is the difference between the selling price of an item and its replacement cost at the time of sale?

    a. Operating margin.
    b. Realized holding gain.
    c. Unrealized holding gain.
    d. Gross margin.

_____ 20. In variable costing (direct costing) for inventories for manufacturing firms, all of the following represent valid characteristics except

    a. Classification of production costs into variable manufacturing costs and fixed manufacturing costs.
    b. Generally accepted use for income tax and financial statements to owners.
    c. Product costs contain only variable costs.
    d. Unusual patterns of income do not result because the number of units produced differs from the number of units sold.

_____ 21. Under this cost flow assumption, the costs assigned to the ending inventory are the costs of the earliest units acquired:

    a. FIFO method.
    b. LIFO method.
    c. Weighted-average method.
    d. Replacement cost method.

_____ 22. This cost flow assumption conforms to most actual physical inventory flows:

    a. FIFO method.
    b. LIFO method.
    c. Weighted-average method.
    d. Replacement cost method.

_____ 23. If this inventory flow assumption is used for income tax purposes, the Internal Revenue Service requires its use for income determination for financial reports to owners:

    a. FIFO method.
    b. LIFO method.
    c. Weighted-average method.
    d. Replacement cost method.

Exercises

1. Place the correct number in the space provided for each of the following.

Beginning Inventory	$ 40,000	$ (c)	$ (e)	$ 45,000	$ (i)
Net Purchase	(a)	40,000	85,000	(g)	275,000
Total Goods Available	$440,000	$45,000	$85,000	$ 245,000	$350,000
Ending Inventory	36,000	(d)	-0-	(h)	90,000
Cost of Goods Sold	$ (b)	$38,000	$ (f)	$ 215,000	$ (j)

a. _____ f. _____

b. _____ g. _____

c. _____ h. _____

d. _____ i. _____

e. _____ j. _____

2. Polly Corp. sells goods on account on March 3, for $300. The goods cost $200. Prepare journal entries to be made at the time of the sale under each condition:

a. When a periodic inventory is used.

b. When a perpetual inventory is used.

3. Brother Prince Company uses LIFO inventory costing. Certain items of information relating to the current inventory operations are listed below:

Replacement cost of goods sold	$ 1,920
Acquisition cost of goods sold	$ 1,800
Replacement cost of ending inventory	$ 4,200
Acquisition cost of ending inventory	$ 3,240
Sales Revenue	$ 3,300

Determine a.   Operating Margin on Sales

b.   Realized Holding Gain

c.   Conventionally Reported Gross Margin

d.   Unrealized Holding Gain

4. The following data were obtained from the inventory records of Austin Company for the month of July:

July 1   Beginning Inventory   2,000   units @ $3 each

July 5   Issued   500   units

July 8   Purchased   1,000   units @ $4 each

July 12 Purchased   300   units @ $3 each

July 15 Issued   400   units

July 20 Issued   800   units

July 25 Issued   500   units

July 30 Purchased   500   units @ $5 each

a. Calculate the cost of July ending inventory assuming a periodic inventory system using the following:

1. · FIFO cost flow assumption.

2. LIFO cost flow assumption.

3. Weighted-average flow assumption.

b. Calculate the cost of goods sold for July assuming a periodic inventory system using the following:

   1. FIFO cost flow assumption.

   2. LIFO cost flow assumption.

c. Calculate the ending inventory and cost of goods sold assuming a perpetual inventory system using the following:

   1. LIFO cost flow assumption.

   2. Weighted-average flow assumption.

5. The following data were obtained from the inventory records of Lois Company for the months of May, June, and July:

Products	Units	Unit Cost	Total Cost
Beginning Inventory, May 1	—	—	—
Purchases, May 3	50	$5.00	$ 250
Purchases, May 23	75	6.00	450
Total Goods Available for Sale	125		$ 700
Withdrawal during May.	100		?
Ending Inventory, May 31, and			
Beginning Inventory, June 1	25		?
Purchases, June 15	100	6.50	650
Purchases, June 19.	150	7.00	1,050
Total Goods Available for Sale	275		?
Withdrawals during June.	225		?
Ending Inventory, June 30, and			
Beginning Inventory, July 1	50		?
Purchases, July 3	225	8.00	1,800
Total Goods Available for Sale	275		?
Withdrawals during July	245		?
Ending Inventory (July 31)	30		?

a. Compute the cost of goods sold (withdrawals) for May, June, and July, using a (1) FIFO, (2) LIFO, and (3) weighted-average cost flow assumption.

b. Compute the effect of the LIFO liquidation on net income before income taxes for the year.

c. Assume the following:

	June 30	July 31
Current assets excluding inventories	$650	$730
Current liabilities	715	712

1. Compute the current ratio for June 30 and July 31 using (a) FIFO, (b) LIFO, and (c) weighted-average cost flow assumption for inventories.

2. Compute the inventory turnover ratio for June and July using (a) FIFO, (b) LIFO, and (c) weighted-average cost flow assumption.

Answers to Questions and Exercises

True/False

1.	F	7.	F	13.	T	19.	F	25.	T
2.	T	8	T	14.	T	20.	F	26.	T
3.	F	9.	F	15.	F	21.	F	27.	T
4.	F	10.	T	16.	T	22.	T	28.	F
5.	T	11.	T	17.	F	23.	T		
6.	F	12.	F	18.	F	24.	F		

Matching

1.	o	6.	q	11.	w	16.	i	21.	t
2.	a	7.	u	12.	h	17.	m	22.	b
3.	r	8.	j	13.	g	18.	d	23.	l
4.	v	9.	p	14.	c	19.	s	24.	e
5.	f	10.	n	15.	x	20.	k		

Multiple Choice

1.	a	6.	d	11.	b	16.	a	21.	b
2.	a	7.	b	12.	c	17.	c	22.	a
3.	b	8.	a	13.	d	18.	c	23.	b
4.	d	9.	d	14.	b	19.	a		
5.	c	10.	d	15.	c	20.	b		

Exercises

1. a. $400,000
    b. $404,000
    c. $ 5,000
    d. $ 7,000
    e.   -0-
    f. $ 85,000
    g. $200,000
    h. $ 30,000
    i. $ 75,000
    j. $260,000

2.

			Dr.	Cr.
a.	3/3	Accounts Receivable	300	
		Sales		300
		To record sales on account.		
b.	3/3	Accounts Receivable	300	
		Sales		300
		To record sales on account.		
	3/3	Cost of Goods Sold	200	
		Merchandise Inventory (or Finished Goods Inventory)		200
		To record cost of goods sold.		

3.

a.	Sales Revenue	$3,300
	Less Replacement Cost of Goods Sold	1,920
	Operating Margin on Sales	$1,380

b.	Replacement Cost of Goods Sold	$1,920
	Less Acquisition Cost of Goods Sold	1,800
	Realized Holding Gain	$ 120

c.	Sales Revenue	$3,300
	Less Acquisition Cost of Goods Sold	1,800
	Conventionally Reported Gross Margin	$1,500
	(Sum of a + b above)	

d.	Replacement Cost of Ending Inventory	$4,200
	Less Acquisition Cost of Ending Inventory	3,240
	Unrealized Holding Gain	$ 960

4.

a.   1.

	Available	Issued
July 1 Beginning	2,000	
July 5		500
July 8	1,000	
July 12	300	
July 15		400
July 20		800
July 25		500
July 30	500	
Total Available Units	3,800	2,200
Issued Units	2,200	
Units in Ending Inventory	1,600	

	Units	Unit Cost	Total
	500	$5	$ 2,500
	300	3	900
	800	4	3,200
FIFO Ending Inventory	1,600		$ 6,600

2.

	Units	Unit Cost	Total
LIFO Ending Inventory	1,600	$3	$ 4,800

3.

	Units	Unit Cost		Total
	2,000	$3	=	$ 6,000
	1,000	4	=	4,000
	300	3	=	900
	500	5	=	2,500
	3,800			$13,400

$13,400/3,800 = $3.53*/unit

Weighted-Average			
Ending Inventory	1,600 @ $3.53	=	$ 5,648

*Rounded to the nearest cent.

b.   1.

	Units Sold	Unit Cost	Total
	2,000	$3	$6,000
	200	4	800
FIFO Cost of Goods Sold	2,200		$6,800

2.

	500	$5	$2,500
	300	3	900
	1,000	4	4,000
	400	3	1,200
LIFO Cost of Goods	2,200		$8,600

c.   1.

	Purchased			Issued			Balance		
Date	Units	Cost	Amount	Units	Cost	Amount	Units	Cost	Amount
7/1							2,000	$3	$6,000
7/5				500	$3	$1,500	1,500	3	4,500
7/8	1,000	$4	$4,000				1,500	3	4,500
							1,000	4	4,000
7/12	300	3	900				1,500	3	4,500
							1,000	4	4,000
							300	3	900
7/15				300	3	900	1,500	3	4,500
				100	4	400	900	4	3,600
7/20				800	4	3,200	1,500	3	4,500
							100	4	400
7/25				100	4	400			
				400	3	1,200	1,100	3	3,300
7/30	500	5	2,500				1,100	3	3,300
							500	5	2,500
				2,200	$7,600		1,600		$5,800

Perpetual LIFO Ending Inventory   1,600 units $5,800 cost

Perpetual LIFO Cost of Goods Sold   2,200 units $7,600 cost

2.

Date	Purchased			Issued			Balance		
	Units	Cost	Amount	Units	Cost	Amount	Units	Cost	Amount
7/1							2,000	$3	$6,000
7/5				500	$3	$1,500	1,500	3	4,500
7/8	1,000	$4	$4,000				2,500	3.40	8,500
7/12	300	3	900				2,800	3.36*	9,400
7/15				400	3.36	1,344	2,400	3.36	8,056
7/20				800	3.36	2,688	1,600	3.36	5,368
7/25				500	3.36	1,680	1,100	3.36	3,688
7/30	500	5	2,500				1,600	3.87*	6,188
				2,200		$7,212	1,600		$6,188

Perpetual Weighted-Average Ending Inventory   1,600 units $6,188 cost

Perpetual Weighted-Average Cost of Goods Sold   2,200 units $7,212 cost

*Rounded to the nearest cent.

5.

a.

Products	Units	Unit Costs	Total Cost FIFO	LIFO	Weighted Average
Beginning Inventory, May 1					
Purchases, May 3	50	$5.00	$ 250	$ 250	$ 250
Purchases, May 23	75	6.00	450	450	450
Total Goods Available for Sale	125		$ 700	$ 700	$ 700
May Withdrawals	100		550a	575c	560e
Ending Inventory, May 31, and					
Beginning Inventory, June 1	25		$ 150b	$ 125d	$ 140f
Purchases, June 15	100	6.50	650	650	650
Purchases, June 19	150	7.00	1050	1050	1050
Total Goods Available for Sale	275		$1850	$1825	$1840
June Withdrawals	225		1500g	1538i	1505k
Ending Inventory, June 30,					
Beginning Inventory, July 1	50		$ 350h	$ 287j	335l
Purchases, July 3	225	8.00	1800	1800	1800
Total Goods Available for Sale	275		$2150	$2087	$2135
July Withdrawals	245		1910m	1930o	1902q
Ending Inventory, July 31	30		$ 240n	$ 157p	$ 233r

a.   (50 @ $5.00) + (50 @ $6.00) = $550

b.   25 × $600 = $150

c.   (75 @ $6.00) + (25 @ $5.00) = $575

d.   25 × $5.00 = $125

e.   ($700/125) × 100 - $560

f.   ($700/125) × 25 = $140

g.   (25 @ 6.00) + (100 @ 6.50) + (100 @ 7.00) = $1500

h.   50 @ $7.00 = $350

I.   (150 @ $7.00) + (75 @ $6.50) = $1,538 (rounded)

j.   (25 @ $5.00) + (25 @ $6.50) = $287 (rounded)

k.   ($1,840/275) × 225 = $1,505 (rounded)

l.   ($1,840/275) × 50 = $335

m.   (50 @ $7.00) + (195 @ $8.00) = $1,910

n.   30 @ $8.00 = $240

o.   (225 @ 8.00) + (20 @ $6.50) = $1930

p.   (25 @ $5.00) + (5 @ $6.50) = $157 (rounded)

q.   ($2,135/275) × 245 = $1,902 (rounded)

r.   ($2,135/275) × 30 - $233 (rounded)

b. 20 × ($8.00 - $6.50) = $30

c. 1.

June 30	FIFO	LIFO	Weighted Average
($650 + $350)/$715	1.40		
($650 + $287)/$715		1.31	
($650 + $335)/$715			1.38

July 31			
($730 + $240)/$712	1.36		
($730 + $157)/$712		1.25	
($730 + $233)/$712			1.35

2.

June			
$1,500/.5($150 + $350)	6.00		
$1,538/.5($125 + $287)		7.47	
$1,505/.5($140 + $335)			6.34

July			
$1,910/.5($350 + $240)	6.47		
$1,930/.5($287 + $157)		8.69	
$1,902/.5($335 + $233)			6.70

Chapter 9

Plant, Equipment, and Intangible Assets: The Source of Operating Capacity

Chapter Highlights

1. Plant assets refer to long-lived assets used in operations of trading, service, and manufacturing enterprises and include land, buildings, machinery, and equipment.

2. Amortization is the general process of allocating the cost of long-lived assets over the several accounting periods of benefit.

3. Depreciation refers to amortization of plant assets (other than land).

4. Depletion denotes the amortization of the cost of natural resources, called wasting assets.

5. The general name amortization refers to the process of writing off the cost of all intangible assets.

6. The cost of a plant asset includes all charges necessary to prepare it for rendering services. For an asset such as equipment, the total cost would include the invoice price (less any discount), transportation costs, installation charges, and any other costs before the equipment is ready for use.

7. When a firm constructs its own building or equipment, the asset's costs include the costs of material, labor, and overhead during construction. In addition FASB Statement No. 34 requires the firm to capitalize interest paid during construction. The amount capitalized is the portion of interest cost incurred during the asset's construction periods that theoretically could have been avoided if the asset had not been constructed.

8. If there is a specific borrowing in connection with a self-constructed asset, the interest rate on that borrowing is used. If expenditures on plant exceed the specific borrowing, the interest rate to be applied to the excess is a weighted average of rates applicable to other borrowings of the enterprise. The total amount of interest to be capitalized cannot exceed the total interest costs for the period.

9. The cost of an asset with a limited life is the price paid for a series of future benefits—a purchase of so many hours or units of service. The plant asset accounts, other than land, are therefore similar in many respects to prepaid rent or insurance—payments in advance for benefits to be received in the future. As the firm uses asset in each period, it treats a portion of the investment in the asset as a cost of the benefits received. Depreciation accounting allocates the cost of an asset over its useful life in a reasonable and orderly fashion.

199

10. The determination of the amount of depreciation for any year is not an exact process, since the cost of the plant asset is a joint cost of several periods. Each period of the asset's use benefits from the services, but there is usually no single correct way to allocate a joint cost. Depreciation accounting attempts to assign reasonable periodic charges that reflect systematic calculations.

11. Depreciation is frequently characterized as a decline in the market value of assets. While there is certainly a decline in value of an asset from the time it is acquired until it is retired from service, the yearly decline in value is an unsatisfactory description of the charge for depreciation made to the operations of each accounting period. Depreciation is a process of cost allocation and not one of valuation.

12. Many factors lead to the retirement of assets from service, but the causes of decline in service potential result from either physical or functional causes. Physical factors include the normal wear and tear, decay, and deterioration from use. The most important functional cause is obsolescence. Identification of specific causes of depreciation can help when estimating the useful life of an asset.

13. There are three principal accounting problems in allocating the cost of an asset over time. They are (a) measuring the depreciable basis of the asset, (b) estimating its useful service life, and (c) deciding on the pattern of expiration of services over the useful life.

14. Historical cost accounting bases depreciation charges on the difference between acquisition cost and the asset's estimated salvage value (or net residual value). Salvage value represents the estimated proceeds on disposition of an asset less all removal and selling costs.

15. The estimate of service life must take into consideration both the physical and functional causes of depreciation. Past experience with similar assets, corrected for differences in the planned intensity of use or alterations in maintenance policy, is usually the best guide for the estimate.

16. Income tax laws allow shorter lives to be used in computing depreciation for tax reporting (called the Accelerated Cost Recovery System), but when these lives are shorter than the economic lives of the assets, the economic lives must be used for financial reporting.

17. There are five basic patterns for the allocation of the total depreciation charges to specific years when depreciation is based on the passage of time:

    (a) Straight-line depreciation.
    (b) Accelerated depreciation.
    (c) Decelerated depreciation.
    (d) Immediate expensing.
    (e) No depreciation.

18. The following specific depreciation methods will be discussed:

    (a) Straight-line (time) method.
    (b) Production or use (straight-line use) method.
    (c) Declining-balance methods.
    (d) Sum-of-the-years'-digits method.
    (e) Accelerate Cost Recovery System (ACRS).

19. Financial reporting most commonly uses the straight-line method, which provides a uniform pattern of depreciation per year. The annual depreciation is determined in the following manner:

$$\text{Annual Depreciation} \ = \ \frac{\text{Cost Less Estimated Salvage Value}}{\text{Estimated Life in Years}}.$$

20. Many assets are not used uniformly over time, as straight-line depreciation implies. Where assets are not likely to receive the same amount of use in each month or year of their lives, the straight-line method may result in an illogical charge for such assets. Instead, a depreciation charge based on actual usage during the period may be justified. The production method uses a uniform cost per unit of activity that is multiplied by the units of production for the period. The depreciation cost per unit of activity is as follows:

$$\text{Depreciation Cost Per Unit} \ = \ \frac{\text{Cost Less Estimated Salvage Value}}{\text{Estimated Number of Units}}.$$

21. The efficiency and earning power of many plant assets decline as the assets grow older. These assets provide more and better services in early years, with increasing amounts of maintenance as the assets grow older. These cases justify an accelerated method in which depreciation charges in early years are greater than in later years. Declining balance and sum-of-the-years' digits are two types of accelerated methods.

22. In the declining-balance method, the depreciation charge results from multiplying the net book value of the asset at the start of each period (cost less accumulated depreciation) by a fixed rate. The depreciation charge is then subtracted from the net book value in determining the depreciation base for the subsequent year. The salvage is not subtracted from the cost in making this depreciation calculation. However, the total depreciation taken over an asset's useful life cannot exceed the asset's cost less salvage value.

23. Firms sometimes use the 200 percent declining-balance method, in which the rate multiplied times the net book value is 200 percent of the straight-line rate.

24. Under declining-balance methods, the firm switches to straight-line depreciation of the remaining book value when the straight-line depreciation charge is higher than the declining-balance charge for depreciation.

25. Another accelerated method is sum-of-the-years' digits. Under this method, the depreciation charge results from applying a fraction, which diminishes from year to year, to the cost less salvage value of the asset. The numerator of the fraction is the number of periods of remaining life at the beginning of the year for which depreciation is being computed. Thus, the numerators for years 1–5 of an asset with a 5-year life would be 5, 4, 3, 2, 1, respectively. The denominator of the fraction, which remains the same for each year, is the sum of all such numbers. For an asset with a 5-year life, the denominator would be 15 = (1 + 2 + 3 + 4 + 5). The formula $n(n+1)/2$, where n is the asset's depreciable life, is useful in determining the sum-of-the-year's digits denominator.

26. For income tax reporting, firms generally use Accelerated Cost Recovery System (ACRS), sometimes abbreviated MACRS when the M means "modified," which specifies accelerated depreciation charges based on the class of asset. Under ACRS, almost all assets are grouped in one of seven classes of write-off periods. They are as follows:

    (a)   3 years—Some racehorses; almost no others.
    (b)   5 years—Cars, trucks, some manufacturing equipment, research and development property.
    (c)   7 years—Office equipment, railroad cars, locomotives.
    (d) 10 years—Vessels, barges, land improvements.
    (e) 20 years—Municipal sewers.
    (f) 27.5 years—Residential rental property.
    (g) 31.5 years—Nonresidential buildings.

27. ACRS is an accelerated method for three reasons. First, the depreciable lives specified by class of asset are generally shorter than the economic lives. Second, the rates employed for assets other than buildings are similar to the 150 percent and 200 percent declining-balance methods, which are more rapid than straight-line. Third, ACRS allows salvage to be ignored in calculating depreciation, therefore the entire depreciable basis can be written off.

28. The goal in financial reporting for long-lived assets is to provide a statement of income that is realistic in measuring the expiration of these assets. In order to accomplish this purpose, the depreciation reported and the method selected should report depreciation charges based upon reasonable estimates of asset expirations.

29. The goal in depreciation accounting for tax purposes should be to maximize the present value of the reductions in tax payments from deducting depreciation. Earlier deductions are worth more than later ones (if tax rates do not change) because a dollar saved today is worth more than a dollar saved later. For tax purposes, the asset should be written off as soon as possible. Use of ACRS will accomplish this purpose.

30. The journal entry to record depreciation involves a debit either to depreciation expense, or, in the case of a manufacturer, to a product cost account and a credit to a contra asset account, Accumulated Depreciation. The Accumulated Depreciation account is shown on the balance sheet as a deduction from the asset account to which it relates. The term "book value" refers to the difference between the balance of the asset account and the balance of its accumulated depreciation account.

31. The original depreciation schedule for a particular asset may require changing due to previously incorrect estimates of the asset's useful life or salvage value. If the misestimate is material, corrective action must be taken. The generally accepted procedure for handling this problem is to make no adjusting entry for the past misestimate but to spread the undepreciated balance less the revised estimate of the salvage value over the revised estimate of the remaining service life of the asset.

32. Depreciation is not the only cost of using a depreciating asset. There will almost always be some repair and maintenance costs incurred during the life of the asset. Repairs are the small adjustments and replacements of parts whose effect does not extend estimated service life of an asset materially or otherwise increase productivity capacity. Maintenance includes routine costs such as cleaning and adjusting. Repair and maintenance costs are charged to expense as costs are incurred.

33. Improvements involve making an asset subsequently better by improving its productive capacity. Whereas repairs maintain or restore service potential, improvements extend service beyond what was originally anticipated. Accountants treat costs of improvements as an asset acquisition.

34. When an asset is retired, an entry should be made to bring depreciation up to date. Then the cost of the asset and its related accumulated depreciation must be removed from the books. The difference between the proceeds received on retirement and the book value (cost less accumulated depreciation) is either a gain (if positive) or a loss (if negative).

35. Instead of selling an asset, a firm may trade it in on a new one. The trade-in transaction can be viewed as a sale of an old asset followed by the purchase of a new asset. The accounting for trade-in transactions determine simultaneously the gain or loss on disposal of the old asset and the acquisition costs recorded for the new asset.

36. Property, plant, and equipment accounts appear in the balance sheet among the noncurrent assets. Firms generally disclose the assets' cost and accumulated depreciation in one of three ways: (a) the balance sheet contains the original cost less accumulated depreciation; (b) the balance sheet omits the original costs, presenting the accumulated depreciation and book value; and (c) the balance omits the original cost and accumulated depreciation, presenting only the book value (details appear in notes).

37. Depreciation expense appears in the income statement, sometimes disclosed separately and sometimes, particularly for manufacturing firms, as part of cost of goods sold expense.

38. The costs of finding natural resources and preparing to extract them should be capitalized and amortized. There are two acceptable treatments for capitalizing exploration costs: full costing and successful efforts.

39. Full costing capitalizes the costs of all exploration (both successful and unsuccessful) so long as the expected benefits from the successful explorations will more than cover the cost of all explorations.

40. Successful efforts costing capitalizes only the costs of successful efforts; the cost of unsuccessful exploration efforts become expenses of the period when the fact becomes apparent that the efforts will not result in productive sites.

41. Depletion is the name for amortization of natural resources. The depletion method most often employed for financial accounting statements is the units-of-production method, which is comparable to the production method of depreciation.

42. In special circumstances, tax laws permit computation of depletion for measuring taxable income by the percentage-depletion method, which is not generally acceptable for financial accounting. In financial accounting, depletion charges off the cost of the natural resources as it is consumed. Under percentage depletion, a firm may deduct from taxable income an amount equal to a specified percentage of the revenues earned from the sale of natural resources, regardless of the cost of the natural resources.

43. Intangible assets provide future benefits without having physical form. Examples are research costs, advertising costs, patents, trademarks, and copyrights. The first problem with intangibles is to decide whether the expenditures have future benefits and should be capitalized and amortized over time or whether they have no measurable future benefits and should be expensed in the period incurred. The second problem is how to amortize the cost if they are capitalized. Amortization of capitalized intangibles usually uses the straight-line method, but other methods can be used if they seem appropriate.

44. Firms incur research and development costs to develop a new product or process, to improve present products or processes, or to develop new information that may be useful at some future date. Whatever the reason, nearly all research costs will yield their benefits, if any, in future periods. The accounting issue, therefore, is whether to expense these costs immediately when incurred or to capitalize them and amortize them over future periods. Theoretically, the research costs should be matched with the benefits produced by their expenditure through the capitalization procedure with amortization over the benefitted

periods. Generally accepted accounting principles, however, require immediate expensing in all cases because of the uncertainty of future benefits and conservatism.

45. A patent is a right obtained from the federal government to exclude others from the use of the benefits of an invention. A firm amortizes purchased patent costs over the shorter of (a) the remaining legal life (as long as 17 years) or (b) the estimated economic life. A firm expenses internally developed patent costs as required for all research and development costs.

46. Firms incur advertising expenditures to increase sales of the period in which they are made. There is a lag, however, between the incurrence of these costs and their impact, probably extending into subsequent periods. Even though advertising often benefits more than merely the period of expenditure, common practice is to immediately expense these costs.

47. Goodwill is an intangible asset that arises from the purchase of one company by another company and is the difference between the amount paid for the acquired company as a whole and the current value of its individual identifiable net assets. The amount of goodwill acquired is recognized only on the books of the company making the acquisition. Goodwill is not recognized by a company that has internally developed goodwill. Generally accepted accounting principles require that goodwill be amortized over a period not exceeding 40 years.

48. In most developed countries accounting for plant assets, depreciation, and intangible assets parallels that in the United States. One recent change in the Great Britain is that firms now place a valuation on their brand names and include this item among the assets on the balance sheet.

49. The statement of cash flows reports the cash used for the acquisition of plant and intangible assets and cash provided by their retirement among the investing activities. The investing section of the statement shows all the proceeds from the sale of plant and intangible assets. On the statement of cash flows using the indirect approach, the net income is the starting point in computing cash flow from operations. If plant or intangible assets are sold at an amount different from their book value then a gain or loss results. Since this sale is nonoperating, any loss is added back and any gain is deducted from net income in deriving operating cash flows. The statement shows adjustments for depreciation and amortization in deriving cash from operations. Depreciation and amortization are added back to net income in deriving cash from operations.

Questions and Exercises

True/False. **For each of the following statements, place a T or F in the space provided to indicate whether the statement is true or false.**

_____ 1. The term "accelerated depreciation method" implies that the amount of depreciation per year decreases as the asset becomes older.

_____ 2. A firm is not required to use the same method of depreciation for financial accounting and income tax purposes.

_____ 3. The goal of a firm when choosing a depreciation method for tax purposes should be to maximize the present value of the tax savings attributable to the depreciation charge.

_____ 4. Depreciation can be recorded as a product cost or an expense.

_____ 5. The goal for computing depreciation is the same for tax purposes and financial accounting even though different methods may be used.

_____ 6. Common practice is to expense advertising costs even though the benefits extend beyond the period of expenditure.

_____ 7. The useful life of an asset for computing depreciation should be the total number of years for which the asset is physically capable of performing.

_____ 8. Intangible assets lack physical substance.

_____ 9. When calculating depreciation for tax reporting, salvage is ignored.

_____ 10. A major difficulty in ACRS depreciation is determining the useful life of the asset.

_____ 11. The production method is a type of straight-line method.

_____ 12. The recognition of goodwill when one company acquires another should be made on the books of the company that developed the goodwill.

_____ 13. Patent costs must be amortized over the legal life of the patent—17 years.

_____ 14. When a depreciable asset is disposed of, an entry should be made to bring depreciation up to date before making the entry to remove the asset from the books.

_____ 15. When the estimated useful life of an asset is revised, it is necessary to correct the books for misstated depreciation in previous years.

_____ 16. Property, plant, and equipment accounts appear in the balance sheet among the financing items.

_____ 17. When the efficiency and earning power of assets decline as the assets grow older, it may be appropriate to employ an accelerated depreciation method.

_____ 18. Firms expense all research and development costs when incurred for financial accounting purposes.

_____ 19. The usual entry to record depreciation on a building is to debit Depreciation Expense and credit Building.

_____ 20. The most common depletion method for financial accounting purposes is the units-of-production method.

_____ 21. Declines in the service potential of an asset are due to both physical and functional factors.

_____ 22. Under full costing, the full cost of successful efforts are capitalized and the full cost of unsuccessful efforts are expensed.

_____ 23. The book value of an asset is the difference between the balance of the asset account and its salvage value.

_____ 24. Accumulated depreciation is a contra asset account used to house the total amount written off through depreciation.

_____ 25. The percentage-depletion method is permitted for tax purposes but is not acceptable for financial accounting.

_____ 26. When the proceeds from the sale of an asset exceed the net book value, there is a gain on the sale.

_____ 27. The cost of testing a newly acquired piece of equipment, prior to initial use, should be expensed.

_____ 28. The depreciation method most commonly used for financial statement purposes is the straight-line method.

_____ 29. When the rate of usage of an asset varies from period to period, a depreciation charge based upon actual usage during the period may be justified.

_____ 30. Expenditures made to repair an asset should be capitalized.

_____ 31. The amount of expenses in any one year is the same whether interest during construction is capitalized or not.

_____ 32. Identifying the specific cause of depreciation is not essential for measuring it.

_____ 33. Salvage value can never be negative.

_____ 34. Interest costs incurred during construction of a plant asset should be capitalized.

_____ 35. Amortization of intangible assets is called depletion.

_____ 36. Expenditures made on an asset to maintain the service level anticipated should be expensed when incurred, but costs to improve an asset should be capitalized.

_____ 37. In the depreciation calculation, the task of estimating service lives is no problem due to the abundant data from experience.

_____ 38. If the current value of a depreciable asset rises instead of falls over a year, the income statement would report an appreciation gain rather then depreciation expense.

_____ 39. The main purpose underlying depreciation accounting is to record the decline in market values of assets over their useful life.

_____ 40. Since the investment in a depreciable asset is the price paid for a series of future benefits, the asset is similar in many respects to prepayments for rent or insurance.

_____ 41. Theoretically, research and development costs should probably be capitalized and amortized over future periods.

_____ 42. The sum-of-the-years' digits depreciation method applies a constant rate per year times the declining book value of the asset.

_____ 43. Since the cost of a plant asset is a joint cost of many benefitted periods, there is no single correct way to determine the amount of periodic depreciation charge.

_____ 44. The 150 percent declining-balance method is one of several decelerated methods.

_____ 45. Since 1981, firms generally use ACRS method of depreciation for financial reporting.

Matching. From the following list of terms, select that term which is most closely associated with each of the descriptive phrases or statements that follows and place the letter for that term in the space provided.

a. Accelerated Methods
b. Accelerated Cost Recovery System
c. Accumulated Depreciation
d. Advertising
e. Book Value
f. Building under Construction
g. Compound Interest Depreciation Method
h. Cost Allocation
i. Deferral Method
j. Depletion
k. Depreciation
l. Expense
m. Full Costing Method

n. Goal of Depreciation Accounting for Financial Statement Purposes
o. Goodwill
p. Improvements
q. Intangible Assets
r. Obsolescence
s. n(n+1)/2
t. Patent
u. Percentage Depletion
v. Repairs
w. Salvage Value
x. Self-Constructed Assets
y. Trade-in Allowance
z. Work-in-Process Inventory

_____ 1. Account debited if depreciation is a production cost.

_____ 2. Interest is capitalized for these items.

_____ 3. Depreciation is not a decline in value; it is a process of _____ .

_____ 4. Amortization of natural resources.

_____ 5. Small adjustments and replacement to plant assets with little or no effect on useful life.

_____ 6. Proceeds upon disposition of an asset at the end of its useful life.

_____ 7. Matching of costs with the benefits derived from the use of an asset.

_____ 8. A cost normally expensed when incurred even though future benefits exist.

_____ 9. A cost allocation of wasting assets method that is only allowed for tax reporting.

_____ 10. An intangible that appears on the balance sheet only when one company is acquired by another.

_____ 11. All exploration costs are capitalized so long as the expected benefits from successful explorations will more than cover the cost of all explorations.

_____ 12. Cost less accumulated depreciation.

_____ 13. Proper accounting for all research and development costs when incurred.

_____ 14. Assets that can provide future benefits without having physical form.

_____ 15. Groups assets into one of seven classes for tax depreciation.

_____ 16. A functional factor in determining depreciation.

_____ 17. Sum-of-the-years' digits is an example of one.

_____ 18. The account credited for depreciation.

_____ 19. Denominator of the sum-of-the-years' digits fraction.

_____ 20. Legal right to future benefits of an invention.

Multiple Choice. Choose the best answer for each of the following questions and enter the identifying letter in the space provided.

_____ 1. Which of the costs listed below would not be included in the cost of the machinery?

    a. Invoice price.
    b. Installation costs.
    c. Testing of machinery prior to its intended use.
    d. All of the above would be included.

_____ 2. In the statement of cash flows using the indirect method, the following would be added to net income in deriving operating cash flows:

    a. Amortization.
    b. Depreciation.
    c. Loss on retirement of a plant asset.
    d. All of the above.

_____ 3. In the statement of cash flows using the indirect method, the following would be deducted from net income in deriving operating cash flows:

    a. Gain on retirement of a plant asset.
    b. Depreciation.
    c. Loss on retirement of a plant asset.
    d. None of the above.

_____ 4. In the statement of cash flows using the indirect method, the following would be included in the cash flows from investing activities:

    a. Proceeds from the retirement of plant assets.
    b. Amortization.
    c. Depreciation.
    d. Net Income.

_____ 5. The generally accepted procedure for corrective action for material misestimates involving depreciation is

    a. To spread the remaining undepreciated balance less the new estimate of salvage value over the new estimate of remaining service life of the asset.
    b. To make an adjustment for the past misestimate.
    c. Either a or b.
    d. Neither a or b.

_____ 6. The text describes five basic patterns for allocations of fixed assets:

    E – Expense immediately.
    S – Straight-line depreciation.
    A – Accelerated depreciation.
    D – Decelerated depreciation.
    N – No depreciation.

    Which basic pattern would be appropriate for land?

    a. E.
    b. S.
    c. D.
    d. N.

_____ 7. Referring to the question above, which pattern would be appropriate for most intangibles?

    a. E.
    b. S.
    c. A.
    d. N.

_____ 8. Which term below is used when referring to the write-off of intangible assets?

    a. Amortization.
    b. Depreciation.
    c. Depletion.
    d. Write-off.

_____ 9. Grouping assets into one of seven life classes is a characteristic of which of the following:

    a Sum-of-the-years' digits method.
    b. Accelerated cost recovery system.
    c. Declining-balance method.
    d. None of the above.

_____ 10. Which of the factors listed below is an example of a functional cause of depreciation?

    a. Wear and tear.
    b. Inadequate size to meet current needs of the company.
    c. Rust or decay.
    d. Deterioration from wind and rain.

_____ 11. The Foschee Co. owns machinery having a cost of $100,000 and accumulated depreciation of $60,000 on January 1, 1995. On July 1, 1995, the machinery is sold for $43,000. The straight-line depreciation method has been used during the previous 6 years of life. How much gain or loss will be recorded on the sale?

    a. $ 3,000 gain.
    b. $13,000 gain.
    c. $22,000 loss.
    d. $ 8,000 gain.

_____ 12. In selecting the best depreciation method for tax purposes, which statement below would not be correct?

    a. The goal should be to maximize the present value of the tax savings from the depreciation deductions.
    b. The asset should be written off as soon as possible.
    c. Earlier depreciation deductions are more valuable than later ones.
    d. A decelerated depreciation method should be employed.

_____ 13. Colleen Co. acquired a machine for $20,000 in 1994 and has depreciated it on the straight-line basis (no salvage value) for 2 years based upon an estimated 10-year life. In 1996 it was determined that the remaining life was only 4 years instead of 8. What amount of depreciation should be recorded for 1996, based upon generally accepted accounting principles?

    a. $5,000.
    b. $4,000.
    c. $3,333.
    d. $2,000.

_____ 14. Which cost below is capitalized for a self-constructed asset?

    a. Interest prior to construction.
    b. Interest during construction.
    c. Interest after construction.
    d. All of the above.

_____ 15. For which method below may salvage be ignored in calculating depreciation?

    a. Straight-line.
    b. Sum-of-the-years' digits.
    c. Production method.
    d. ACRS.

_____ 16. For which depreciation method below is the estimate of useful life not required?

    a. Straight-line.
    b. Sum-of-the-years' digits.
    c. 200-percent declining-balance.
    d. ACRS.

_____ 17. Tiny Tim Co. purchased a machine that cost $20,000 and has a $2,000 salvage value and a 5-year life. What should be the depreciation charge for the first year under the sum-of-the-years' digits method?

    a. $1,200.
    b. $6,000.
    c. $6,667.
    d. $8,000.

_____ 18. Anna Co. buys a building on April 1, 1995, for $100,000. The building has a physical life of 50 years, but Anna anticipates using the building for 30 years. At the end of 50 years, the building will have no disposal value, but it will have a disposal value of $5,000 in 30 years. How much depreciation would be recorded on December 31, 1995, if the straight-line method is used?

    a. $3,167.
    b. $2,000.
    c. $1,500.
    d. $2,375.

_____ 19. The Allison Company on January 1, 1996, has machinery on the books that originally cost $200,000. During 1996, the following expenditures were made:

Minor Repairs	$ 5,000
Improvements	10,000
Additions	37,000

How much would be recorded in the machinery account on December 31, 1996?

    a. $252,000.
    b. $247,000.
    c. $235,000.
    d. $225,000.

_____ 20. Shamaine Co. purchases a piece of equipment on January 1, 1995, at a cost of $100,000. The equipment has a 5-year useful life and can be sold for $10,000 at the end of 5 years. How much depreciation would be recorded in the second year if Shamaine Co. uses the 150 percent declining-balance depreciation method?

    a. $21,000.
    b. $20,000.
    c. $18,900.
    d. $27,000.

_____ 21. Michelle Co. has spent $250,000 on research and development during 1995 to generate new product lines. Of the five projects being worked on, one resulted in a patented item while the other four were considered unsuccessful. According to generally accepted accounting principles, how much of the $250,000 should be recognized as an expense in 1995?

    a. $250,000.
    b. $ -0-.
    c. $200,000.
    d. $ 50,000.

_____ 22. Each of the following methods are generally accepted for financial reporting for wasting assets except

    a. Full costing method.
    b. Successful-effort method.
    c. Units-of-production method.
    d. Percentage-depletion method.

_____ 23. When the ACRS method of depreciation is employed, which life would be used for automobiles?

    a. 3 years.
    b. 5 years.
    c. 10 years.
    d. 15 years.

_____ 24. Which statement is not true concerning ACRS depreciation?

    a. It is an accelerated method.
    b. It is used for tax reporting.
    c. Salvage cannot be ignored.
    d. It assumes that all purchases take place at midyear.

_____ 25. When the rate of usage for an asset varies greatly from period to period, the depreciation method that would best match the cost with expected benefits would be which of the following?

    a. Straight-line method.
    b. Production method.
    c. Declining-balance method.
    d. Sum-of-the-years' digits method.

_____ 26. Volley Co. reports its net assets at a book value of $150,000. Recent investigation revealed that the net assets had a market value of $175,000. In addition, Volley had been offered $220,000 for the company by Conglomerate Corp. What is the amount of goodwill that should be recorded on the books of Volley?

    a. $ -0-.
    b. $25,000.
    c. $45,000.
    d. $70,000.

_____ 27. Firms generally disclose in the balance sheet property, plant, and equipment, and related accumulated depreciation by displaying which of the following?

    a. The original cost less accumulated depreciation.
    b. The accumulated depreciation and the book value.
    c. The book value and by providing the detail of cost and accumulated depreciation in the notes.
    d. All of the above are used.

_____ 28. Natural resources are called

    a. Intangible assets.
    b. Plant assets.
    c. Wasting assets.
    d. None of the above.

Exercises

1. The Williams Corp. purchased some equipment on April 1, 1995, for $78,000. The freight costs were $1,500. Upon receipt, the following expenditures were incurred:

Major repair prior to use	$ 2,300
Rearrangement of other machinery to accommodate new machine	2,000
Rewiring for new machine	500
Installation	650
Testing prior to productive use	
Labor	500
Materials	200
Operating costs after start of productive operations	29,000
Minor repair during operational period	820
Depreciation in first year of use	1,500

Determine the costs that should be assigned to the equipment account. Include how any items excluded from this account would be properly handled.

2. The Lois Company has the following relevant debt and equity structure:

Long-term debt, at 13 percent	$5,000,000
Capital Stock	6,000,000
Retained Earnings	2,500,000

Lois is constructing a building for its own productive use, which is being financed with long-term debt. During the year the average balance in the construction accounts was $6,000,000. A construction loan for $4,000,000 was taken out at the beginning of the year, requiring the payment of interest at 14 percent.

Determine the amount of interest to be capitalized for the year.

3. Journalize the following transactions. All of the transactions are related to the same machine.

   a. A machine is purchased for $4,000 on account.
   b. Depreciation of $500 for one year is recorded.
   c. The machine is sold for $800 cash. At the time of the sale, the Accumulated Depreciation account shows a balance of $2,500. Depreciation of $500 for the current year (asset is sold at the end of the year) has not been recorded.

4. A truck is purchased for $8,000 and is expected to have a 5-year useful life and a $1,000 salvage value at the end of that time. The truck is further expected to be operable for a total of 1,400 hours during the 5 years. Calculate the depreciation expense in each of the 5 years for the following depreciation methods.

   a. The straight-line method.

b. The sum-of-the-years' digits method.

c. The 150 percent declining-balance method.

d. The hours of production method, if the production hours in years 1–5 were 240, 280, 360, 320, and 200, respectively.

e. The ACRS method (for tax purposes).

5. Prince Company purchased land with a building on it as a site for a new plant it planned to construct. Classify the expenditures listed below into either the Land account, the Plant account, or neither Land nor Plant.

   a. Cost of building permit. _____

   b. Cost of property taxes assumed by Prince accrued to date of purchase of land. _____

   c. Proceeds from sale of salvage material from old building. _____

   d. Interest incurred to finance construction. _____

   e. Property taxes accrued since date of land acquisition. _____

   f. Cost of land and old building. _____

   g. Legal fees in connection with land purchase. _____

   h. Cost of construction of plant by independent contractor. _____

   i. Cost of repairing a construction truck damaged in an accident by a careless worker. _____

6. On July 1, 1995, the Phylis Company purchased a machine for $20,000, having an estimated life of 8 years and a salvage value of $2,000.

   In early 1996, a major improvement to the machine took place, costing $2,500. As a result the annual capacity was expanded, but its estimated life remained unchanged.

   During 1997, Phylis revised its estimated useful life to be only 3 remaining years and its salvage value to be $1,000.

   Calculate the depreciation for 1995, 1996, and 1997 using the straight-line method.

7. Give correcting journal entries for the following situation. Assume each case is independent and the firm uses straight-line depreciation. You are making the correction at year-end prior to the company closing its books.

a. A piece of store equipment was purchased for $1,000 at the beginning of the year. The equipment had an estimated life of 5 years, with no salvage value. The bookkeeper made the following entry to record the transaction:

Supplies Expense	1,000	
Cash		1,000

b. A used truck was sold for $4,000. At the time of the sale, the truck's related accumulated depreciation (properly recorded) was $5,000. Its original cost was $8,000. The bookkeeper made the following entry to record the transaction:

Cash	4,000	
Truck		4,000

Answers to Questions and Exercises

True/False

1.	T	11.	T	21.	T	31.	F	41.	T
2.	T	12.	F	22.	F	32.	T	42.	F
3.	T	13.	F	23.	F	33.	F	43.	T
4.	T	14.	T	24.	T	34.	T	44.	F
5.	F	15.	F	25.	T	35.	F	45.	F
6.	T	16.	F	26.	T	36.	T		
7.	F	17.	T	27.	F	37.	F		
8.	T	18.	T	28.	T	38.	F		
9.	T	19.	F	29.	T	39.	F		
10.	F	20.	T	30.	F	40.	T		

Matching

1.	z	5.	v	9.	u	13.	l	17.	a
2.	x	6.	w	10.	o	14.	q	18.	c
3.	h	7.	n	11.	m	15.	b	19.	s
4.	j	8.	d	12.	e	16.	r	20.	t

Multiple Choice

1.	d	7.	b	13.	b	19.	b	25.	b
2.	d	8.	a	14.	b	20.	a	26.	a
3.	a	9.	b	15.	d	21.	a	27.	d
4.	a	10.	b	16.	d	22.	d	28.	c
5.	a	11.	d	17.	b	23.	b		
6.	d	12.	d	18.	d	24.	c		

Exercises

1. The Cost of Equipment:

Purchase price	$78,000
Freight	1,500
Major repair	2,300
Rearrangement of machinery	2,000
Rewiring	500
Installation	650
Testing	700
	$85,650

The operating expenses, minor repair and depreciation, would be in the operating expense section of the 1995 income statement.

2. The interest capitalized for Lois Company is as follows:

$$.14 \times \$4,000,000 = \$560,000$$
$$.13 \times \ \ 2,000,000 = \ \ \underline{260,000}$$
$$\$820,000$$

3.

	Dr.	Cr.
a. Machinery	4,000	
Accounts Payable		4,000
Purchased machine on account.		
b. Depreciation Expense	500	
Accumulated Depreciation		500
To record annual depreciation.		
c. Depreciation Expense	500	
Accumulated Depreciation		500
To record annual depreciation.		
Cash	800	
Accumulated Depreciation	3,000	
Loss on Sale of Machine	200	
Machinery		4,000
To record sale of machine.		

4. a.

$$\text{Depreciation per year} = \frac{\$8,000 - \$1,000}{5} = \$1,400$$

b.

Year	Depreciation Fraction		Cost Less Salvage	Depreciation
1	5/15*	×	$7,000	$2,333
2	4/15	×	7,000	1,867
3	3/15	×	7,000	1,400
4	2/15	×	7,000	933
5	1/15	×	7,000	467
				$7,000

*(1 + 2 + 3 + 4 + 5 = 15)

c.

Year	Book Value at Beginning of Year		Depreciation Rate	Depreciation
1	$8,000	×	.30	$2,400
2	5,600	×	.30	1,680
3	3,920	×	.30	1,176
4	2,744	×	.30	823
5	1,921	×	.30	576*
End	1,345			
				$6,655

*Since the book value was still $1,345 at the end of Year 5, an additional depreciation of $345 may have been taken to reduce the book value to the $1,000 salvage value.

d.

Year	Hours Produced	Depreciation Rate*	Depreciation
1	240	$5	$1,200
2	280	5	1,400
3	360	5	1,800
4	320	5	1,600
5	200	5	1,000
			$7,000

*($8,000 - $1,000)/1,400 = $5/hour.

220

e.

Year*	ACRS %		Cost	Depreciation
1	20.0%	×	$8,000	$1,600
2	32.0	×	8,000	2,560
3	19.2	×	8,000	1,536
4	11.5	×	8,000	920
5	11.5	×	8,000	920
6	5.8	×	8,000	464
				$8,000

*An asset in the 5-year property class for ACRS will have depreciation charges in 6 calendar years.

5. a. Plant
   b. Land
   c. Land (deduction)
   d. Plant
   e. Other (expense)
   f. Land
   g. Land
   h. Plant
   i. Other (loss or expense)

6.

1995: $$\text{Depreciation} = \frac{\$20,000 - \$2,000}{8} = \frac{\$18,000}{8} \times 1/2 \text{ year} = \underline{\underline{\$1,125}}$$

1996:

Original Cost	$20,000
Less: Depreciation in 1995	(1,125)
Plus: Improvement	2,500
Book Value, Depreciation before 1996	$21,375
Less: Salvage	2,000
Depreciable Basis	$19,375
Remaining Life	÷ 7.5 years
Depreciation, 1996	$ 2,583

1997:

Book Value, before 1996 Depreciation	$21,375
Less: Depreciation in 1996	2,583
Book Value, 1/1/97	$18,792
Less: Revised Salvage	1,000
Depreciable Basis	$17,792
Remaining Life (Revised)	÷ 3
Depreciation, 1997	$ 5,931

7.

	Dr.	Cr.
a. Equipment	1,000	
Depreciation Expense	200	
Supplies Expense		1,000
Accumulated Depreciation		200
To correct error in recording equipment purchase.		
b. Accumulated Depreciation	5,000	
Truck		4,000
Gain on Sale of Truck		1,000
To correct error in recording sale of truck.		

Chapter 10

Liabilities: Introduction

Chapter Highlights

1. An obligation is generally recognized as a liability of an entity if it has three essential characteristics: (a) the obligation involves a probable future sacrifice of resources at a specified or determinable date and the cash-equivalent value of resources to be sacrificed can be measured with reasonable precision; (b) the firm has little or no discretion to avoid the transfer; (c) the transaction or event giving rise to the obligation has already occurred.

2. Obligations which are recognized as liabilities include (a) obligations with fixed payment dates and amounts, such as notes payable; (b) obligations with fixed payment amounts but estimated payment dates, such as accounts payable; (c) obligations for which both timing and amount of payment must be estimated, such as warranties payable; and (d) obligations arising from unexecuted contracts and agreements, such as rental fees received in advance.

3. Obligations under mutually unexecuted contracts (such as purchase commitments) and contingent obligations (such as unsettled lawsuits) are generally not recognized as liabilities.

4. Liabilities are generally classified on the balance sheet as current or noncurrent. Current liabilities are normally those due within one year. Most current liabilities are shown on the balance sheet at the amount payable. Examples of current liabilities include accounts payable, short-term notes payable, and taxes payable. Noncurrent liabilities are shown on the balance sheet at the present value of payments to be made in the future. The historical interest rate (the interest rate that the borrower was required to pay at the time the liability was incurred) is used in computing the present value of the liability.

5. A contingent liability is a potential future obligation that arises from an event that has occurred in the past but whose outcome is not now known. A future event will determine whether or not the item becomes an obligation. An estimated loss from a contingency should be recognized in the accounts if "Information available prior to the issuance of the financial statements indicates that it is probable that an asset had been impaired or that a liability had been incurred..." and "The amount of the loss can be reasonably estimated." The term "contingent liability" is used only when the item is not recognized in the accounts. Contingent liabilities are disclosed in the footnotes to the financial statements.

6. Businesses organized as corporations must pay federal income tax based on their taxable income from business activities. In contrast, the income earned by a partnership or sole proprietorship is taxed to the individual partners or the sole proprietor.

7. A current liability arises from advance payments by customers for goods or services to be delivered in the future. In other words, cash is received before the goods or services are furnished to the customer. Examples of this type of transaction include the advance sale of theater tickets and the collection in advance for magazine subscriptions. Another type of deferred performance liability arises when a firm provides a warranty for service or repairs for some period after a sale.

8. The differences between current and noncurrent liabilities, in addition to their maturity dates, are that (a) interest on long-term liabilities is ordinarily paid at regular intervals during the life of the long-term obligation, and (b) either the principal of long-term obligations is paid back in installments or special funds are accumulated by the borrower for retiring the liability.

9. Long-term liabilities are recorded at the present value of all payments to be made using the market interest rate at the time the liability is incurred. A portion of each payment represents interest expense. Any excess of cash payment over interest expense is used to reduce the borrower's liability for the principal amount.

10. An example of a long-term liability is a mortgage contract in which the lender (mortgagee) is given legal title to certain property of the borrower (mortgagor), with the provision that the title reverts to the borrower when the loan is repaid in full. The mortgaged property is collateral for the loan.

11. Firms often finance the acquisition of buildings, equipment, and other fixed assets using interest-bearing notes. If the borrowing arrangement does not state an explicit interest rate, the principal of the note includes implicit interest. To determine the present value of the future cash payments, an imputed interest rate is used in the discounting process. The imputed interest rate is the interest rate appropriate for the particular borrower at the time it incurs the obligation, given the amount and terms of the borrowing arrangement.

12. The computation of the present value of the liability and the amount of imputed interest can be based on the market value of the asset acquired. If the asset's current market value is not known, the present value of the liability can be computed based on the interest rate the firm would have to pay for a similar loan in the open market at the time that it acquired the asset. Regardless of how the present value of the liability and the imputed interest is computed, the total expense over the combined lives of the liability and the asset—interest plus depreciation—is the same.

13. When large amounts of funds are needed, a firm may borrow from the general investing public through the use of a bond issue. The distinctive features of a bond issue are (a) a bond indenture, or agreement, is drawn up that shows in detail the terms of the loan; (b) bond certificates are issued, each one representing a portion of the total loan; (c) a trustee is named to hold title to any property serving as collateral for the loan and to act as the representative of the bondholders; (d) an agent is appointed to act as registrar and disbursing agent; (e) some bonds have coupons for the interest payments attached to the bond certificate; and (f) the entire bond issue is usually sold by the borrower to an investment banking firm, or a group of bankers, which assumes the responsibility of reselling the bonds to the investing public.

14. The most common type of corporate bond is the debenture bond, which carries no special collateral; instead, it is issued on the general credit of the business. To give added protection to the bond holders, the bond indenture usually includes provisions that limit the dividends that the borrower can declare, or the amount of subsequent long-term debt that it can incur. Mortgage bonds and collateral trust bonds are examples of bonds collateralized by property of the issuer. Convertible bonds are debentures that the holder can exchange, after some specified period of time has elapsed, for a specific number of shares of common or, perhaps, preferred stock.

15. Most bonds provide for the payment of interest at regular intervals, usually semiannually. The amount of interest is usually expressed as a percentage of the principal or face value of the bond. The amount of funds received by the borrower may be more or less than the par (face) value of the bonds issued. The difference arises because the coupon interest rate stated in the bond indenture differs from the interest, or discount, rate the market considers appropriate for the issuer.

16. The price at which a firm issues bonds depends on (a) the future cash payments that the bond indenture requires the firm to make and (b) the discount rate that the market deems appropriate given the risk of the borrower and the general level of interest rates in the economy. If the coupon rate is less than the market interest rate, the bond will sell at a discount (the bond will sell for less than its face amount). If the coupon rate is higher than the market interest rate, the bond will sell at a premium (the bond will sell for more than its face amount). If the coupon rate equals the market interest rate, the bond will sell at its face amount.

17. When a bond is issued for less than par value, the difference between the face value and the amount of the proceeds represents additional interest, which will be paid as a part of the face value at maturity. This additional interest plus the periodic payments of interest will be charged to the periods during which the bond is outstanding. Therefore, the periodic interest expense includes the interest payment plus a portion of the discount. The process of allocating the discount as additional interest expense over the life of the bond is called amortization. The Discount on Bonds Payable account is a contra liability account and should be shown on the balance sheet as a deduction from the liability account, Bonds Payable.

18. A premium on bonds, like a discount on bonds, represents an adjustment of the cost of borrowing. The effect of amortizing the premium will be to reduce the interest expense below the cash actually paid for interest. Over the life of the bonds, the interest expense will be less than the amount of cash actually paid for interest by the principal lent but not repaid at maturity. The Premium on Bonds Payable is an adjunct to a liability account and should be shown on the balance sheet as an addition to Bonds Payable.

19. Generally accepted accounting principles require the effective-interest method of recognizing interest expense. Under the effective-interest method (a) interest expense each period is equal to the market interest rate at the time the bonds were issued (the historical interest rate) multiplied by the book value of the liability at the beginning of the interest period; (b) the interest expense on the income statement will be a constant percentage of the recorded liability at the beginning of each interest period (for a bond issued at a discount, interest expense on the income statement will be an increasing amount each period because the book value amount of the liability increases each period, and for a bond issued at a premium, interest expense on the income statement will be a decreasing amount each period because the book value amount of the liability decreases each period); and (c) the bonds will be stated on the balance sheet at the present value of the remaining cash outflows discounted at the market rate of interest when the bonds were issued.

20. Bonds may remain outstanding until their stated maturity date or a firm may enter the marketplace and purchase its own bonds before they mature. As market interest rates change, the market price of a bond issue will change. For example, assume that a company issues a 6 percent bond at par (the market rate of interest is also 6 percent). The issuing company records the bonds at par, using the historical cost convention. If market interest rates rise, the market price of the bond issue will decrease. If market interest rates drop, the market price of the bond issue will increase. In other words, there is an inverse relationship between the market interest rate and the market price of the bond. If market interest rates rise and the market price of the bond issue decreases, the issuing company can go into the marketplace and repurchase its bonds and record a gain from the retirement of the bonds. The gain actually occurred as interest rates increased. Under historical cost accounting, the gain is realized in the period the bond is retired.

21. The FASB requires that all gains and losses on bond retirements be reported in the income statement as extraordinary items. Such a gain or loss results because the bond issue is recorded at historical cost amounts and changes in the bond's market price are not recorded.

22. Two types of provisions for bond retirements are frequently encountered. One provides that certain portions of the principal amount will come due on a succession of maturity dates; the bonds of such issues are known as serial bonds. The other major type of retirement provision stipulates that the firm must accumulate a fund of cash or other assets (commonly known as a sinking fund) that will be used to retire the bonds. The sinking fund appears on the balance sheet of the borrower as a noncurrent asset in the Investments section.

23. Some bond issues make no provision for installment repayment or for accumulating funds for the payment of the bonds when they come due. In such situations, the bond liability either may be paid at maturity out of cash available at that time, or the bond issue may be refunded (new bonds issued to obtain the funds to retire the old ones when they come due). A common provision gives the company that issued the bonds the right to retire (call) portions of the bond issue before the bond's maturity date. The bond indenture usually provides that the bonds shall be callable at specified prices. The call price is usually set a few percentage points above the par value and declines as the maturity date approaches.

24. Long-term liabilities are reported at the present value of the future payments. The present value is computed using the historical rate of interest—the market interest rate on the date the obligation was incurred. Interest expense is computed by multiplying the book value of the liability by the historical interest rate. The difference between interest expense and the cash payment increases or decreases the book value of the liability for the next accounting period.

25. When a firm uses the indirect method of deriving cash flows from operations, the statement of cash flows (a) must, for bonds issued at a discount, add back to net income the difference between the interest expense recorded and the interest paid in cash and (b) must, for bonds issued at a premium, subtract from net income the difference between the interest expense recorded and the interest paid in cash.

26. When a firm retires a bond for cash, it reports that cash in the financing section of the statement of cash flows. If there is a gain or loss on the bond retirement transaction, the gain must be subtracted or the loss added back to net income in the operations section of the statement of cash flows to derive operating cash flows.

Questions and Exercises

True/False. For each of the following statements, place a T or F in the space provided to indicate whether the statement is true or false.

_____ 1. Footnotes to the financial statements may be employed to report contingent liabilities.

_____ 2. Contingent liabilities are liabilities that are known to exist, but that are uncertain in amount.

_____ 3. For a bond sold at a premium, the annual cash payment for interest exceeds the annual interest expense.

_____ 4. If a liability can be retired for an amount that is less than the amount owed, a loss would be reported by the party paying off the liability.

_____ 5. A debenture is a bond contract that shows in detail the terms of the loan.

_____ 6. One difference between current and noncurrent liabilities is that either the principal of long-term obligations is paid back in installments or special funds are accumulated by the borrower for retiring the liability.

_____ 7. Another difference between current and noncurrent liabilities is that interest on short-term liabilities is ordinarily paid at regular intervals during the life of the short-term obligation.

_____ 8. Upon retiring bonds that were originally issued at a discount, the appropriate portion of the unamortized discount also must be retired.

_____ 9. When bonds are issued at a premium, the dollar amount of interest expense will remain constant each period.

_____ 10. The allowance method of accounting for warranties may be used for tax reporting purposes.

_____ 11. The balance in the Warranty Liability account represents an estimate of the cost of repairs to be made under outstanding warranties.

_____ 12. Bond indentures usually limit the borrower's right to declare dividends.

_____ 13. For a bond, the contractual amount of interest payable is the product of the bond's interest rate and the bond's principal amount.

_____ 14. Liabilities are generally classified on the balance sheet as current or indeterminate term.

_____ 15. Current liabilities are valued on the balance sheet at their present value at that date and not at the amount that will be paid.

_____ 16. Amortization of bond discount or premium by the effective-interest method results in a changing rate of interest each period.

_____ 17. Under the effective-interest method, interest expense each period is equal to the historical interest rate times the recorded book value of the liability at the beginning of the interest period.

_____ 18. Bonds sold at a discount have a higher effective rate of interest than bonds sold at a premium.

_____ 19. Bonds that are due on a succession of maturity dates are known as serial bonds.

_____ 20. For a bond sold at a discount, the amount of cash paid for interest will be more than the amount of interest expense recorded.

_____ 21. In mortgage contracts, the lender is known as the mortgagee, and the borrower is known as the mortgagor.

_____ 22. If a bond's interest rate is higher than the market interest rate, the bond will sell at a discount.

_____ 23. Coupon bonds have coupons for the interest payments attached to the bond certificate.

_____ 24. Current liabilities are those due within the current operating cycle, normally one year.

_____ 25. The process of issuing new bonds to obtain funds to retire old bonds as they come due is known as calling the old bond issue.

_____ 26. Discount on Bonds Payable should be classified as a contra account to Bonds Payable.

_____ 27. A manufacturing company guarantees its product against defects for one year. Since the amount due and the due date are not known with certainty, the liability for the warranty need not be disclosed.

_____ 28. Under the effective-interest method of recognizing interest expense, a bond liability would be shown on the balance sheet at the present value of future cash outflows discounted at the historical market rate of interest.

_____ 29. The terms "face value" and "par value" are synonymous and refer to the principal amount of a bond.

_____ 30. When a company has the right to retire portions of a bond issue before the bond's maturity date, the bond is said to be callable.

_____ 31. For a bond issued at a discount, the amount of interest expense reported on the income statement each period will be decreasing under the effective-interest method of recognizing interest expense.

_____ 32. When the market rate of interest exceeds the interest rate stated on a bond, the bond will sell at a premium.

_____ 33. The historical interest rate is the market interest rate at the time the debt was initially issued.

_____ 34. A fund of cash or other assets that will be used to retire bonds is commonly known as a sinking fund.

_____ 35. When bonds are sold at a discount, the difference between the face value and the amount of the proceeds represents additional interest, which will be paid as a part of the face value at maturity.

_____ 36. Long-term liabilities are recorded initially at the present value of all payments.

_____ 37. The premium on bonds payable represents additional interest that will be paid at the bond's maturity.

_____ 38. The effect of amortizing the discount on bonds payable is to increase the interest expense over the amount actually paid as interest.

Matching. From the list of terms below, select the term which is most closely associated with each of the descriptive phrases or statements that follows and place the letter for that term in the space provided.

a. Bond Principal
b. Contingent Liability
c. Debenture Bond
d. Discount on Bonds Payable
e. Effective-Interest Method
f. Historical Interest Rate
g. Imputed Interest Rate

h. Liability
i. Mortgage
j. Premium on Bonds Payable
k. Refunding
l. Serial Bonds
m. Sinking Fund
n. Unexecuted Contracts

_____ 1. An obligation that involves a probable future sacrifice of resources, results from a past transaction or event, and for which the entity has little or no discretion to avoid the transfer.

_____ 2. Contract in which the lender is given legal title to certain property of the borrower, with the provision that the title reverts to the borrower when the loan is repaid in full.

_____ 3. New bonds are issued to obtain the funds to retire the old bonds when they come due.

_____ 4. A potential future obligation that arises from an event that has occurred in the past but whose outcome is not now known.

_____ 5. Face value or par value.

_____ 6. When allocated over the life of the bond, interest expense is increased.

_____ 7. When allocated over the life of the bond, interest expense is decreased.

_____ 8. Cash or other assets are accumulated and used to pay the bonds when they mature.

_____ 9. This method of interest expense recognition results in an interest charge each period that results in a constant interest rate.

_____ 10. Portions of the principal amount come due on a succession of maturity dates.

_____ 11. The market interest rate at the time the debt was issued.

_____ 12. This type of bond carries no specific collateral; instead, it is issued on the general credit of the business.

_____ 13. An interest rate appropriate for a borrower at the time it incurs an obligation, given the amount and terms of the borrowing arrangement.

_____ 14. An obligation arising from a transaction with a customer, such as rental fees received in advance.

Multiple Choice. Choose the best answer for each of the following questions and enter the identifying letter in the space provided.

_____ 1. White, Inc., issued bonds on 1/1, Year 1, which mature in 10 years. The $100,000 bonds, which pay 8 percent interest annually on 12/31, were issued at a time when the market interest rate was 10 percent. The bonds were issued for $87,710. What amount of bond interest expense would White report in Year 2?

   a. $10,000.
   b. $ 8,000
   c. $ 8,771.
   d. $ 8,848.

_____ 2. On March 1, Year 1, Richardson issued $100,000, 9 percent bonds, which mature on January 1, Year 10. The bonds pay interest semiannually on January 1 and July 1. The bonds were sold on March 1 and cash of $101,500 was received. Which of the following statements is correct?

   a. The bonds sold at par.
   b. The bonds sold at a discount.
   c. The bonds sold at a premium.
   d. No conclusion about the selling price of the bonds can be determined from the information given.

_____ 3. Huffman issued an 8 percent bond when the market interest rate was also 8 percent. The Huffman bonds should have sold

   a. At a discount.
   b. At par.
   c. At a premium.
   d. Cannot be determined with information given.

_____ 4. Smith Corporation guarantees its product against defects for one year. In what year should the corporation report the warranty expense?

   a. In the year that the product is sold.
   b. In the year that the product becomes defective and is repaired or replaced.
   c. The cost of the warranty is included in the product's selling price, and therefore warranty expense is never recorded.
   d. None of the above.

_____ 5. Pritz Corporation sold 10-year, 10 percent coupon bonds, face amount $100,000 on January 1, Year 1, for 97 percent of their face value. Over the bonds' 10-year life, how much interest expense, in total, will Pritz report in its income statements?

   a. $ 97,000.
   b. $100,000.
   c. $103,000.
   d. $200,000.

_____ 6. Christian Co. issued 10-year, 10 percent bonds, face amount $100,000 on 1/1, Year 1, when the market rate was 12 percent. On its Year 1 income statement, Christian reports bond interest expense of $10,644. For what amount were the bonds issued on 1/1, Year 1?

    a. $88,700.
    b. $93,560.
    c. $90,000.
    d. $80,000.

_____ 7. Which of the following accounts would usually be classified as a long-term liability?

    a. Warranty Liability.
    b. Premium on Bonds Payable.
    c. Magazine Subscription Fees Received in Advance.
    d. Federal Withholding Taxes Payable.

_____ 8. Both the employer and employee must make contributions for which of the following taxes?

    a. Social Security Taxes.
    b. Federal Unemployment Compensation Taxes.
    c. State Unemployment Compensation Taxes.
    d. All of the above.

_____ 9. Hudson Company had sales of personal computers totaling $50,000 for the year ending 12/31, Year 1. Hudson provides free warranty service for 18 months after the sale and estimates warranty costs to be 6 percent of sales. For the year, expenditures made for warranty repairs totaled $500. What should be the balance in the warranty liability account on the 12/31, Year 1, Balance Sheet?

    a. $ 500.
    b. $2,500.
    c. $3,000.
    d. None of the above.

_____ 10. Lang, Inc., issued bonds on 1/1, Year 1, which mature in 10 years. The $100,000 bonds, which pay 9 percent interest annually on 12/31, were issued at a time when the market interest rate was 11 percent. The bonds were issued for $88,220. At the end of Year 1, after adjusting entries have been recorded, the Discount on Bonds Payable account would have a balance of

    a. $11,780.
    b. $10,602.
    c. $11,076.
    d. $12,484.

_____ 11. The Lanier Corporation sold a $1-million bond issue at 103 percent of its par value. If the company recognizes interest expense by the effective interest method

    a. Interest expense on the bond issue will increase each year.
    b. Interest expense on the bond issue will decrease each year.
    c. Interest expense on the bond issue will be the same amount each year.
    d. None of the above.

_____ 12. Blanchard Corporation purchased land for $15,000 and signed an 8 percent mortgage note for $10,000. Mortgage payments are $200 per month. Which of the following statements is false?

    a. A portion of each payment represents interest expense.
    b. The interest expense portion of each payment increases over the mortgage term.
    c. Any excess of cash payment over interest expense is used to reduce the principal.
    d. The interest expense portion of the first monthly payment will be $66.67.

_____ 13. If the Williams Company issued bonds due in 10 years at a discount, this indicates that

    a. The market rate of interest exceeded the bond's interest rate at the time the bonds were issued.
    b. The bond's interest rate exceeded the market rate at the time the bonds were issued.
    c. The bond's interest rate equaled the market rate of interest at the time the bonds were issued.
    d. None of the above.

_____ 14. If bonds are issued at a discount, the net long-term liability reported on the balance sheet

    a. Increases each year during the life of the bond issue.
    b. Decreases each year during the life of the bond issue.
    c. Remains at the maturity value throughout the life of the bond issue.
    d. Remains at the issue price throughout the life of the bond issue.

_____ 15. Johns, Inc., issued bonds on 1/1, Year 1, which mature in 10 years. The $100,000 bonds, which pay 15 percent interest annually on 12/31, were issued at a time when the market interest rate was 12 percent. The bonds were issued for $116,950. Over the 10-year life of the bonds, how much interest expense will Johns report?

    a. $150,000.
    b. $166,950.
    c. $133,050.
    d. $120,000.

_____ 16. The account, Premium on Bonds, should be shown on the balance sheet as a(an)

    a. Contra account to Bonds Payable.
    b. Current liability.
    c. Adjunct account to Bonds Payable.
    d. None of the above.

_____ 17. On July 1, Year 1, Borders, Inc., which publishes a weekly news magazine, sold 4,000 2-year subscriptions for $10 each. On its income statement for the year ending December 31, Year 1, what amount from the July 1 transaction should be reported as revenue?

    a. $ 2,500.
    b. $ 5,000.
    c. $10,000.
    d. $20,000.

_____ 18. If bonds are issued at a premium and interest expense is recognized under the effective-interest method

    a. The amount of premium amortized each year will increase.

    b. The amount of the liability reported on the balance sheet will increase each year.

    c. The amount of interest expense reported on the income statement will increase each year.

    d. All of the above are true statements.

_____ 19. Rose, Inc., issued bonds on 1/1, Year 1, which mature in 10 years. The $100,000 bonds, which pay 12 percent interest annually on 12/31, were issued at a time when the market interest rate was 11 percent. The bonds were issued for $105,890. At the end of Year 1, how much of the premium should be amortized?

    a. $352.

    b. $589.

    c. $707.

    d. $884.

_____ 20. These bonds can be exchanged for a specific number of shares of common stock.

    a. Mortgage Bonds.

    b. Debenture Bonds.

    c. Convertible Bonds.

    d. Collateral Trust Bonds.

_____ 21. Regina Corporation issued a 7 percent, $100,000 bond issue at a price to yield the market interest rate of 8 percent. The bond pays interest semiannually. How much cash would be paid by Regina at the first interest payment date?

    a. $3,500.

    b. $4,000.

    c. $7,000.

    d. $8,000.

_____ 22. Which of the following is not an example of a mutually unexecuted contract?

    a. Purchase commitments.

    b. Contingent liability on unsettled lawsuit.

    c. Rental fees received in advance.

    d. None of the above is an example of a mutually unexecuted contract.

_____ 23. Graham Inc., issued bonds on 1/1, Year 1, which mature in 10 years. The bonds were issued at a premium. Over the 10-year term of the bond issue, Graham, Inc., will record

    a. Increasing amounts of interest expense each year.

    b. Decreasing amounts of interest expense each year.

    c. An unchanging amount of interest expense each year.

    d. The question cannot be answered with the information given.

_____ 24. A bond that is issued on the general credit of the business is commonly known as a

    a. Mortgage bond.
    b. Collateral trust bond.
    c. Debenture bond.
    d. None of the above.

_____ 25. The Herring Company issued bonds on 1/1, Year 1, which mature in 10 years. The $100,000 bonds, which pay 12 percent interest annually on 12/31, were issued at a time when the market interest rate was 10 percent. The bonds were issued for $112,290. At what amount would the long-term liability be reported on 12/31, Year 2?

    a. $109,732.
    b. $111,061.
    c. $111,519.
    d. $110,671.

_____ 26. The Fuller Corporation issued 10 percent, 10-year bonds several years ago when the market interest rate was 8 percent. The market interest rate is now 12 percent and Fuller purchases its own bonds in the market and retires them. Fuller would report

    a. A gain on the transaction.
    b. A loss on the transaction.
    c. Neither a gain nor a loss.
    d. Cannot be determined from the information given.

_____ 27. The balance in the Estimated Warranty Liability account at the end of the period

    a. Represents the costs incurred for repairs made.
    b. Represents the estimated cost of repairs to be made under warranties in effect at that time.
    c. Should be identical to the balance in the Warranty Expense account.
    d. Should be closed to Retained Earnings so that warranty costs and revenues will be matched.

_____ 28. The Carlson Corporation issued a 10 percent, 10-year, $100,000 bond at a time when the market interest rate was 15 percent. The bond was issued for $74,910. The Carlson bond pays interest annually on December 31. On December 31 of the current year the bond liability is carried on the balance sheet at $79,204. How many years has the bond issue been outstanding?

    a. 2 years.
    b. 3 years.
    c. 4 years.
    d. None of the above.

_____ 29. Which of the following would be an example of an unexecuted contract?

    a. A company sold a 1-year subscription to its publication and received the subscription price in cash.
    b. A customer purchased merchandise on account.
    c. A company issued 10-year bonds for cash.
    d. A company borrowed money from a bank to purchase a delivery van.

_____ 30. When a bond issue is sold, the proceeds from the sale of the bonds equal

    a. The present value of the maturity amount.

    b. The present value of all the future interest payments during the life of the bond issue.

    c. The sum of a and b above.

_____ 31. On October 1, Year 1, Johnson Company issued $1 million, 12 percent bonds at par. The bonds pay interest semiannually on January 1 and July 1. For the year ending December 31, Year 1, Johnson would report how much interest expense from this bond issue on its income statement?

    a. $120,000.

    b. $ 60,000.

    c. $ 30,000.

    d. Interest expense on this bond issue for Year 1 cannot be determined from the information given.

_____ 32. The Ashcraft Company issued $200,000 par-value bonds several years ago. On January 1, Year 8, the bond premium account has a balance of $12,000 when $50,000 of the bonds are called at 104. What is the amount of the gain or loss on the retirement of the bonds?

    a. $1,000 gain.

    b. $2,000 gain.

    c. $4,000 gain.

    d. $4,000 loss.

_____ 33. Refer to Question 32. The balance in the bond premium account on January 1, Year 8, after the retirement of the $50,000 of bonds would be

    a. $ -0-.

    b. $6,000.

    c. $9,000.

    d. None of the above.

_____ 34. The Clamma Corporation issued a 10 percent, $100,000 bond on April 1, Year 1 at par. Interest is paid semiannually on July 1 and January 1. On its Year 1 Income Statement, Clamma would report Interest Expense of

    a. $10,000.

    b. $ 5,000.

    c. $ 7,500.

    d. $ 6,667.

_____ 35. On its 12/31, Year 1 Balance Sheet, St. Charles reported an Estimated Warranty Liability of $86,000. The company estimates warranty expense to be 3 percent of sales. During Year 2, sales totaled $700,000 and warranty repair expenditures totaling $23,000 were incurred. At what amount should St. Charles report the Estimated Warranty Liability on its 12/31, Year 2 Balance Sheet?

   a. $107,000.
   b. $ 21,000.
   c. $ 84,000.
   d. $ 63,000.

_____ 36. Long-term liabilities are reported on a company's balance sheet at the present value of all promised payments using

   a. The current market interest rate.
   b. A rate of 10 percent.
   c. The market interest rate at the time the liability was incurred.
   d. The prime interest rate.

_____ 37. On 1/1, Year 1, Rogers borrowed $150,000 from Green Mountain Bank. The note calls for five annual installment payments of $40,650 to be paid each year on 12/31. The effective interest rate is 11 percent. How much of the first installment (made on 12/31, Year 1) is payment on the principal amount borrowed?

   a. $30,000.
   b. $40,650.
   c. $16,500.
   d. $24,150.

_____ 38. Bird Company issued a $100,000 bond on July 1, Year 1. The 10-year bond pays interest annually on June 30. On 12/31, Year 1, Bird carries the bond on its Balance Sheet at $96,450 and reports Interest Payable of $5,000 as a current liability. What is the bond's interest rate?

   a. 10 percent.
   b. 5 percent.
   c. 9 percent.
   d. Cannot be determined from the information given.

_____ 39. Walter Company reported a balance of $85,000 in its Liability for Advance Ticket Sales account on its 12/31, Year 1, balance sheet. During Year 2, the company collected $346,000 from customers for additional advance ticket sales. On its income statement for the year ending 12/31, Year 2, the company reported $405,000 on its Revenues from Advanced Ticket Sales account. What balance would Walter report in its Liability for Advanced Ticket Sales account on its 12/31, Year 2, balance sheet?

   a. $235,000.
   b. $ 59,000.
   c. $144,000.
   d. $ 26,000.

_____ 40. Frisco Company gives a 3-year warranty with its product. At the end of its first year of business, the company reported sales of $620,000 and warranty expense of $43,400. On its 12/31, Year 1, balance sheet, the company reported $24,800 on its Estimated Warranty Liability account. During Year 2, sales totaled $750,000 and the company incurred parts and labor costs of $39,500 for warranty work performed. The company used the same warranty expense percentage for both years. The warranty expense for Year 2 and the balance in the Estimated Warranty Liability account at 12/31, Year 2, are, respectively:

    a. $52,500; $37,800.
    b. $30,000; $15,300.
    c. $43,400; $56,400.
    d. $24,800; $13,000.

_____ 41. On January 2, Year 1, Yellowstone Company purchased land and gave in exchange a $50,000 noninterest-bearing note that is due in 5 years. Using a 10 percent imputed interest rate, the land and the note payable were both recorded at $31,050. Assuming that Yellowstone recognizes interest under the effective-interest method, interest expense for Year 2 would be

    a. $3,790.
    b. $3,105.
    c. $3,415.
    d. $5,000.

_____ 42. Refer to the previous question. At what amount would the note payable be recorded on the 12/31, Year 2, balance sheet?

    a. $50,000.
    b. $31,050.
    c. $34,155.
    d. None of the above.

_____ 43. On July 1, Year 1, Mike sold to Ruth an acre of land in exchange for Ruth's $4,000 noninterest-bearing note due in 3 years. The fair market value of the land is determined to be $3,100. What is the present value of Ruth's obligation to Mike on July 1, Year 1?

    a. $3,100.
    b. $3,250.
    c. $4,000.
    d. None of the above.

_____ 44. On 1/1, Year 1, the Colorado Company purchased machinery that had a cash price of $9,860. Colorado gave a $15,000 note that is due in 3 years. The implicit interest rate is 15 percent. What amount of interest expense would Colorado report in its Year 2 Income Statement?

    a. $1,713.
    b. $1,701.
    c. $1,479.
    d. $1,620.

_____ 45. Refer to the previous question. At what amount would the $15,000 note be carried on Colorado's 12/31, Year 1, balance sheet?

   a. $15,000.
   b. $11,573.
   c. $11,339.
   d. $11,561.

Exercises

1. The May Company provides a warranty on its product for one year after sale. Warranty costs are estimated to be 5 percent of the selling price. In Year 3, the company had sales of $150,000, which were subject to the warranty. During January, Year 4, $3,600 in parts were used to make repairs covered under the warranty.

   Prepare entries for Year 3 and Year 4 for the sale and related warranty transactions.

2. The Taylor Company issued $400,000 of 10 percent, 10-year bonds for $354,120 on January 1, Year 1. Interest is paid semiannually on July 1 and January 1.

    Prepare Year 1 entries relative to the bond issue, assuming (a) that the bonds were sold to yield the market interest rate of 12 percent and (b) that interest expense is recognized on an effective-interest basis.

3. Campbell Company has outstanding on December 31, Year 5, $400,000 of 4 percent bonds that mature on December 31, Year 10. The bonds, which were sold on January 1, Year 1, have an unamortized discount of $12,000 on December 31, Year 5, the last interest payment date. On January 1, Year 6, Campbell purchased $100,000 of its bonds in the open market for $82,000 and retired the bonds.

Prepare the January 1, Year 6, entry to record the retirement of the bonds.

4. On July 1, Year 1, Espana Company issued a 10-year $500,000 bond which pays interest semiannually on January 1 and July 1. Fill in the 12 blanks on the amortization schedule below:

Period	Liability at Start of Period	Effective Interest	Coupon Rate	Change in Book Value of Liability	Liability at End of Period
0					601,725
1	____	____	27,500	3,431	____
2	____	____	____	____	594,726
3	____	____	____	____	____

5. Rhonda Company borrowed money and signed a note for $100,000 which is due in 8 years. Fill in the 10 blanks on the amortization schedule below:

Period	Loan Balance at Start of Period	Interest Expense	Change in Book Value of Note	Liability at End of Period
0				54,000
1	____	4,320	____	58,320
2	____	____	____	____
3	____	____	____	____

6. On January 1, Year 1, Ramon Company financed the purchase of some land with a 5-year note which calls for payments of $25,000 every 6 months with the first payment due on July 1, Year 1. Fill in the 12 blanks on the amortization schedule below:

Period	Loan Balance at Start of Period	Interest Expense	Payment	Principal Reduction	Liability at End of Period
1/1/1					160,442
7/1/1					
1/1/2	149,882	13,489			
7/1/2	138,371				

7. On January 2, Year 1, Lander Company purchased machinery and gave in exchange a $90,000 noninterest-bearing note due in 3 years. Assuming that a 14 percent interest rate has been imputed for this transaction, the present value of the note on January 2, Year 1, is $60,750. Lander recognizes interest expense under the effective-interest method.

Record the appropriate entries for the note from January 2, Year 1, until the note is paid upon maturity on January 2, Year 4.

8. On January 1, Year 1, Rodney Wainwright purchased equipment that had a cash price of $35,589. In lieu of paying cash, Wainwright gave a 3-year noninterest-bearing note with a face amount of $50,000. The implicit interest rate is 12 percent per year.

   a. What is the cost of the equipment?

   b. What amount of interest expense would Wainwright report for the first year?

   c. What is the carrying value of the obligation at the end of the second year?

   d. What amount of interest expense would Wainwright report for the third year?

Answers to Questions and Exercises

True/False

1.	T	9.	F	17.	T	25.	F	33.	T
2.	F	10.	F	18.	F	26.	T	34.	T
3.	T	11.	T	19.	T	27.	F	35.	T
4.	F	12.	T	20.	F	28.	T	36.	T
5.	F	13.	T	21.	T	29.	T	37.	F
*6.	T	14.	F	22.	F	30.	T	38.	T
7.	F	15.	F	23.	T	31.	F		
8.	T	16.	F	24.	T	32.	F		

Matching

1.	h	4.	b	7.	j	10.	l	13.	g
2.	i	5.	a	8.	m	11.	f	14.	n
3.	k	6.	d	9.	e	12.	c		

Multiple Choice

1.	d	10.	c	19.	a	28.	b	37.	d
2.	a	11.	b	20.	c	29.	a	38.	a
3.	b	12.	b	21.	a	30.	c	39.	d
4.	a	13.	a	22.	c	31.	c	40.	a
5.	c	14.	a	23.	b	32.	a	41.	c
6.	a	15.	c	24.	c	33.	c	42.	d
7.	b	16.	c	25.	d	34.	c	43.	a
8.	a	17.	c	26.	a	35.	c	44.	b
9.	b	18.	a	27.	b	36.	c	45.	c

Exercises

1.

		Dr.	Cr.
Year 3	Cash (or Accounts Receivable)	150,000	
	Warranty Expense	7,500	
	Sales		150,000
	Estimated Warranty Liability		7,500
	To record sale and warranty liability.		
Year 4	Estimated Warranty Liability	3,600	
	Parts Inventory		3,600
	To record parts used in performing warranty work.		

2.

		Dr.	Cr.
1/1 Year 1	Cash	354,120	
	Discount on Bonds Payable	45,880	
	Bonds Payable		400,000
	To record sale of bonds at a discount.		
7/1 Year 1	Interest Expense	21,247	
	Discount on Bonds Payable		1,247
	Cash		20,000
	To record interest expense and amortization of discount.		
	Interest expense: $354,120 \times .06 = \$21,247$		
12/31 Year 1	Interest Expense	21,322	
	Discount on Bonds Payable		1,322
	Interest Payable		20,000
	To record interest expense and amortization of discount.		
	Interest expense: $(\$354,120 + \$1,247) \times .06 = \$21,322$.		
3. 1/1 Year 6	Bonds Payable	100,000	
	Gain on Retirement of Bonds		15,000
	Discount on Bonds Payable		3,000
	Cash		82,000
	To record retirement of bonds.		

4.

Period	Liability at Start of Period	Effective Interest	Coupon Rate	Change in Book Value of Liability	Liability at End of Period
0					601,725
1	601,725	24,069	27,500	3,431	598,294
2	598,294	23,932	27,500	3,568	594,726
3	594,726	23,789	27,500	3,711	591,015

5.

Period	Loan Balance at Start of Period	Interest Expense	Change in Book Value of Note	Liability at End of Period
0				54,000
1	54,000	4,320	4,320	58,320
2	58,320	4,666	4,666	62,986
3	62,986	5,039	5,039	68,025

6.

Period	Loan Balance at Start of Period	Interest Expense	Payment	Principal Reduction	Liability at End of Period
1/1/1					160,442
7/1/1	160,442	14,440	25,000	10,560	149,882
1/1/2	149,882	13,489	25,000	11,511	138,371
7/1/2	138,371	12,453	25,000	12,547	125,824

7.

		Dr.	Cr.
1/2 Year 1	Machinery	60,750	
	Note Payable		60,750
	To record purchase of machine in exchange for a noninterest-bearing note.		
12/31 Year 1	Interest Expense	8,505	
	Note Payable		8,505
	To record interest expense for Year 1. Interest = .14 × .$60,750 = $8,505.		
12/31 Year 2	Interest Expense	9,696	
	Note Payable		9,696
	To record interest expense for Year 2. Interest = .14 × ($60,750 = $8,505) = $9,696.		
12/31 Year 3	Interest Expense	11,049	
	Note Payable		11,049
	To record interest expense for Year 3. Interest = $90,000 − $60,750 − $8,505 − $9,696 = $11,049.		
1/2 Year 4	Note Payable	90,000	
	Cash		90,000
	To record payment of note at maturity.		

8.
  a. $35,589
  b. $4,271   ($35,589 × .12)
  c. $44,643   ($35,589 + $4,271 + $4,783)
  d. $5,357   ($44,643 × .12)

Chapter 11

Liabilities: Off-Balance Sheet Financing, Leases, Deferred Income Taxes, and Retirement Benefits

Chapter Highlights

1. The rationale for off-balance sheet financing is to obtain funds without recording a liability. The objective is to show fewer liabilities on the balance sheet and improve the debt ratios that analysts use to assess the financial risk of a firm

2. Reasons cited for off-balance sheet financing include (a) the cost of borrowing is lowered and (b) the violation of debt covenants is avoided.

3. To be an accounting liability, a firm must incur an obligation for a past or current benefit received—the event or transaction must already have happened. If the firm will receive the benefit in the future, accounting treats the obligation as an executory contract and typically does not recognize a liability. Off-balance sheet financing emphasizes that mutual performance will occur in the future and therefore a liability is not recorded.

4. Firms create innovative financing schemes to keep debt off the balance sheet. Leasing assets, using purchase commitments to obtain loans and selling accounts receivable or inventory are transactions which may result in keeping debt off the balance sheet. When the entity needing financing enjoys the economic benefits and bears the economic risk of the transaction, a liability is usually recognized on the balance sheet. When the entity providing the financing enjoys the economic benefits and bears the economic risk, the debt does not appear as a liability on the balance sheet of the firm needing financing. As a result of off-balance sheet financing, ratios (such as the debt-equity ratio) will appear more favorable, which may favorably affect future credit ratings and future borrowing costs.

5. There are two approaches to accounting for leases: the operating-lease method and the capital-lease method. In an operating lease, the lessor transfers only the rights to use the property to the lessee for specified periods of time. At the end of the lease period, the property is returned to the lessor. The lessee merely records annual rent expense when the lease payment is made. Under the capital-lease method, the lease is judged to be a form of borrowing to purchase the property. This treatment recognizes the signing of the lease as the acquisition of a long-term asset, called a leasehold, and the incurring of a long-term liability for lease payments. The lessee must amortize the leasehold over its useful life and must recognize each lease payment as part payment of interest on the liability and part reduction of the liability itself.

247

6. One difference between the operating-lease method and the capital-lease method is the timing of the expense recognition. Another difference is that the capital-lease method recognizes both the asset (lease-hold) and the liability on the balance sheet. Most lessees prefer to use the operating-lease method because the reported income is higher in the earlier years of the lease than it would be under the capital-lease method. Also, with an operating-lease, the asset and related liability are not shown on the lessee's balance sheet.

7. A firm must account for a lease as a capital lease if the lease meets any one of four conditions. A lease is a capital lease (a) if it transfers ownership to the lessee at the end of the lease term (b) if transfer of ownership at the end of the lease term seems likely because the lessee has a "bargain purchase" option, (c) if it extends for at least 75 percent of the asset's life, or (d) if the present value of the contractual minimum lease payments equals or exceeds 90 percent of the fair market value of the asset at the time the lessee signs the lease.

8. The four criteria attempt to identify whether the lessor or lessee enjoys the economic benefit and bears the economic risk of the leased asset. For example, if the leased asset becomes the property of the lessee at the end of the lease period, then the lessee enjoys all of the economic benefits of the asset and incurs all risks of ownership.

9. A bargain purchase option gives the lessee the right to purchase the asset for a price less than the predicted fair market value of the asset when the option is exercised.

10. Generally, the lessor uses the same criteria as does the lessee for classifying a lease as a capital lease or an operating lease. When the lessor and lessee sign a capital lease, the lessor recognizes revenue in an amount equal to the present value of all future lease payments and recognizes expenses in an amount equal to the book value of the leased asset. The lessor records the lease receivable at the present value of the future cash flows. Lessors tend to prefer the capital-lease method because it enables them to recognize income on the "sale" of the asset on the date the lease is signed.

11. The amount that a firm reports as book income usually differs from the amount of taxable income appearing on the income tax return. The difference arises because of permanent differences and temporary differences.

12. Permanent differences result from book income including revenues or expenses that taxable income never includes. Temporary differences result from book income including revenues or expenses in a different accounting period than when they appear in taxable income.

13. Income taxes <u>payable</u> are based on taxable income which excludes permanent differences and uses the accounting methods a firm selects for income tax purposes.

14. Income tax <u>expense</u> could be based on taxable income and equal income taxes actually payable each period. Or, income tax <u>expense</u> could be equal to income taxes actually payable each period plus the income taxes a firm expects to pay (or minus the income taxes a firm expects to save) in the future when temporary differences reverse. Generally accepted accounting principles require firms to follow the second approach. Thus, income tax expense includes income taxes payable currently plus income taxes deferred because of temporary differences.

15. Generally accepted accounting principles require that the measurement of the deferred portion of income tax expense use a balance sheet approach. Using this basis, firms (a) identify temporary differences between the book basis and tax basis of assets and liabilities at the beginning and end of the year and (b)

248

multiply these temporary differences by the income tax rate applicable to the period when the firm expects the temporary differences to reverse. The change in the deferred tax account on the balance sheet between the beginning and end of the year equals the deferred portion of income tax expense.

16. FASB Statement 109 sets forth a five-step procedure for computing income tax expense:

    (a) Identify at each balance sheet date all differences between the book basis and the tax basis of assets and liabilities.

    (b) Eliminate permanent differences (differences that will not have a future tax consequence).

    (c) Separate temporary differences into those that give rise to future tax deductions and those that give rise to future taxable income.

    (d-1) Multiply temporary differences that give rise to future tax deductions by the enacted income tax rate expected to apply in the future periods of the deductions. The result is a deferred tax asset.

    (d-2) Multiply temporary differences that will result in future taxable income by the enacted income tax rate expected to apply in the future period of the taxable income. The result is a deferred tax liability.

    (e) Assess the likelihood that the firm will realize the benefits of deferred tax assets in the future. If the probability of realization of the benefits of deferred tax assets is less than 50 percent, the deferred tax asset must be reduced by a valuation allowance to the amount the firm expects to realize in tax savings in the future.

17. The result of following the five-step procedure is a deferred tax asset and a deferred tax liability at each balance sheet date. Income tax expense each period equals (a) income taxes currently payable on taxable income plus (b) the credit change in the deferred tax asset and the deferred tax liability (or minus the debit change in the deferred tax asset and the deferred tax liability) between the beginning and end of the period.

18. Notes on the financial statements provide additional information regarding a firm's income tax expense. Firms report four items of information: (a) components of income before taxes, which indicates the amount of book income before income taxes that a firm derives from domestic and foreign operations; (b) components of income tax expense, which indicates the amount of income taxes currently payable and the amount deferred because of temporary differences; (c) a reconciliation from statutory to effective tax rates, which indicates why the effective tax rate differs from the statutory tax rate, and (d) components of deferred tax assets and liabilities, which discloses the types of temporary differences that result in the deferred tax asset and the deferred tax liability on the balance sheet each period.

19. The accounting for deferred income taxes has been the subject of much criticism. The economic benefit of deferring tax payments and the economic cost of temporary differences that require an immediate cash net flow are ignored. Another criticism is that deferred taxes are neither an asset nor a liability. A third criticism is that, unlike all other long-term liabilities which are reported on the balance sheet at the present value of future cash payments, deferred tax liabilities are reported as undiscounted amounts.

20. Most employers provide retirement benefits to their employees. Typical benefits include pensions, health insurance, and life insurance. The employer's cost of these retirement benefits is an expense in measuring net income. The accounting issue is whether firms should recognize the expense during the years while employees render services or later, when they receive the benefits during retirement. The matching convention of accrual accounting requires that firms recognize the expense during the employees's working years because those labor services generate revenues.

21. Under a pension plan, an employer promises to make payments to employees after they retire. The employer sets up a pension plan, specifying the eligibility of employees, the type of promises to employees, the method of funding, and the pension plan administrator.

22. The pension plan set up by the employer may be a defined contribution plan or a defined benefit plan. In a defined contribution plan, the amounts to be contributed to the pension plan by the employer are defined, but the benefits to be received by retired employees are not defined (they depend on investment performance). Under a defined benefit plan, the amounts to be paid to an employee upon retirement are based on a formula that usually takes into account the employee's length of service and average earnings. The employer must contribute sufficient amounts to the pension plan so that those contributions plus earnings from investments made with those contributions will be sufficient to pay the specified benefit.

23. The employer computes pension expense each period and transfers cash to a separate pension fund according to some formula. If cumulative pension expenses exceed cumulative pension funding, a pension liability appears on the employer's balance sheet. If cumulative pension funding exceeds cumulative pension expense, a pension asset appears on the employer's balance sheet. Additionally, Statement No. 87 requires firms to report a pension liability on the balance sheet if the present value of pension commitments to employees exceeds the assets in the pension fund.

24. The employer's pension expense for a defined contribution plan is the amount contributed to the pension fund.

25. Pension expense for a defined benefit plan consists of (a) interest cost on the increase in the projected benefit obligation and (b) service cost, which is the increase in the projected benefit obligation because of an additional year of employee service. Pension expense for a defined benefit plan is reduced by (c) the expected return on pension investments. The return from these investments reduces pension expense because it reduces the amount the employer must contribute. The fourth component of pension expense for a defined benefit plan is (d) the amortization of actuarial and performance gains and losses. For example, the actual return from pension investments might exceed or fall short of the expected return or the firm may improve, or sweeten, pension benefits. Statement No. 87 requires firms to smooth the effect of these items on pension expense for a defined benefit plan by amortizing them over some period of years.

26. The pension plan receives cash each period from the employer and invests the cash to generate income. Also, the pension plan pays cash to retired employees each period. The assets in the pension plan do not appear on the balance sheet of the employer.

27. The pension plan computes the amount of the pension liability each period. The pension liability for a defined contribution plan equals the assets in the pension plan. The pension liability for a defined benefit plan is the present value of the expected amounts payable to employees and is based on the pension benefit formula underlying the pension plan. The typical benefit formula takes into account the employee's length of service and some measure of average earnings.

28. Statement No. 87 defines two measures of the pension liability of the pension plan. Accumulated benefit obligation is the present value of amounts expected to be paid to employees during retirement based on accumulated service and current salary at the time of measuring the pension liability. Projected benefit obligation is the present value of amounts expected to be paid to employees during retirement based on accumulated service to date but using the level of salary expected to serve as a base for computing pension benefits. The difference between accumulated benefit obligation and the projected benefit obligation relates to future salary increases.

29. Statement No. 87 requires firms to disclose both the accumulated benefit obligation and the projected benefit obligation. If the accumulated benefit obligation exceeds the assets in the pension fund, the firm must report the underfunded accumulated benefit obligation on its balance sheet as a liability.

30. Requiring firms to report a liability based on the underfunded accumulated benefit obligation rather than on the larger underfunded projected benefit obligation reflects the political nature of the standard-setting process. Most firms have overfunded accumulated benefit obligations but some firms have significantly, underfunded projected benefit obligations. The latter firms claimed that they would discontinue granting pension benefits if the FASB required the recognition of the underfunded projected benefit obligation as a liability.

31. Health care insurance and other benefits are similar in concept to pension benefits. The present value of these commitments represents an economic obligation of the employer. FASB Statement No. 106 requires firms beginning in 1993 to recognize liabilities for their unfunded obligations for health care and similar benefits. Firms may recognize the full liability in one year or recognize it piecemeal over several years.

32. When firms account for leases as operating leases, the amount reported as rent revenue or rent expense usually equals the lessee's cash payment. No adjustment is needed to net income in deriving cash flows from operations.

33. A lease accounted for as a capital lease is an investing and a financing activity that does not affect cash. As the leased asset is depreciated, depreciation expense is added to net income in deriving cash flows from operations. The portion of the lease payment representing interest expense requires no adjustment to net income in deriving cash flows from operations. The portion of the lease payment representing repayment of the lease liability is a financing activity which uses cash.

34. When income tax expense exceeds income tax paid in cash, the difference is added back to net income in deriving cash flows from operations. When income taxes paid in cash exceed income tax expense, the difference is subtracted from net income in deriving cash flows from operations.

35. If pension expense exceeds pension funding, the difference is added back to net income in deriving cash flows from operations. If pension expense is less than pension funding, the difference is subtracted from net income in deriving cash flows from operations.

Questions and Exercises

True/False. For each of the following statements, place a T or F in the space provided to indicate whether the statement is true or false.

_____ 1. A liability is usually recognized on the balance sheet if the entity needing financing enjoys the economic benefits and bears the economic risk of the transaction.

_____ 2. When the lessor and the lessee sign a capital lease, the lessor recognizes revenue in an amount equal to the book value of the leased asset.

_____ 3. The amounts to be contributed to the pension plan by the employer are defined in a defined-benefit plan.

_____ 4. A visitor in Florida who rents a car for 2 weeks rents the auto under an operating lease arrangement.

_____ 5. If an employer's cumulative pension expenses exceed the employer's cumulative pension funding, the employer will report a pension asset on its balance sheet.

_____ 6. If a pension plan is funded, cash is set aside to pay the future liability.

_____ 7. Many firms prefer the operating-lease method because the reported income is higher in the earlier years of the lease than it would be under the capital-lease method.

_____ 8. Income tax expense includes income taxes payable currently plus income taxes deferred because of temporary differences.

_____ 9. Service cost is the present value of pension liabilities generated by employees' service during the period.

_____ 10. If a lease is considered to be in substance an installment purchase of property, then the property and the unpaid obligation should be accounted for under the operating-lease method.

_____ 11. Under a defined benefit plan, total corporate pension expense consists only of service costs.

_____ 12. In an operating lease, the lessor transfers the rights to use the property to the lessee for a specified period of time.

_____ 13. The existence of a bargain purchase option in a noncancelable lease would require that the lease be accounted for as a capital lease.

_____ 14. A temporary difference that will require income tax allocation between periods will result when a company reports interest revenue on an investment in tax-exempt municipal bonds.

_____ 15. Deferred income taxes result from permanent differences between book income and taxable income.

_____ 16. If the lease term extends for at least 75 percent of the leased asset's life, the lease should be accounted for as an operating lease.

_____ 17. In a defined-contribution plan, the benefits to be received by retired employees are not defined.

_____ 18. Like other long-term liabilities, deferred income taxes are reported on the balance sheet at the present value of future cash payments.

_____ 19. The recognition of a lease asset and obligation on the books of the lessee will increase the lessee's debt-equity ratio.

_____ 20. For an employer with a defined contribution plan, pension expense is the amount contributed to the pension fund.

_____ 21. A transaction, in which income from credit sales is recognized in the year of sale for book purposes and is recognized in the year cash is collected for tax purposes, creates a temporary difference that requires income tax allocation.

_____ 22. Off-balance sheet financing is preferred by lessees because the leased asset and corresponding obligation is left off the balance sheet.

_____ 23. The difference between accumulated benefit obligation and projected benefit obligation is that the computation of the projected benefit obligation considers future salary levels.

_____ 24. The concept of temporary differences implies that income taxes which are postponed come due later. In reality, the notion of temporary differences later reversing is questionable.

_____ 25. The capital-lease method recognizes expenses later than does the operating-lease method.

_____ 26. In computing pension expense for a defined benefit plan, pension expense is increased by the expected return on pension investments.

_____ 27. Under the capital-lease method, the lessee merely records annual rent expense when the lease payment is made.

_____ 28. Lessors prefer to account for a lease as an operating lease because it enables the recognition of income from the "sale" of the leased asset.

_____ 29. Generally accepted accounting principles require that income tax expense used in financial reporting be based on actual taxes payable.

_____ 30. A capital lease would be recorded if the present value of the lease payments equals or exceeds 90 percent of the leased asset's fair market value.

_____ 31. Income tax expense refers to an amount on the income statement while the amount of income taxes payable results from a tax return computation.

_____ 32. The capital lease method permits a company's management to recognize expenses later rather than sooner for financial reporting and results in a lower debt-equity ratio for the company.

253

Matching. From the list of terms below, select the term which is most closely associated with each of the descriptive phrases or statements that follows and place the letter for that term in the space provided.

a.	Accumulated Benefit Obligation	k.	Lessee
b.	Bargain Purchase Option	l.	Lessor
c.	Capital Lease Method	m.	Off-Balance Sheet Financing
d.	Debt-Equity Ratio	n.	Operating-Lease Method
e.	Deferred Tax Asset	o.	Pension Expense
f.	Deferred Tax Liability	p.	Permanent Difference
g.	Defined Benefit Plan	q.	Projected Benefit Obligation
h.	Defined Contribution Plan	r.	Service Cost
i.	Income Tax Expense	s.	Temporary Differences
j.	Income Tax Payable		

_____ 1. This equals the income taxes actually payable each period plus the income taxes a firm expects to pay (or minus the income taxes a firm expects to save) in the future when temporary differences reverse.

_____ 2. The amounts to be paid to an employee upon retirement are based on a formula that usually takes into account the employee's length of service and average earnings.

_____ 3. The present value of amounts expected to be paid to employees during retirement based on accumulated service and current salary levels.

_____ 4. Results in more favorable debt-equity ratios and may favorably affect future credit ratings and future borrowing costs.

_____ 5. This results when temporary differences that give rise to future tax deductions are multiplied by the enacted income tax rate expected to apply in the future periods of the deduction.

_____ 6. Under this method, the owner, or lessor, merely sells the rights to use the property to the lessee for specified periods of time.

_____ 7. Tenant.

_____ 8. These result when revenues and expenses for book purposes are reported in a different period than for tax purposes.

_____ 9. The present value of amounts expected to be paid to employees during retirement based on accumulated service to date and future salary levels.

_____ 10. Differences between book income and taxable income that never reverse.

_____ 11. This results when temporary differences that will lead to future taxable income are multiplied by the enacted income tax rate expected to apply in the future period of the taxable income.

_____ 12. Gives the lessee the right to purchase the asset for a price less than the predicted fair market value of the asset when the option is exercised.

_____ 13. The amounts to be contributed to the pension plan by the employer are defined but the benefits to be received by retired employees are not defined.

_____ 14. Landlord.

_____ 15. This treatment recognizes the signing of a lease as the simultaneous acquisition of a long-term asset and the incurring of a long-term liability.

_____ 16. Cost assigned annually for the pension benefits earned during a given year.

_____ 17. This amount results from a computation on the tax return.

_____ 18. Most managements prefer not to show an asset and a related liability on the balance sheet because of the increase in this computation which makes the company appear more risky.

_____ 19. In a defined benefit plan, this consists of interest cost on the increase in the projected benefit obligation plus service cost minus the expected return on pension investments plus (or minus) the amortization of actuarial and performance gains and losses.

Multiple Choice. Choose the best answer for each of the following questions and enter the identifying letter in the space provided.

_____ 1. Arizona Company purchased a machine early in Year 1. For book purposes, Arizona uses straight-line depreciation. For tax purposes, ACRS is followed. Excess depreciation for tax purposes in Year 1 was $60,000. Assuming a tax rate of 30 percent will apply in the future period of taxable income, determine the amount of income taxes deferred in Year 1.

    a. $60,000.
    b. $42,000.
    c. $18,000.
    d. None of the above.

_____ 2. Refer to the previous question. For Year 2, excess depreciation for tax purposes was $30,000. Assuming that a tax rate of 30 percent will apply in the future period of taxable income, determine the balance in the deferred tax liability account at end of Year 2.

    a. $27,000.
    b. $51,000.
    c. $39,000.
    d. $ 9,000.

_____ 3. Refer to the two previous questions. In Year 2, Arizona reported a current liability for income taxes of $65,000. What amount of income tax expense did Arizona report on its Year 2 Income Statement?

    a. $65,000.
    b. $74,000.
    c. $56,000.
    d. $83,000.

_____ 4. On 1/1, Year 1, Utah Company leased some equipment from Dixie Tool Supply under an operating lease for 4 years. Lease payments of $5,000 are payable at the end of each year. The first payment is due on 12/31, Year 1. Using an interest rate of 11 percent, the present value of the four payments is $15,500 on 1/1, Year 1. What expenses would Utah report on its Year 1 Income Statement related to this lease?

    a. Interest Expense of $1,705 and Depreciation Expense of $3,875.
    b. Rent Expense of $5,000.
    c. Interest Expense of $1,125 and Depreciation Expense of $3,875.
    d. Interest Expense of $1,705 and Depreciation Expense of $5,000.

_____ 5. This method of recording leases recognizes the signing of the lease as the acquisition of a long-term asset and the incurring of a long-term liability for lease payments.

    a. Operating-lease method.
    b. Capital-lease method.
    c. Rental-lease method.
    d. None of the above.

_____ 6. In which of the following situations would the lessee enjoy the economic benefits and bear the economic risk of leasing an asset?

    a. An asset with an economic life of 10 years is leased for 4 years.
    b. The lease agreement contains a bargain purchase option.
    c. At the end of the lease term, the lessee returns the leased asset to the lessor.
    d. The present value of the lease payments is $70,000 and the fair market value of the leased asset is $95,000.

_____ 7. Which of the following statements is not descriptive of a defined contribution pension plan?

    a. This plan defines the employer's contribution to the plan.
    b. The amounts to be received by employees depend on the investment performance of the pension plan.
    c. Pension benefits received during retirement are based on wages earned and number of years of employment.
    d. The employer's pension expense equals the amount contributed to the pension fund.

_____ 8. On January 1, Year 1, Wyoming Company leased a building and recorded the leasehold asset and the liability at $42,124, which is the present value of five end-of-year payments of $10,000 each discounted at 6 percent. The asset has a useful life of 5 years and a zero salvage value. On December 31, Year 1, when the first lease payment is made, Wyoming would record interest expense of

    a. $ -0-.
    b. $1,575.20.
    c. $7,876.
    d. None of the above.

_____ 9. Refer to the previous question. Assuming straight-line amortization, on December 31, Year 1, Wyoming would report the book value of the leasehold asset on its balance sheet in the amount of

    a. $50,000.
    b. $33,699.
    c. $42,124.
    d. $32,124.

_____ 10. Lessees prefer operating leases for several reasons. Which of the following is such a reason?

    a. Capital leases result in an increased debt-equity ratio.
    b. Capital leases result in earlier recognition of expenses.
    c. Operating leases result in the nonrecognition of lease assets and lease liabilities.
    d. All of the above are reasons for lessees preferring operating leases.

_____ 11. Under this method of recording leases, the lessee must amortize the leasehold over its useful life and must recognize each lease payment as part payment of interest and part principal.

    a.   Operating-lease method.
    b. Capital-lease method.
    c. Rental-lease method.
    d. None of the above.

_____ 12. Teton Corporation reported book income of $180,000 for Year 1. Included in the computation of the $180,000 was Warranty Expense of $20,000. For tax purposes, warranty costs are not deductible until incurred. Actual expenditures for warranty costs during Year 1 totaled $12,000. The tax rate for Year 1 is 30 percent. What amount should Teton report as a current liability for Income Tax Payable on its 12/31, Year 1, balance sheet?

    a. $48,000.
    b. $50,400.
    c. $54,000.
    d. $56,400.

_____ 13. Refer to the previous question. Regarding Teton's operations in Year 1,

    a. Book income exceeded taxable income.
    b. Taxable income exceeded book income.
    c. Book income equaled taxable income.
    d. The difference between book income and taxable income is due to a permanent difference.

_____ 14. Generally, the accounting treatment for leases favored by lessors and lessees is

    a. Both generally prefer operating leases.
    b. Both generally prefer capital leases.
    c. Lessors prefer capital leases while lessees prefer operating leases.
    d. Lessors prefer operating leases while lessees prefer capital leases.

_____ 15. Which of the following is not an example of a temporary difference and which, therefore, would not result in a deferred income tax account being debited or credited?

   a. A company uses straight-line depreciation for book purposes and ACRS for tax purposes.
   b. Estimated warranty costs are expensed in the year of sale but warranty costs are deducted for tax purposes in the year when repairs are made.
   c. In its financial reports, a company reports interest revenue earned on tax-exempt municipal bonds held as assets.
   d. For book purposes, a company uses the percentage-of-completion basis but uses the completed contract basis for tax purposes.

_____ 16. Nevada Corp. reported a current liability for income tax payable of $60,000 on its 12/31, Year 2, balance sheet. During the year, the corporation's Deferred Tax Liability account increased by $18,000 based on a tax rate of 40 percent applying to the future period of taxable income. The tax rate for Year 2 was 30 percent. What was Nevada's book income for Year 2?

   a. $200,000.
   b. $245,000.
   c. $260,000.
   d. $195,000.

_____ 17. Refer to the previous question. Regarding Nevada's operations in Year 2,

   a. Book income exceeded taxable income.
   b. Taxable income exceeded book income.
   c. Book income equaled taxable income.
   d. The difference between book income and taxable income is due to a permanent difference.

_____ 18. Montana Corporation's reported book income is $200,000 and income for tax purposes is $190,000. The $10,000 difference is caused by the use of ACRS for tax purposes. Assuming that the current tax rate is 35 percent and that a tax rate of 40 percent will apply to the future period of taxable income, determine the amount of taxes currently payable.

   a. $70,000.
   b. $ 4,000.
   c. $66,500.
   d. $70,500.

_____ 19. Which of the following is not a perceived advantage of off-balance sheet financing?

   a. The debt-equity ratio will be higher.
   b. Future credit ratings might be higher.
   c. Future borrowing costs might be lower.
   d. All of the above are perceived advantages of off-balance sheet financing.

_____ 20. A lease must be accounted for as a capital lease if it meets any one of four conditions. Which of the following is not one of the conditions?

    a. The lease contains a bargain purchase option.

    b. The lease transfers ownership of property to lessee.

    c. The lease term is 90 percent or more of the estimated economic life of the leased property.

    d. All of the above are conditions that (if any one is met) would cause the lease to be capitalized.

_____ 21. An entry such as the one that follows indicates that the lessee has accounted for the lease in what manner?

Interest Expense	xx	
Liability-Present Value of Lease Obligation	xx	
Cash		xx

    a. Sales type lease.

    b. Operating lease.

    c. Capital lease.

    d. None of the above.

_____ 22. Estes Park Company reported book income of $120,000 and taxable income of $150,000 (the $30,000 difference is attributed to goodwill amortization). The statutory tax rate is 30 percent and the company reports a current liability for income taxes payable of $45,000 on its Year 1 Balance Sheet. In its Income Statement the company reports income tax expense at an effective rate of 37.5 percent. What amount of Income Tax Expense did Estes Park report for Year 1?

    a. $45,000.

    b. $36,000.

    c. $28,800.

    d. $56,250.

_____ 23. Refer to the previous question. The difference between the statutory tax rate and the effective tax rate is due to

    a. A temporary difference that resulted in book income exceeding taxable income.

    b. A temporary difference that resulted in taxable income exceeding book income.

    c. A permanent difference resulting in book income exceeding taxable income.

    d. A permanent difference resulting in taxable income exceeding book income.

_____ 24. Which of the following is not a criticism of the accounting for deferred income taxes?

    a. Payment of deferred taxes may be deferred indefinitely.

    b. The amount on the balance sheet for deferred income taxes is not an obligation.

    c. Deferred taxes result in the effective tax rate being different than the statutory tax rate.

    d. The amount on the balance sheet for deferred income taxes is an undiscounted amount.

_____ 25. Cheyenne Company included in its book income $25,000 of interest on municipal bonds. The company reported a current liability of $90,000 for income tax payable on its Balance Sheet. The tax rate is 30 percent. What net income will Cheyenne report on its Income Statement?

    a. $235,000.
    b. $300,000.
    c. $325,000.
    d. $210,000.

_____ 26. On 1/1, Year 1, Lake Powell Co. leased equipment under a capital lease that calls for five payments of $5,000 each at the end of each year. The first payment is due on 12/31, Year 1. Using 12 percent interest, the present value of the lease liability is $18,000 on 1/1, Year 1. How much of the first payment of $5,000 is interest expense?

    a. $2,160.
    b. $1,400.
    c. $3,000.
    d. $2,000.

_____ 27. Refer to the previous question. At what amount would Lake Powell Co. report the lease liability on its 12/31, Year 1, balance sheet?

    a. $15,840.
    b. $16,600.
    c. $20,000.
    d. $15,160.

_____ 28. An employee is likely to prefer this type of pension plan because it reduces the employee's risk in planning for retirement.

    a. Nonvesting plan.
    b. Defined contribution plan.
    c. Nonfunded plan.
    d. Defined benefit plan.

_____ 29. On 1/1, Year 1, the Colorado Springs Medical Clinic leased some diagnostic equipment under a capital lease for 6 years. Using 10 percent interest, the present value of the lease liability was $30,500 on 1/1, Year 1. After the first lease payment is made on 12/31, Year 1, the clinic reports a lease liability of $26,550. What is the amount of each lease payment?

    a. $5,867.
    b. $3,950.
    c. $7,000.
    d. $5,083.

_____ 30. Under a defined benefit pension plan, the present value of the pension liability generated by employees' service during the period is called

a. Service costs.
b. Funded costs.
c. Vested costs.
d. None of the above.

_____ 31. In computing its income tax expense for the current year (its first year of operations), Nevada Corporation had a $30,000 temporary difference. It is assumed that a tax rate of 35 percent will apply to the future period of taxable income. The company's income for tax purposes is $470,000 and the current tax rate is 40 percent. What amount would Nevada Corp. report as income tax expense for the current year?

a. $198,500.
b. $200,000.
c. $176,000.
d. $177,500.

_____ 32. Refer to the previous question. For the current year, how would Nevada Corp report the tax effect of the temporary difference on its balance sheet?

a. A Deferred Tax Asset of $12,000 would be reported on its balance sheet.
b. A Deferred Tax Liability of $12,000 would be reported on its balance Sheet.
c. A Deferred Tax Asset of $10,500 would be reported on its balance sheet.
d. A Deferred Tax Liability of $10,500 would be reported on its balance sheet.

The following information relates to Questions 33–37. Vermont Company reports income tax expense of $280,000 on its income statement for the year ending December 31, Year 4. Included in Year 4's income was interest revenue of $50,000 from some tax exempt municipal bonds that the company owns. Additionally, in computing its income tax expense of $280,000, the company had a temporary difference of $100,000, which will result in a future tax deduction. It is assumed that a tax rate of 30 percent will apply to the future tax deduction. The tax rate for Year 4 (the company's first year of operations) is 40 percent.

_____ 33. What amount would Vermont Company report as current income tax payable on its Year 4 balance sheet?

a. $280,000.
b. $310,000.
c. $260,000.
d. None of the above.

_____ 34. For the current year, how would Vermont Company report the tax effect of the temporary difference on its balance sheet?

a. A Deferred Tax Asset of $30,000 would be reported on its balance sheet.
b. A Deferred Tax Liability of $30,000 would be reported on its balance sheet.
c. A Deferred Tax Asset of $40,000 would be reported on its balance sheet.
d. A Deferred Tax Liability of $40,000 would be reported on its balance sheet.

261

_____ 35. What is Vermont Company's taxable income for Year 4?

    a. $700,000.

    b. $775,000.

    c. $650,000.

    d. None of the above.

_____ 36. For the current year, how would Vermont Company report the tax effect of the permanent difference on its balance sheet?

    a. A Deferred Tax Asset of $20,000 would be reported on its balance sheet.

    b. A Deferred Tax Liability of $20,000 would be reported on its balance sheet.

    c. Nothing is reported on the balance sheet because a permanent difference has no effect on deferred taxes.

    d. None of the above.

_____ 37. What is Vermont Company's effective tax rate for Year 4?

    a. $280,000/$725,000 = .386.

    b. $280,000/$825,000 = .339.

    c. $280,000/$775,000 = .361.

    d. None of the above.

Exercises

1.   The Jackson Hole Company reports the book basis and tax basis of its asset and liabilities for Years 1– 4 as follows:

Date	Book Basis	Tax Basis	Temporary Difference
12/31, Year 1			
Assets	$ 400,000	$ 240,000	$160,000
Liabilities	200,000	200,000	—
12/31, Year 2			
Assets	760,000	520,000	240,000
Liabilities	220,000	220,000	—
12/31, Year 3			
Assets	1,060,000	840,000	220,000
Liabilities	250,000	250,000	—
12/31, Year 4			
Assets	1,340,000	1,220,000	120,000
Liabilities	280,000	280,000	—

Assume that the company's taxable income is $500,000 in each of the 4 years and that the tax rate is 35 percent for each of the 4 years.

a. Compute the amount of income tax expense for Years 1–4.

b. Record the appropriate entries for income tax allocation at the end of each of the 4 years.

c. What is the balance in the deferred tax liability account at 12/31, Year 4?

2. On January 2, Year 1, the LaVeta Company leased a machine for 4 years from Specialty Products Co. Annual rentals of $25,000 are to be paid at the end of each calendar year. The present value on January 2, Year 1, of the four lease payments, discounted at 8 percent, is $82,800. The asset's useful life is 4 years, and its salvage value is zero.

    Prepare all Year 1 entries relative to the lease of the machine if LaVeta records the lease by the capital-lease method. Also, prepare the Year 2 entry for the lease payment.

3. Refer to Exercise 2 above. Prepare all Year 1 entries relative to the lease of the machine on the books of Specialty Products Co. Assume that Specialty Products manufactured the machine at a cost of $75,000 and that the company treats the lease as a capital-lease. Also, prepare the Year 2 entry for the receipt of the lease payment.

4. On January 1, Year 1, Phoenix Company leased some equipment for 3 years. The lease calls for the first annual payment to be made on December 31, Year 1.

a. Fill in the 13 blanks on the lease amortization schedule below:

Year	Lease Liability Beginning of Year	Interest Expense for Year	Payment	Reduction of Obligation	Lease Liability End of Year
0	_____	_____	_____	_____	90,000
1	_____	7,200	_____	_____	_____
2	_____	_____	34,924	_____	_____
3	_____	_____	_____	_____	_____

b. If Phoenix treated the lease as a capital lease and amortized the leased asset on a straight-line basis over the 3-year lease term, how much expense, in total, would the company report each year relating to the lease transaction? If the lease were treated as an operating lease, how much expense would the company report each year?

5. On its 12/31, Year 3, balance sheet, the EAJ Corporation reports a deferred tax asset of $85,000 and a deferred tax liability of $53,000.

For Years 4 and 5, EAJ Corporation's income statement and balance sheet reported the following:

	Year 4	Year 5
Taxable Income	$900,000	$750,000
Total Deferred Tax Assets	104,000	121,000
Total Deferred Tax Liabilities	65,000	95,000

The tax rate for Years 3–5 was 40 percent.

Prepare entries for Year 4 and Year 5 to record income taxes for each of the 2 years.

6. Given below are disclosures regarding the pension plan of Calspa Company. The company reported pension expense of $40,000 for Year 5.

	1/1/5	12/31/5
Funded Status of Pension Plan		
Accumulated Benefit Obligation	$530,000	$520,000
Effect of Salary Increases	143,000	128,000
Projected Benefit Obligation	$673,000	$648,000
Plan Assets at Market Value	625,000	640,000
(Over) Underfunded Projected Benefit Obligation	$ 48,000	$ 8,000
Unrecognized Actuarial Gain	(100,000)	(70,000)
Prepaid Pension Asset on Balance Sheet	$ (52,000)	$ (62,000)

Record the 12/31, Year 5, journal entries for pension expense and pension funding.

Answers to Questions and Exercises

True/False

1.	T	7.	T	13.	T	19.	T	25.	F	31.	T
2.	F	8.	T	14.	F	20.	T	26.	F	32.	F
3.	F	9.	T	15.	F	21.	T	27.	F		
4.	T	10.	F	16.	F	22.	T	28.	F		
5.	F	11.	F	17.	T	23.	T	29.	F		
6.	T	12.	T	18.	F	24.	T	30.	T		

Matching

1.	i	5.	e	9.	q	13.	h	17.	j
2.	g	6.	n	10.	p	14.	l	18.	d
3.	a	7.	k	11.	f	15.	c	19.	o
4.	m	8.	s	12.	b	16.	r		

Multiple Choice

1.	c	8.	d	15.	c	22.	a	29.	c	36.	c
2.	a	9.	b	16.	b	23.	d	30.	a	37.	a
3.	b	10.	d	17.	a	24.	c	31.	a		
4.	b	11.	b	18.	c	25.	a	32.	d		
5.	b	12.	d	19.	a	26.	a	33.	b		
6.	b	13.	b	20.	c	27.	d	34.	a		
7.	c	14.	c	21.	c	28.	d	35.	b		

Exercises

1.

   a. <u>Year 1</u>

Income Tax Payable: .35 × $500,000	$175,000
Increase in Deferred Tax Liability: .35 × $160,000	56,000
Income Tax Expense	$231,000

      <u>Year 2</u>

Income Tax Payable: .35 × $500,000	$175,000
Increase in Deferred Tax Liability: .35 ($240,000 - $160,000)	28,000
Income Tax Expense	$203,000

Year 3

Income Tax Payable: .35 × $500,000	$175,000
Decrease in Deferred Tax Liability: .35 ($220,000 − $240,000)	(7,000)
Income Tax Expense	$168,000

Year 4

Income Tax Payable: .35 × $500,000	$175,000
Decrease in Deferred Tax Liability: .35 ($120,000 − $220,000)	(35,000)
Income Tax Expense	$140,000

			Dr.	Cr.
b.	12/31, Year 1	Income Tax Expense	231,000	
		Income Tax Payable		175,000
		Deferred Tax Liability		56,000
		To record income taxes for Year 1.		
	12/31, Year 2	Income Tax Expense	203,000	
		Income Tax Payable		175,000
		Deferred Tax Liability		28,000
		To record income taxes for Year 2.		
	12/31, Year 3	Income Tax Expense	168,000	
		Deferred Tax Liability	7,000	
		Income Tax Payable		175,000
		To record income taxes for Year 3.		
	12/31, Year 4	Income Tax Expense	140,000	
		Deferred Tax Liability	35,000	
		Income Tax Payable		175,000
		To record income taxes for Year 4.		

c.

Deferred Tax Liability			
		$56,000	(12/31, Year 1)
		$28,000	(12/31, Year 2)
(12/31, Year 3)	$ 7,000		
(12/31, Year 4)	$35,000		
		Balance	$42,000

2.

		Dr.	Cr.
1/2, Year 1	Asset-Machine Leasehold	82,800	
	Liability-Present Value of Lease Obligation		82,800
	To record leasehold asset and liability.		
12/31, Year 1	Amortization Expense	20,700	
	Asset-Machine Leasehold		20,700
	To record amortization of asset leasehold.		
	Amortization = $82,800 ÷ 4 = $20,700.		
12/31, Year 1	Interest Expense	6,624	
	Liability-Present Value of Lease Obligation	18,376	
	Cash		25,000
	To record payment of interest and principal.		
	Interest = .08 × $82,800 = $6,624.		
12/31, Year 2	Interest Expense	5,154	
	Liability-Present Value of Lease Obligation	19,846	
	Cash		25,000
	To record payment of interest and principal.		
	Interest = .08 ($82,800 − $18,376) = $5,154.		

3.

		Dr.	Cr.
1/2, Year 1	Lease Receivable	82,800	
	Sales Revenue		82,800
	To record the sale of a machine.		
	Cost of Goods Sold	75,000	
	Inventory		75,000
	To record the cost of the machine sold.		
12/31, Year 1	Cash	25,000	
	Interest Revenue		6,624
	Lease Receivable		18,376
	To record receipt of first lease payment.		
12/31, Year 2	Cash	25,000	
	Interest Revenue		5,154
	Lease Receivable		19,846
	To record receipt of second lease payment.		

4.   a.

Year	Lease Liability Beginning of Year	Interest Expense for Year	Payment	Reduction of Obligation	Lease Liability End of Year
0					90,000
1	90,000	7,200	34,924	27,724	62,276
2	62,276	4,982	34,924	29,942	32,334
3	32,334	2,590	34,924	32,334	0

b. Annual Expenses:

	Capital Lease				Operating Lease	
Year	Straight-Line Amortization	Interest Expense	Total Expense		Year	Rent Expense
1	30,000	7,200	37,200		1	34,924
2	30,000	4,982	34,982		1	34,924
3	30,000	2,590	32,590		3	34,924

5.

		Dr.	Cr.
12/31, Year 4	Income Tax Expense	353,000	
	Deferred Tax Asset	19,000	
	Deferred Tax Liability		12,000
	Income Tax Payable		360,000
	To record Year 4 taxes.		
12/31, Year 5	Income Tax Expense	313,000	
	Deferred Tax Asset	17,000	
	Deferred Tax Liability		30,000
	Income Tax Payable		300,000
	To record Year 5 taxes.		

6.

		Dr.	Cr.
12/31, Year 5	Pension Expense	40,000	
	Pension Liability		40,000
	To record pension expense for Year 5.		
12/31, Year 5	Pension Liability	40,000	
	Prepaid Pension Asset	10,000	
	Cash		50,000
	To record pension funding for Year 5.		

Chapter 12

Shareholders' Equity

Chapter Highlights

1. When owners provide funds, the source of these funds appear on the balance sheet as owners' equity, or in the context of corporations, as shareholders' equity.

2. The corporation is a widely used form of business organization in the United States for at least three reasons:

   a. The corporate form provides the owner, or shareholder, with limited liability. The assets of the individual owners are not subject to the claims of the corporation's creditors. Comparatively, creditors of partnerships and sole proprietorships have a claim on both the owners' business and <u>personal</u> assets to settle firms' debts.

   b. The corporate form facilitates raising owners' capital by the sale of shares of capital stock to the general public.

   c. Transfers of ownership interest may take place relatively easily without interfering with the ongoing management of the business.

3. Corporations have a separate legal existence. Individuals or other entities make capital contributions under a contract between themselves and the corporation. Because those who contribute capital funds are usually issued certificates for shares of stock, they are known as stockholders or shareholders. State laws, articles of incorporation (or charter) an agreement between the firm and the state in which the business is incorporated), the corporation bylaws, and the stock contract govern the rights and obligations of shareholders. Corporate charters often authorize the issue of more than one class of stock, each representing ownership in the corporation. Most shares issued are either common or preferred. Each class of shares appears separately on the balance sheet, with a short description of the major features of the shares.

4. Preferred shares are granted special privileges. These privileges or rights vary from issue to issue. Generally preferred shares have a senior claim on the assets in the event of bankruptcy relative to common shareholders. Preferred shareholders usually are entitled to dividends at a certain rate which must be paid by the firm prior to paying dividends to common shareholders. Preferred shares may be cumulative, callable, or convertible. If preferred shares are cumulative, then all current and previously postponed preferred dividends must be paid before dividends can be distributed to common shareholders. The corporation may reacquire callable preferred stock at a specified price, which may vary according to a predetermined time schedule. Convertible preferred shares may be exchanged by their owner into a specified amount of common shares at specified times. Some preferred stock issues carry mandatory redemption

features requiring the issuing firm to repurchase the shares from their holders, paying a specified dollar amount at a specified future time.

5. Firms may or may not issue preferred stock. All firms must issue common shares. Common shares, frequently the only voting shares, have a residual claim on earnings and assets after commitments to creditors and preferred shareholders have been satisfied.

6. Shares of stock often have a par or stated value per share specified in the articles of incorporation and printed on the face of the stock certificates. Par value of common shares has little economic significance, but it is separated for legal reasons from other contributed capital amounts on the balance sheet . The par value rarely denotes the worth of the shares except perhaps at the date of issue. Par value of preferred shares is more meaningful. Both the dividend rate and preference as to assets in dissolution are almost always based on the par value of the preferred shares.

7. Balance sheet accounts contain information about capital contribution, retained earnings and dividends, and treasury stock activity related to common shareholders' equity. These three components are the equity of the common shareholders. The book value of a common share is the total common stockholders' equity divided by the number of shares outstanding.

8. When shares of stock are issued, the corporation credits the Capital Stock account (either Preferred Stock or Common Stock) with the par value or stated value of the shares issued. When shares are issued for amounts greater than par (or stated) value, the corporation credits the excess to an account called Additional Paid-in Capital. Other titles for this account include Capital Contributed in Excess of Par (Stated) Value and Premium on Capital Stock.

9. Corporations give various individuals or entities the right, or option, to acquire common shares at a price that is less than the market price of the shares at the time they exercise the option.

10. Under a stock option plan, employees may purchase, at some time within a specified number of years in the future, shares in their company at a specified price, usually the market price of the stock on the day the option is granted. If on the date of the grant of the option the exercise price is equal to or exceeds the fair market price, then generally accepted accounting treatment results in no entry being made. When the options are exercised an entry is made to treat the transaction simply as an issue of stock at the option price. The expiration of an option without being exercised requires no entry. If the exercise price is less than the market price of the stock on the grant date, then compensation expense may have to be recognized under some circumstances. An alternative, currently unacceptable but under FASB consideration, recognizes the value of the stock option at the grant date as compensation expense. The terms of options and the number granted, outstanding, and exercised during the period must be disclosed in the financial statements or their related notes.

11. Corporations may grant opportunities to buy shares of stock through stock rights and stock warrants. Stock rights are similar to stock options. Corporations grant stock options to employees as a form of compensation. Firms issue stock rights to current stockholders. The rights usually trade in public markets. Firms grant rights without cost to stockholders, therefore no journal entry is required at the issuance date. When the rights are exercised, the entry is like the one to record the issue of new shares at the price paid.

12. On the other hand, firms issue stock warrants to the general investing public for cash. The warrants allow the holder to acquire additional shares at a specified amount within a specified period. At the date of the sale of the warrants the entry is a debit to Cash and a credit to Common Stock Warrants. When the rights are exercised, the firm debits cash for the additional proceeds, debits Common Stock Warrants for the

cost of the warrants, and makes offsetting credits to Common Stock (for par value) and Additional Paid-in Capital. If the warrants expire without the holders exercising them, the firm debits Common Stock Warrants and credits Additional Paid-in Capital. Firms sometimes attach common stock warrants to a bond or preferred stock. When the accountant can measure objectively the value of the warrant and the value of the associated bond or preferred stock, the accounting allocates the issue price between the two securities.

13. Convertible bonds and convertible preferred stock allow the holder of the bond or preferred stock to convert or "trade in" the bond for shares of common stock. The bond or preferred stock specifies the number of shares to be received when converted into stock, the dates when conversion can occur, and other details. The owner can hold the security as a bond or preferred stock or convert to common stock equity should the company be so successful that its common stock rises in price on the stock market. Although some accountants argue that some of the original proceeds from the issuance of convertible debt or preferred stock should be allocated to the conversion feature, currently firms following generally acceptable accounting principles attribute all the proceeds to the debt or preferred stock with an entry which includes a debit to Cash for the proceeds and a credit to either Convertible Bond Payable or Preferred Stock. Upon conversion the usual entry ignores current market prices and merely shows a swap of common stock for bonds or preferred stock at their book value. An acceptable alternative recognizes the market value of the shares of common stock issued, and a firm records the difference between that market value and the book value of the bonds or preferred stock as a gain or loss on conversion.

14. Treasury shares or treasury stock are shares of stock reacquired by the issuing corporation. Firms reacquire their own shares to use in various option arrangements, invest excess cash, and to defend against unfriendly takeover bids. When stock is reacquired, the corporation debits an account, Treasury Shares, with the total amount paid to reacquire the shares. If the corporation reissues the shares, it debits cash for the amount received and credits the Treasury Shares account with the cost of the shares. If the reissue price is greater than the acquisition price, the corporation credits the difference to the Additional Paid-in Capital account to make the entry balance. If the reissue price is less than the amount paid, the debit to make the entry balance is usually to Additional Paid-in Capital, as long as there is a sufficient credit balance in that account. If there is not, the additional balancing debit goes directly to Retained Earnings. Corporations present the Treasury Shares account as a contra account to total stockholders' equity on the balance sheet. A corporation does not report profit or loss on transactions involving its own shares.

15. The Retained Earnings account increases (decreases) each period by the amount of net income (net loss) and decreases for dividends declared. The income statement reports revenues from the sale of products to customers and the expenses for the resources used to generate these revenues. Firms sometimes engage in transactions that are peripherally related to their customary revenue generating operations, nonrecurring, or relate to measurements of income of prior periods. The reporting issue for these peripheral transactions is whether they should be reported on the income statement of the current period or added (credited) or deducted (debited) directly in retained earnings, bypassing the income statement. Generally accepted accounting principles usually require disclosures of all items on the income statement before their transfer to retained earnings. Others advocate reporting peripheral transactions directly in retained earnings providing only the current periods' usual recurring transactions on the income statement.

16. Net income for the period which is closed to Retained Earnings may contain various income components: (a) income from continuing operations; (b) income gains, and losses from operations to be discontinued; (c) income from extraordinary items; and (d) adjustments to income resulting from changes in accounting principles.

17. A prior period adjustment causes the total of retained earnings to change other than transactions reported in the income statement for that period and dividends. A firm records a prior period adjustment when it corrects errors of previous accounting periods by making either a debit or a credit to Retained Earnings. Examples of such errors are miscounting inventories or arithmetic mistakes.

18. Changes in accounting estimates occur as time passes and new information becomes available. Examples of changes in estimates include the amount to recognize as uncollectible accounts and the useful lives of depreciable assets. The effects of changes in estimates are reported in the income statements of the current and future periods, not through retained earnings as a prior period adjustment.

19. Profitable companies generate additional owners' equity from undistributed earnings. These undistributed earnings are the accumulated periodic net incomes in excess of dividends that have been declared. One misconception about net income is that it represents a fund of cash available for distributions or expansion. Although earnings from operations generally involve cash at some stage, the only certain statement that can be made about the effect of retaining earnings is that it results in increased net assets (excess of all assets over all liabilities).

20. Most publicly held firms distribute a portion of the assets generated by earnings as a dividend to shareholders. The board of directors declares these dividends periodically. The directors, in considering whether or not to declare cash dividends, must conclude both (a) that the declaration of a dividend is legal and (b) that it would be financially expedient. In other words, the directors should carefully examine the statutory restrictions on dividends, the contractual restrictions on dividends, and the corporate financial policy in regard to dividends.

21. State corporation laws generally provide that dividends "may not be paid out of capital" but must be "paid out of earnings." "Capital" is usually defined as the total paid in capital. In some states, dividends may be paid out of current earnings even though there is an accumulated deficit from previous periods. Balance sheet disclosure should provide the user with information to determine any legal restrictions on dividend payment. For example, state statutes can provide that "treasury shares may be acquired only in amounts less than retained earnings."

22. Contracts with bondholders, preferred shareholders, and lessors often place restrictions upon dividend payments and thereby compel the retention of earnings.

23. Some of the reasons why the directors may decide to allow the retained earnings to increase as a matter of corporate financial policy are (a) the earnings may not reflect a corresponding increase of available cash, (b) a restriction of dividends in prosperous years may permit the continued payment of dividends in poor years, (c) a corporation may need funds for expansion of working capital or plant and equipment, and (d) the firm may consider the reduction of indebtedness desirable rather than the declaration of all or most of the net income as dividends.

24. Firms may pay dividends in cash, other assets, or shares of its common stock. When cash dividends are declared, the entry is a debit to Retained Earnings and a credit to Dividends Payable. At the date of payment, Dividends Payable is debited and Cash is credited.

25. A distribution of a corporation's assets other than cash to its shareholders is a dividend in kind or a property dividend. The amount debited to Retained Earnings is the fair market value of the assets distributed. Any gain or loss is recognized as part of income for the period.

26. A stock dividend is a distribution of additional shares to stockholders in proportion to their existing holdings without any additional contributions. In the accounts, a stock dividend requires a transfer from

274

retained earnings to the contributed capital accounts. Generally accepted accounting principles require that the amount transferred from retained earnings be equal to the market value of the shares issued. Therefore, the resulting entry generally is a debit to Retained Earnings (for fair market value) and credits to the Common Stock account (for par value) and to the Additional Paid-in Capital account for the excess of fair market value over the par value. Following the stock dividend, a stockholder has additional shares, but the stockholder's proportionate interest in the capital of the corporation and proportionate voting power have not changed.

27. A stock split (or more technically, split-up) is a distribution of additional shares of stock to shareholders in proportion to their existing holdings without additional contributions. Although difficult to distinguish, the primary difference between a stock dividend and a stock split is that in a stock split the par or stated value of all stock in the issued class is reduced proportionately to the additional shares issued. A stock split usually does not require a journal entry. Large stock dividends are generally treated as stock splits. Stock splits (or large stock dividends) usually reduce the market value per share in reverse proportion to the split (or dividend). Stock splits have been used by management to keep the market prices per share from rising to an unacceptable price level.

28. Accountants calculate earnings per share of common stock by dividing net income attributable to common shareholders by the weighted-average number of shares of common stock outstanding during the period. Earnings-per-share calculations become more complicated when a firm has outstanding securities that if exchanged for common stock would decrease earnings per share. Stock options, stock rights, warrants, and convertible bonds all have the potential of reducing earnings per share and must be taken into account in calculating earnings per share.

29. The annual report to shareholders must explain the changes in all shareholders' equity accounts. The reconciliation of retained earnings may appear in the balance sheet, in an income statement and retained earnings statement, or in a separate statement of shareholders' equity.

30. The accounting for stockholders' equity in most developed countries closely parallels that in the United States. One major difference is the use of "reserve" accounts. In many other countries the use of the reserve account is to disclose a portion of retained earnings that is either permanently or temporarily not available for future dividends. A second use of reserve accounts relates to revaluations of assets. Accounting regulations in the Great Britain and France permits firms to revalue periodically their plant and other assets.

31. Most transactions (with the exception of net income) affecting shareholders equity accounts appear in the statement of cash flows as financing activities. Example transactions include cash received from the issue of common stock, preferred stock, and stock under options, rights, or warrants arrangements. Cash dividends paid appear as outflows in the financing activities section of the statement of cash flows, significant shareholder equity transactions not involving cash are disclosed in a supplementary schedule or note to the financial statements.

Questions and Exercises

True/False. For each of the following statements, place a T or F in the space provided to indicate whether the statement is true or false.

_____ 1. Cumulative preferred stock entitles the holder to receive all current and previously postponed dividends before common stock dividends can be distributed.

_____ 2. Many state laws carry mandatory redemption features, requiring the issuing firm to repurchase the shares from their holders.

_____ 3. The cost of treasury stock is presented in the Investment section of the balance sheet with other securities owned by the company.

_____ 4. The book value of common stock while not equal to fair market value is almost always equal to the par value or stated value of the shares.

_____ 5. Stock options and stock rights are similar, but stock options are nontransferable while stock rights are traded in the open market.

_____ 6. At the end of an accounting period, a well-managed company will always have an increase in cash at least equal to the net income for the period.

_____ 7. Net assets refers to the excess of all assets over all liabilities.

_____ 8. For most companies the amount and timing of dividend declarations are determined by the shareholders at their annual meeting.

_____ 9. Corporations in most cases pay out dividends equal to net income unless specific restrictions (either legal or financial) are stated in the annual report.

_____ 10. A stock dividend is often referred to as a dividend in kind.

_____ 11. In a stock split the par or stated value of all stock in the issued class is reduced in proportion to the additional shares issued.

_____ 12. Cash received from the issuance of stock to an employee exercising a stock option is reported in the financing section of the statement of cash flows.

_____ 13. Stock rights cannot be traded in the open market since they are exclusively for employees.

_____ 14. Stock options, often a part of compensation plans, offer employees the opportunity to purchase, at some time within a specified number of years in the future, shares in their company at a specified price.

_____ 15. Corrections of errors result in either a debit or credit to Retained Earnings.

_____ 16. It is difficult to raise large amounts of funds for corporations because so many shares of relatively small value must be sold.

_____ 17. Common shareholders have the claim to earnings of the corporation after commitments to creditors and preferred shareholders have been satisfied.

_____ 18. Preferred stock is frequently the only voting stock of the company.

_____ 19. State corporation laws generally provide that dividends must be "paid out of earnings."

_____ 20. The corporate form provides the owner, or shareholder with unlimited liability.

_____ 21. Convertibility is generally a feature of common stock allowing the holder to convert shares into preferred stock at some specified time in the future.

_____ 22. Par value and stated value have basically the same effect on the recording in the accounts of the issue of capital stock.

_____ 23. Additional Paid-in Capital, Capital Contributed in Excess of Par (Stated) Value, and Premium on Capital Stock are three titles referring to the same type of account.

_____ 24. Premium on Common Stock is amortized in the same manner as Premium on Bonds.

_____ 25. Treasury Stock refers to shares of stock reacquired by the issuing corporation.

_____ 26. Bondholder agreements often place restrictions upon dividend payments.

_____ 27. Stock splits and stock dividends are accounted for in the same manner.

_____ 28. Changes in accounting estimates are reported in income statements of the current and future periods.

_____ 29. Accounting regulations permit the use of a reserve account for plant revaluation in the United States, the United Kingdom, and France.

_____ 30. Changes in shareholdings' equity usually are not reported in annual reports but are provided to the SEC.

Matching. From the list of terms below, select that term which is most closely associated with each of the descriptive phrases or statements that follows and place the letter for that term in the space provided.

a. Additional Paid-in Capital
b. Callable Preferred Stock
c. Common Stock
d. Contractual Restriction on
e. Convertible Bonds
f. Convertible Preferred Stock
g. Corporate Charter
h. Cumulative Preferred Stock
i. Net Assets
j. Par Value

k. Preferred Stock
l. Prior-Period Adjustment
m. Redeemable Preferred Stock
n. Reserve Accounts Dividends
o. Stock Dividends
p. Stock Options
q. Stock Rights
r. Stock Splits
s. Stock Warrants
t. Treasury Shares

_____ 1. An example would be a restriction of dividends imposed by an agreement between bondholders and the corporation.

_____ 2. Type of preferred shares which may be reacquired by the corporation at a specified price, which may vary according to a predetermined time schedule.

_____ 3. A nominal value per share specified in the articles of incorporation and printed on the face of the stock certificates.

_____ 4. Class of stock usually entitling the holder to dividends at a certain rate which must be paid before dividends can be declared and paid to common shareholders.

_____ 5. Used in many countries to disclose a portion of retained earnings that is either permanently or temporarily not available for future dividends.

_____ 6 Shares of stock reacquired by the issuing corporation.

_____ 7. The agreement between the firm and the state in which the business is incorporated.

_____ 8. Type of shares that must receive all current and previously postponed dividends before dividends may be issued to other classes of stock.

_____ 9. Account title used to designate contributed capital by owners paid in excess of par or stated value.

_____ 10. An issue of additional shares of stock to shareholders in proportion to existing holdings without any additional contributions but with a proportional reduction of the par or stated value of all the stock in the issued class.

_____ 11. An issue of an additional number of shares to shareholders in proportion to their existing holdings without any additional contribution and without a change in the par value per share of stock.

_____ 12. The voting class of stock which also has a residual claim to earnings.

_____ 13. Issued to the general public for cash allowing the holder to buy shares of stock in the future at a specified price.

_____ 14. Granted to current stockholders, usually at no cost, allowing the holder to buy shares of stock at a specified price in the future.

_____ 15. Securities with a feature which allows the stockholder to convert the shares into a specified amount of common shares at specified times.

_____ 16. Preferred stock issues which have some characteristics of debt, i.e., required repurchase features or repurchase at the option of the holder.

_____ 17. Correction of an error as a direct adjustment of retained earnings at the beginning of the period.

_____ 18. Part of an employee compensation plan which under generally accepted accounting principles usually does not require a journal entry at the date of grant.

_____ 19. Type of bonds which may be exchanged for common shares at specified times at the option of its owner.

_____ 20. Excess of all assets over all liabilities of a firm.

Multiple Choice. Choose the best answer for each of the following questions and enter the identifying letter in the space provided.

_____ 1. The owners' equity account with a normal debit balance is

    a. Additional Paid-in Capital.
    b. Common Stock.
    c. Retained Earnings.
    d. Treasury Shares.

_____ 2. The corporate charter (or articles of incorporation) is

    a. The contract between the firm and the state in which the business is incorporated.
    b. The corporation laws of the state in which incorporation takes place.
    c. The bylaws of the corporation.
    d. The stock contract.

_____ 3. One feature that is generally not associated with preferred stock is the

    a. Cumulative feature.
    b. Callable feature.
    c. Voting right.
    d. Conversion right.

_____ 4. Which of the following enables the holder to become a common stockholder?

    a. Callable preferred shares.
    b. Redeemable preferred shares.
    c. Convertible preferred shares.
    d. None of the above.

_____ 5. Which of the following is usually sold to the general public for cash?

    a. Stock options.
    b. Stock rights.
    c. Stock warrants.
    d. None of the above.

_____ 6. Which of the following does not generally require a journal entry?

    a. Issue shares in a stock split.
    b. Issue shares in a stock dividend.
    c. Reissue treasury shares.
    d. Issue stock warrants.

_____ 7. Which of the following increases total shareholders' equity?

    a. Issue shares in a stock split.
    b. Issue shares in a stock dividend.
    c. Reissue treasury shares.
    d. None of the above.

_____ 8. Which of the following generally requires a debit to retained earnings?

    a. Stock dividend.
    b. Stock split.
    c. Both (a) and (b) above.
    d. None of the above.

_____ 9. When a corporation reissues treasury shares for a price above their acquisition price, the amount above the acquisition price is credited to

    a. Additional Paid-in Capital.
    b. Treasury Stock.
    c. Gain on Sale of Treasury Stock.
    d. Retained Earnings.

_____ 10. The Treasury Shares account should be disclosed in the balance sheet as a

    a. Short-term investment.
    b. Contra to total shareholders' equity.
    c. Deferred charge.
    d. Stock investment account.

_____ 11. Which of the following distributions usually does not require a debit to retained earnings?

    a. Cash dividend.
    b. Dividend in kind.
    c. Stock dividend.
    d. Stock split.

_____ 12. Which of the following is usually associated with employee compensation plans?

    a. Stock options.
    b. Stock rights.
    c. Stock warrants.
    d. None of the above.

_____ 13. Which of the following entries are correct when a company issues convertible bonds?

    a. Debit Cash, credit Convertible Bonds Payable.
    b. Debit Cash, credit Convertible Bonds Payable and Additional Paid-in Capital.
    c. Neither entry is correct.
    d. Both entries are correct.

_____ 14. Which of the following require direct adjustments to retained earnings?

    a. Extraordinary items.
    b. Gain or loss from discontinued operations.
    c. Prior period adjustments.
    d. None of the above.

_____ 15. A corporation usually recognizes a gain or loss when

    a. It reissues treasury stock for an amount less than or greater than its par value.

    b. It reissues treasury stock for an amount less than or greater than its cost to acquire the stock.

    c. It issues stock to employees at a price specified in a stock option plan.

    d. None of the above.

_____ 16. When a company issues its capital stock for an amount in excess of the par value the excess amount is credited to

    a. Additional Paid-in Capital.

    b. Capital Contributed in Excess of Par Value.

    c. Premium on Capital Stock.

    d. All three account titles in a, b, and c are acceptable.

_____ 17. The following should be accounted for in current and future income statements:

    a. Prior Period Adjustments.

    b. Changes in Accounting Estimates.

    c. Error corrections.

    d. All of the above.

_____ 18. The following should be presented in the statement of cash flows as an inflow from financing activities:

    a. Payment of cash dividends.

    b. The receipt of cash from the reissue of treasury shares.

    c. The purchase of treasury shares using cash.

    d. None of the above.

_____ 19. All of the following should be presented in the financing activities section of the statement of cash flows except

    a. Issue of common shares for cash.

    b. Issue of preferred shares for cash.

    c. Sale of investment in stock for cash.

    d. Payment of cash dividends.

_____ 20. Income statement prepared under generally accepted accounting principles may contain the following components except

    a. Income from extraordinary items.

    b. Corrections of errors.

    c. Adjustments for changes in accounting principles.

    d. Income, gains, and losses from discontinued operations.

Exercises

1. From the following accounts, indicate in the space provided the correct debit and credit entries corresponding to the transactions described. Credit entries should be shown in parentheses. The first is answered as an example.

a.	Additional Paid-in Capital		h.	Preferred Stock
b.	Cash		i.	Retained Earnings
c.	Common Stock		j.	Redeemable Preferred Stock
d.	Common Stock Warrants		k.	Treasury Stock
e.	Dividends Payable		l.	Some Account Not Listed
f.	Inventory		m.	No Formal Journal Entry
g.	Investments			

b, (c)
_____ 1. Issued common stock at par value for cash.

_____ 2. A stock dividend is declared and distributed at a time when the market value is above the par value.

_____ 3. The board of directors authorize the distribution of a 2 for 1 stock split.

_____ 4. Stock warrants to acquire common stock are issued for cash to the public.

_____ 5. One-half of the warrants in transaction 4 are submitted for redemption with the appropriate cash (the amount exceeds the par value of the stock).

_____ 6. The remaining warrants from transaction 4 expire without having been exercised.

_____ 7. Closed Income Summary (credit Balance) to Retained Earnings.

_____ 8. The board of directors declared a cash dividend to be distributed in 3 weeks.

_____ 9. Cash dividend from transaction 8 is paid.

_____ 10. Preferred stock is issued for cash in excess of the par value of the shares issued.

_____ 11. A stock option is granted to employees when the option price was equal to the market price.

_____ 12. The option in transaction 11 above is exercised. The option price is above par value.

_____ 13. Preferred stock is "retired." The price paid to retire is in excess of the original issue price (which was above par value).

_____ 14. A declaration and distribution of a dividend in kind, distributing shares of another company held as an investment. The investment cost is equal to its fair market value at the time of the declaration.

_____ 15. Common shares previously issued are reacquired by the corporation, which gives cash in excess of the price for which the shares were initially sold.

_____ 16. One-half of the shares in transaction 11 are reissued at an amount which exceeds one-half the purchase price.

_____ 17. The remaining one-half of the treasury shares are reissued at an amount which is less than one-half the purchase price.

_____ 18. An error was discovered in which the inventory at the end of the previous period was understated by $15,000.

2. Record the following entries in the books of Prince-Williams Corporation.

   a. Issued 1,000 shares of common stock for $15 cash per share. The common shares had a $10 par value per share.

   b. A 10 percent common stock dividend was declared and issued. At the time of issuance there were 100,000 shares outstanding, and each share was currently trading on the open market for $16 per share.

   c. Reacquired 1,000 shares of common stock (treasury shares) paying $14,000.

   d. Reissued 250 shares obtained in transaction c above, receiving $13 per share.

e. Reissued 250 shares obtained in transaction c above, receiving $15 per share.

f. Issued 400 shares of preferred stock for $50 cash per share. The preferred stock had a $40 par value per share.

g. Reacquired 300 shares of preferred stock (treasury shares) from transaction f above paying $52 per share.

h. Reacquired 100 shares of preferred stock from transaction f above paying $52 per share and formally "retired" these shares.

i. Reissued 200 shares of preferred stock (treasury shares) from transaction g above receiving $52 per share.

j. Retired 100 shares of preferred stock (treasury shares) from transaction g above.

k. Declared a cash dividend to shareholders totaling $200,000.

l. Granted a common stock option to employees to acquire 3,000 shares at $15 a share, which is the current market price.

m. Employees exercised stock options in Exercise 1 to acquire 2,000 shares.

n. The remaining stock option in Exercise 1 lapse.

o. The firm issues at par $50,000 of 20-year bonds, 12 percent semiannual coupon bonds, each $1,000 bond convertible into 40 shares of the company's $10 par value common stock. The bonds without the convertible feature would have sold for $47,000.

p. Paid cash dividend declared in transaction k above.

q. Declares and distributes a dividend in kind.Prince-Williams owns 1,000 shares of Stephens, which had a cost of $10 per share. The shares have a $12 per share fair market value at the time of the dividend. The Stephens shares are distributed as a dividend.

r. Issued stock warrants to the public containing rights to purchase 2,000 common shares for $15 each and received $2,500 cash for the warrants.

s. Issued 500 shares of treasury stock (from transaction transaction c above) as the rights for 500 common shares in transaction r above were exercises.

t. The rights for 1,000 common shares in transaction r above were exercised and common stock issued. The market price was $16.

u. The remaining rights in transaction r above expire without being exercised.

v. The firm acquired a truck 2 years ago. The truck cost $40,000 and had a $5,000 estimated salvage value. The firm had recorded depreciation correctly for the past 2 years based on an estimated 7-year life using straight-line depreciation. The firm now estimates the total life will be 4 years. Record depreciation for this year (third year of asset's life) and any required adjustments to depreciation of previous years. Assume the estimated salvage value to remain $5,000.

w. Net income of $300,00 (balance in Income Summary) is closed to Retained Earnings.

Answers to Questions and Exercises

True/False

1.	T	7.	T	13.	F	19.	T	25.	T
2.	F	8.	F	14.	T	20.	F	26.	T
3.	F	9.	F	15.	T	21.	F	27.	F
4.	F	10.	F	16.	F	22.	T	28.	T
5.	T	11.	T	17.	T	23.	T	29.	F
6.	F	12.	T	18.	F	24.	F	30.	F

Matching

1.	d	5.	n	9.	a	13.	s	17.	l
2.	b	6.	t	10.	r	14.	q	18.	p
3.	j	7.	g	11.	o	15.	f	19.	e
4.	k	8.	h	12.	c	16.	m	20.	i

Multiple Choice

1.	d	5.	c	9.	a	13.	a	17.	b
2.	a	6.	a	10.	b	14.	c	18.	b
3.	c	7.	c	11.	d	15.	d	19.	c
4.	c	8.	a	12.	a	16.	d	20.	b

Exercises

1.
1.	b,(c)	7.	l,(i)	13.	h,a,i,(b)
2.	i,(c),(a)	8.	i,(e)	14.	i,(g)
3.	m	9.	e,(b)	15.	k,(b)
4.	b,(d)	10.	b,(h),(a)	16.	b,(k),(a)
5.	b,d,(c),(a)	11.	m	17.	b,i,(k), or b,a,(k)
6.	d,(a)	12.	b,(c),(a)	18.	f,(i)

2.

		Dr.	Cr.
a.	Cash	15,000	
	Common Stock		10,000
	Additional Paid-in Capital		5,000
	To issue 1,000 shares of common stock for $15 per share.		
b.	Retained Earnings	160,000	
	Common Stock		100,000
	Additional Paid-in Capital		60,000
	To issue a 10 percent stock dividend.		
c.	Treasury Shares—Common	14,000	
	Cash		14,000
	To reacquire 1,000 shares of common stock.		
d.	Cash	3,250	
	Additional Paid-in Capital*	250	
	Treasury Shares—Common		3,500
	To reissue 250 treasury shares.		

*Debit to Retained Earnings would be appropriate if balance insufficient in Additional Paid-in Capital.

		Dr.	Cr.
e.	Cash	3,750	
	Treasury Shares—Common		3,500
	Additional Paid-in Capital		250
	To reissue 250 treasury shares.		
f.	Cash	20,000	
	Preferred Stock		16,000
	Additional Paid-in Capital		4,000
	To issue 400 shares of preferred stock for $50 per share.		
g.	Treasury Shares—Preferred	15,600	
	Cash		15,600
	To reacquire 300 shares of preferred stock.		
h.	Preferred Stock	4,000	
	Additional Paid-in Capital	1,000	
	Retained Earnings	200	
	Cash		5,200
	To retire 100 shares of preferred stock paying $52 per share.		
i.	Cash	10,400	
	Treasury Shares—Preferred		10,400
	To reissue 200 shares of preferred stock.		

		Dr.	Cr.
j.	Preferred Stock	4,000	
	Additional Paid-in Capital	1,000	
	Retained Earnings	200	
	Treasury Shares—Preferred		5,200
	To retire 100 shares of preferred stock held in treasury.		
k.	Retained Earnings	200,000	
	Dividends Payable		200,000
	To declare $200,000 cash dividend.		
l.	No Formal Journal Entry		
m.	Cash	30,000	
	Common Stock		20,000
	Additional Paid-in Capital		10,000
	To issue 2,000 shares under stock option plan.		
n.	No Formal Journal Entry		
o.	Cash	50,000	
	Convertible Bonds Payable		50,000
	To issue $50,000 par 20-year, 12 percent semiannual coupon bonds convertible into 40 shares of common stock for each $1,000 bond.		
p.	Dividend Payable	200,000	
	Cash		200,000
	To pay cash dividend.		
q.	Retained Earnings	12,000	
	Investments		10,000
	Gain on Disposition of Investments		2,000
	To issue dividend in kind when shares of investment had a fair market value in excess of cost.		
r.	Cash	2,500	
	Common Stock Warrants		2,500
	To issued stock warrants.		
s.	Cash	7,500	
	Common Stock Warrants	625	
	Treasury Shares—Common		7,000
	Additional Paid-in Capital		1,125
	Treasury shares issued for the exercise of stock warrants for 500 shares.		

		Dr.	Cr.
t.	Cash	15,000	
	Common Stock Warrants	1,250	
	Common Stock		10,000
	Additional Paid-in Capital		6,250
	Stock warrants for 1,000 shares exercised.		
u.	Common Stock Warrants	625	
	Additional Paid-in Capital		625
	To record warrants expiration.		
v.	Depreciation Expense	12,500	
	Accumulated Depreciation		12,500
	Original annual depreciation:		
	($40,000 – 5,000)/7 = $5,000.		
	Book value after 2 years		
	= $30,000 ($40,000 – $10,000).		
	Current depreciation		
	is $12,500 [($30,000 – 5,000)/2].		
w.	Income Summary	300,000	
	Retained Earnings		300,000
	To close net income to Retained Earnings.		

Chapter 13

Long-Term Investments in Corporate Securities

Chapter Highlights

1. For a variety of reasons, corporations often acquire the stock of other corporations. Long-term investments in corporate securities are typically classified as "Investments" on the Balance Sheet. The accounting for long-term investments depends on the purpose of the investment and on the percentage of voting stock that one corporation owns of another.

2. Three types of long-term investments can be identified: (1) minority, passive investments, (2) minority, active investments, and (3) majority, active investments.

3. Minority, passive investments are shares of capital stock of another corporation viewed as a good long-term investment and are acquired for the dividends and capital gains. The percentage of shares owned is not so large (less than 20 percent of the voting stock) that the acquiring company can control or exert significant influence over the other company.

4. Minority, active investments are shares of another corporation acquired so that the acquiring corporation can exert significant influence over the other company's activities. Generally accepted accounting principles view investments of 20 percent to 50 percent of the voting stock of another company as minority, active investments "unless evidence indicates that significant influence cannot be exercised."

5. Majority, active investments are shares of another corporation acquired so that the acquiring corporation can control the other company. Ownership of more than 50 percent of the voting stock of another company implies an ability to control, unless there is evidence to the contrary.

6. In the following discussion the firm owning shares will be referred to as Company P. Company S will be used to refer to the firm whose shares are owned.

7. The market value method is used for minority, passive investments (Company P owns less than 20 percent of the stock of Company S). Under the market value method, Company P will (a) initially record investments at acquisition cost, including costs of acquisition, such as brokerage fees and commissions, (b) report as income each period its share of the dividends declared by Company S, (c) adjust the book value of each investment to its market value and make an offsetting entry to an Unrealized Holding Gain or Unrealized Holding Loss on Investment in Securities account (this account typically appears between additional Paid-In Capital and Retained Earnings), and (d) recognize gains and losses on the income

statement from holding the stock of Company S only at the time the shares are sold. This realized gain or loss is the difference between selling price and original cost.

8. Generally accepted accounting principles require the use of the equity method for minority, active investments (Company P owns 20 percent or more of the voting stock of Company S, but not more than 50 percent). Under the equity method, the purchase of stock is recorded at acquisition cost. However, Company P treats as income each period its proportionate share of the periodic earnings of Company S. The entry to record this income is a debit to the account, Investment in Stock of S, and a credit to Equity in Earnings of Affiliate. Dividends paid by Company S to Company P are treated by Company P as a reduction in its investment in Company S. The entry to record dividends received is a debit to Cash and a credit to Investment in Stock of S.

9. One complication using the equity method arises when the acquisition cost of P's shares exceeds P's proportionate share of the book value of the net assets (assets minus liabilities), or stockholders' equity, of S at the date of acquisition. Under the equity method, the excess is generally goodwill. Goodwill must be amortized over a period not greater than 40 years.

10. Under the equity method, the amount shown in the noncurrent section of the balance sheet for Investment in Stock of S will generally be equal to the acquisition cost of the shares plus Company P's share of Company S's undistributed earnings since the date the shares were acquired. On the income statement, Company P shows its share of Company S's net income as revenue each period.

11. Control of one corporation (Company S) by another (Company P) is assured when Company P owns more than 50 percent of Company S's voting stock. The corporation exercising control through stock ownership is the parent, and the one subject to control is the subsidiary.

12. Generally accepted accounting principles require majority investments (over 50 percent) to be reported by the preparation of consolidated statements. Consolidated statements are designed to report the financial position and operations of two or more legally distinct entities as if they were a single, centrally controlled economic entity.

13. When one company controls another, the controlling company could bring the legal existence of the controlled company to an end. However, some important reasons for continued existence of subsidiary companies are (a) to reduce the financial risk of one segment (subsidiary) becoming insolvent, (b) to meet more effectively the requirements of state corporation and tax legislation, (c) to expand or diversify with a minimum of capital investment, and (d) to sell an unwanted operation with a minimum of administrative, legal, and other costs.

14. Generally, consolidated financial statements provide more useful information than would separate financial statements of the parent and each subsidiary or than would be provided using the equity method. The parent, because of its voting interest, can control the use of all of the subsidiary's assets. Consolidation of the individual assets and equities of both the parent and the subsidiary provides a more realistic picture of the operations and financial position of the single economic entity. Consolidated financial statements are generally prepared when the following two criteria are met: (1) the parent owns more than 50 percent of the voting stock of the subsidiary, and (2) there are no important restrictions on the ability of the parent to exercise control of the subsidiary.

15. State laws typically require each legally separate corporation to maintain its own set of books. The consolidation of these financial statements basically involves summing the amounts for various financial statement items across the separate company statements. Adjustment to this summation must be made to

eliminate double counting resulting from intercompany transactions. The eliminations typically appear on a consolidation work sheet and not on the books of any of the legal entities being consolidated.

16. For example, a parent may lend money to its subsidiary. If the separate balance sheets were added together, then the funds would be counted twice—once as the notes receivable on the parent's books and again as cash or other assets on the subsidiary's books. Therefore, an entry is made to eliminate the receivable of the parent and the payable of the subsidiary in preparing consolidated statements. Another example of an elimination entry to avoid double counting relates to the parent's investment account. If the assets of the parent (including the investment account) were added to the assets of the subsidiary, there would be double counting of the subsidiary's assets. At the same time the sources of financing would be counted twice if the shareholders equity accounts of Company S were added to those of Company P. Therefore, an eliminating entry removes the investment account of the parent and, correspondingly, shareholders' equity items of the subsidiary. In addition, Company P's account, Equity in Earnings of Company S, must be eliminated to avoid the double counting of Company S's revenues and expenses.

17. A consolidated income statement is little more than the sum of the income statements of the parent and the subsidiaries. Intercompany transactions such as sales and purchases are eliminated in order to avoid double counting. Thus, the consolidated income statement attempts to show sales, expenses, and net income figures that report the results of operations of the group of companies in their dealings with the outside world.

18. The amount of consolidated net income for a period is the same as the amount that would be reported if the parent company used the equity method of accounting for the intercorporate investment. That is, consolidated net income is equal to parent company's net income plus parent's share of subsidiary's net income minus profit (or plus loss) on intercompany transactions. However, under the equity method for an unconsolidated subsidiary, the parent's share of subsidiary's net income (adjusted for intercompany transactions) appears on a single line, Equity in Earnings of Unconsolidated Subsidiary. The consolidation process combines the individual revenues and expenses of the subsidiary (adjusted for intercompany transactions) with those of the parent, and eliminates the account Equity in Earnings of Unconsolidated Subsidiary, shown on the parent's books.

19. When a parent company owns less than 100 percent of the subsidiary, the minority stockholders continue to have a proportionate interest in the shareholders' equity of the subsidiary as shown in its separate corporate records. The amount of minority interest appearing in the balance sheet results from multiplying the common stockholders' equity of the subsidiary by the minority's percentage of ownership. Typically the minority interest appears among the equities on the consolidated balance sheet between the liabilities and shareholders' equity.

20. The amount of the minority interest in the subsidiary's net income shown on the consolidated income statement is generally the result of multiplying the subsidiary's net income by the minority's percentage of ownership. The consolidated income statement allocates the portion applicable to the parent company and the portion of the subsidiary's income applicable to the minority interest. Typically, the minority interest in the subsidiary's net income appears as a deduction in calculating consolidated net income.

21. Most countries outside the United States account for minority, passive investments using a lower-of-cost-or-market method, instead of the market value method. In recent years the accounting for active investments have become similar to practices in the United States: the equity method for minority, active investments, and consolidation for majority investments.

22. In a corporate acquisition, one corporation acquires all, or substantially all, of another corporation's common stock in a single transaction. Generally accepted accounting principles require the use of one of two methods of accounting for corporate acquisitions: the purchase method and the pooling-of-interests method.

23. The purchase method uses acquisition-cost accounting. The assets and liabilities of the acquired company are reported in the consolidated balance sheet at the date of acquisition at their market values. If Company P purchases Company S paying a price in excess of the market value of the identifiable net assets (assets minus liabilities), the excess is recognized on the consolidated statements as goodwill. Goodwill must be amortized over a period not exceeding 40 years. The consolidated income statement in subsequent periods will show expenses (depreciation and amortization) based on these market values.

24. The pooling of interests method accounts for a corporate acquisition as a uniting of ownership interest of two companies by exchange of equity (common stock) securities. Since the exchange is viewed as a change in form rather than substance, no new basis of accountability arises. Book values of the assets and liabilities of the predecessor companies are carried over to the new combined, or consolidated, enterprise.

25. Generally, if an acquisition qualifies as a purchase, then the reported income of the combined enterprise may be reduced by additional depreciation and amortization expenses. The extra depreciation and amortization expenses result from recognizing increased asset valuations and, perhaps, goodwill. If the acquisition qualifies as a pooling of interest, reported income for the consolidated enterprise will ordinarily be larger than for the same consolidated enterprise accounted for as a purchase.

26. The various methods of accounting for long-term investments in corporate securities have effects on the statement of cash flows. When a firm uses the market value method, dividend revenues generally produce cash. Therefore, calculating cash flow from operations normally requires no adjustment. Changes in the Investment account and the Unrealized Holding Gain or Loss account applying the market method do not appear in the statement of cash flows. However, under the equity method, equity in investee's undistributed earnings is subtracted from net income to derive cash provided from operations of the investor. In consolidated statement of cash flows, the individual sources and uses of cash of the subsidiary are combined with those of the parent.

Questions and Exercises

True/False. For each of the following statements, place a T or F in the space provided to indicate whether the statement is true or false.

_____ 1. Dividends paid to the owner of common shares in an investment accounted for by the equity method are treated as a reduction of the investment account.

_____ 2. When a stockholder owns more than 50 percent of the voting stock of another company, the stockholder is called the majority investor or the parent.

_____ 3. A minority investor owns less than 50 percent of the voting shares of another corporation.

_____ 4. Generally accepted accounting principles require that the equity method be used when a company owns 20 to 50 percent of the voting stock of another company.

_____ 5. When the equity method is used, cash from operations in the statement of cash flows is increased by the amount of dividend received.

_____ 6. Minority interest in net income is a deduction in determining the consolidated net income.

_____ 7. Unlike the purchase method, assets and liabilities do not reflect market values at the date of a pooling-of-interest corporate acquisition on the consolidated balance sheet.

_____ 8. To fully disclose consolidated assets, both the parent's Investment in Subsidiary account and individual assets and liabilities of the subsidiary are presented in the consolidated balance sheet.

_____ 9. Companies with minority, passive investments, classified as investments, could report a balance in Unrealized Holding Loss on Investments in Securities as a negative amount in the shareholders' equity section of the balance sheet.

_____ 10. Under the equity method, the investor company treats as income (or revenue) each period its proportionate share of the periodic earnings of the investee company.

_____ 11. A company is required to use the market value method to account for its investments in securities of another company regardless of its percentage of ownership.

_____ 12. The consolidation method of reporting investments in stocks may be used under the same percentage of ownership as the equity method.

_____ 13. Goodwill appears on the consolidated balance sheet after a business combination has been accounted for as either a purchase or a pooling of interests.

_____ 14. If a company is appropriately using the market value method of accounting for long-term investments in corporate securities, a decline in market value below cost results in a loss to be recognized on the current period income statement.

_____ 15. Consolidated financial statements reflect only transactions between the group of consolidated companies and other entities.

_____ 16. Goodwill is the excess of the cost of an acquisition over the current market value of the net identifiable assets acquired.

_____ 17. Goodwill may be presented on the balance sheet (not expensed) indefinitely or until the board of directors determines there is no value associated with it.

_____ 18. The entries to eliminate intercompany transactions are made on the books of the parent company only.

_____ 19. Generally accepted accounting principles require the parent to combine, or consolidate, the financial statements of majority-owned companies with those of the parent.

_____ 20. A firm's minority, passive investment appears in the firm's balance sheet between the liabilities and shareholders' equity.

_____ 21. Under the market value method the investor firm does not recognize dividends received as income but as a return of investment.

_____ 22. The amount of the minority interest shown on the balance sheet is generally the result of multiplying the common stockholders' equity of the subsidiary by the minority's percentage of ownership.

_____ 23. Dividends can legally be declared only from retained earnings of one corporation.

_____ 24. Subsidiary companies are those which have equal ownership in the common shares of a third corporation.

_____ 25. Most published financial statements report minority interest as a reduction in the cost of the asset, Investment in Stock.

_____ 26. The market value method is used by most countries in a parallel fashion to U.S. firms.

_____ 27. Companies using the market value method normally require no adjustment to net income when calculating cash flow from operations.

Matching. From the list of terms below, select that term which is most closely associated with each of the descriptive phrases or statements that follows and place the letter for that term in the space provided.

a.	Consolidated Financial Statements	g.	Minority, Active Investment
b.	Equity Method	h.	Minority, Passive Investment
c.	Goodwill	i.	Minority Interest
d.	Intercompany Transactions	j.	Parent
e.	Majority, Active Investment	k.	Pooling-of-Interest Method
f.	Market Value Method	l.	Purchase Method
		m.	Subsidiary

_____ 1. The corporate acquisition method that accounts for an acquisition as the uniting of ownership interest of two companies by exchange of equity.

_____ 2. Under this method the investor's share of ownership is between 20 and 50 percent.

_____ 3. The majority investor who owns more than 50 percent of the voting stock of another company.

_____ 4. Statements combining the results of operations, financial position, and statement of cash flow of a parent company and its subsidiaries as if the companies were one economic entity.

_____ 5. The corporate acquisition method that uses acquisition cost accounting.

_____ 6. An investment where the stockholder owns greater than 50 percent of the voting stock of another company.

_____ 7. These would be eliminated in preparing consolidated statements.

_____ 8. An investment where the percentage of the ownership of voting shares is between 20 percent and 50 percent.

_____ 9. The equity of minority stockholders shown in a consolidated balance sheet.

_____ 10. The excess of the cost of the acquisition over the current market value of the net assets acquired.

_____ 11. Companies use this method to account for long-term investments where their ownership is less than 20 percent of the outstanding voting common stock.

_____ 12. The corporation which is subject to control by a parent corporation.

_____ 13. An investment where the percentage of the other corporation's shares owned is not so large that the acquiring company can control or exert significant influence over the other company.

Multiple Choice. Choose the best answer for each of the following questions and enter the identifying letter in the space provided.

_____ 1. This method is required by generally accepted accounting principles for accounting for investment in common stock of 20 percent to 50 percent.

    a. Market value method.
    b. Equity method.
    c. Consolidation method.
    d. All of the above are acceptable.

_____ 2. Which of the following account titles is not associated with the use of the market value method?

    a. Unrealized Holding Loss on Investments in Securities.
    b. Unrealized Holding Gain on Investments in Securities.
    c. Equity in Earnings of Affiliate.
    d. Investment in Securities.

_____ 3. Under the equity method, as the investee company declares dividends the investor company would

    a. Increase the investment account.
    b. Decrease the investment account.
    c. Increase the revenue account.
    d. Decrease the revenue account.

_____ 4. Elimination entry for the parent company's Investment account would typically include debits to the following except

    a. Common Stock (Company S).
    b. Retained Earnings (Company S).
    c. Equity of Earnings of Company S (Company P).
    d. Investments in Stock of Company S (Company P).

_____ 5. If an acquisition qualifies as a pooling of interest, reported income for the consolidated enterprise will ordinarily be

    a. Larger than for the same consolidated enterprise accounted for as a purchase.
    b. Smaller than for the same consolidated enterprise accounted for as a purchase.
    c. Equal to the same consolidated enterprise accounted for as a purchase.
    d. Adjusted for goodwill amortization.

_____   6. The equity method is used to account for

   a. Minority, passive investments.
   b. Minority, active investments.
   c. Majority, active investments.
   d. All of the above.

_____   7. The following are true statements describing the effects of Investments in Securities on the statement of cash flows except

   a. When a company uses the market value method, calculating cash flow from operations normally required no adjustment to net income.
   b. Unrealized Holding Loss is usually added back to net income in calculating cash flow from operations.
   c. When a firm uses the equity method and received dividends less than its share of investee's earnings, normally there is a substraction from net income in calculating cash flow from operations.
   d. All of the above are true.

_____   8. Generally work sheet procedures to prepare consolidated statements include the following steps:

   a. Elimination of the parent company's investment account.
   b. Elimination of intercompany receivables and payables.
   c. Elimination of intercompany sales and purchases.
   d. All of the above.

_____   9. Majority investments are generally reported by

   a. Preparation of consolidated statements.
   b. Application of the equity method.
   c. One-line presentations on the balance sheet (as an investment).
   d. Application of the market value method.

_____   10. One important reason for continued legal existence of subsidiary companies is

   a. To reduce the financial risk of one segment becoming insolvent.
   b. To meet more effectively the requirements of state corporation and tax legislation.
   c. To expand with a minimum of capital investment.
   d. All of the above.

_____   11. The entry to record a decline in value at year-end in a company's marketable equity securities held as long-term investments is

   a. Debit Investment in Securities, credit Unrealized Holding Loss on Investment in Securities.
   b. Debit Unrealized Holding Loss on Investment in Securities, credit Investments in Securities.
   c. Debit Realized Loss on Valuation of Marketable Investments, credit Investment in Securities.
   d. Debit Realized Gain on Valuation of Marketable Equity Investments, credit Investment in Securities.

_____ 12. The market value method is used to account for

    a. Minority, passive investments.
    b. Minority, active investments.
    c. Majority, active investments.
    d. None of the above.

_____ 13. The ownership percentage of voting stock of minority, active investments is usually

    a. Zero to 20 percent.
    b. 20 to 50 percent.
    c. More than 50 percent.
    d. 100 percent.

_____ 14. Goodwill generally is recognized after a business acquisition accounted for under the

    a. Pooling-of-interests method.
    b. Purchase method.
    c. Either pooling-of-interests or purchase method.
    d. Neither pooling-of-interest nor purchase method.

_____ 15. All of the following accounts would be eliminated in the preparation of consolidated financial statements except

    a. Common Stock (Company P).
    b. Common Stock (Company S).
    c. Investment in stock of Company S (Company P).
    d. All of the above.

_____ 16. All of the following accounts would be eliminated in the preparation of consolidated financial statements except

    a. Equity in Earnings of Company S (Company P).
    b. Accounts Receivable (Intercompany).
    c. Sales (Intercompany).
    d. Dividends Declared (Company P).

_____ 17. All of the following statements are true except

    a. Consolidated net income is the same amount as that which results when the parent uses the equity method for an unconsolidated subsidiary.
    b. Consolidated retained earnings is the same amount as that which results when the parent uses the equity method for an unconsolidated subsidiary.
    c. The consolidation process eliminates the account, Equity in Earnings of Subsidiary.
    d. All of the above are true.

_____ 18. The eliminations to remove intercompany transactions are typically made on

    a. Separate books for the consolidated entity.
    b. Company P's books.
    c. A consolidated work sheet.
    d. Company S's books.

_____ 19. Financial statements generally are consolidated for parent and subsidiary companies for

    a. Minority, passive investments.
    b. Minority, active investments.
    c. Majority, active investments.
    d. None of the above.

_____ 20. Consolidated financial statements are generally prepared when the following characteristic is present:

    a. The parent owns more than 50 percent of the voting stock of the subsidiary.
    b. The parent owns 100 percent of the voting stock of a real estate subsidiary.
    c. The parent owns 100 percent of the voting stock of a finance subsidiary.
    d. All of the above.

Exercises

1. Prepare general journal entries for each of the following transactions on the books of the Clio Corporation.

    January 18, 1995:   Purchased 10 percent of the outstanding shares of Franklin Enterprises for $40,000. (Use the market value method.)

    February 12, 1995:   Purchased 30 percent of the outstanding shares of Merritt Company for $75,000. (Use the equity method.)

December 31, 1995: Franklin Enterprises reported $10,000 of net income and Merritt Company reported $5,000 of net income. Franklin Enterprises shares are currently valued at $35,000. (Apply market value method for Franklin Enterprises and the equity method for Merritt Company.)

January 15, 1996: Franklin Enterprises declared and distributed cash dividends totaling $5,000.

January 18, 1996: Merritt Company declared and distributed $3,000 in cash dividends.

January 19, 1996: Clio Corporation sold one-half of its interest in Franklin Enterprises for $18,000.

January 20, 1996: Clio Corporation sold 10 percent of its interest in Merritt Company for $8,000.

December 31, 1996: The remaining Franklin Enterprises shares are currently valued at $19,000. (Apply market value method.)

2. Company P acquired 100 percent of the outstanding shares of Company S for $500,000 cash on January 1, 1995. At the time of acquisition, the book value of the shareholders' equity of Company S was $500,000, comprising the following account balances:

Common Stock	$200,000
Retained Earnings	300,000
Total Stockholders' Equity	$500,000

During 1995, Company S reported net income of $50,000. At December 31, 1995, $5,000 of Company S's accounts receivable represent amounts payable by Company P. During 1995, Company P sold merchandise to Company S for $15,000. None of that merchandise remains in Company S's inventory at year-end. Assuming Company P properly applied the equity method of accounting for its investment in Company S, prepare elimination entries in general journal form for the preparation of the December 31, 1995, financial statements for the following:

a. Elimination of the parent company's investment account.

b. Elimination of intercompany receivables and payable.

c. Elimination of intercompany sales and purchases.

3. Presented below is balance sheet data for Rich Corporation and Segrid Corporation as of January 1, 1995. On this date, Rich Corporation exchanges 3,000 shares of its common stock for all the common stock of Segrid Corporation. The common shares of Rich Corporation were selling for $32 per share on this date.

   a. Prepare a consolidated balance sheet for Rich Corporation and Segrid Corporation on January 1, 1995, using (1) the purchase method and (2) the pooling-of-interests method.

   b. Projected net income without consideration given to the effects of the corporate acquisition is $6,000 for Rich Corporation and $3,500 for Segrid Corporation. The firms amortize any excess acquisition cost allocated to property, plant, and equipment over five years and any excess acquisition cost allocated to goodwill over 40 years. Compute the amount of consolidated net income and earnings per share for Rich Corporation and Segrid Corporation for 1995 using (1) the purchase method and (2) the pooling-of-interests method.

Balance Sheet Data for
Rich Corporation and Segrid Corporation
January 1, 1995

| | Historical Cost | | Current Market Value |
	Rich Corp.	Segrid Corp.	Segrid Corporation
Assets			
Current Assets	$15,000	$12,000	$ 12,000
Property, Plant, and Equipment	40,000	25,000	39,000
Goodwill			60,000
Total Assets	$55,000	$37,000	$111,000
Equities			
Liabilities	$23,000	$15,000	$ 15,000
Common Stock ($2 par value)	2,000	2,000	2,000
Additional Paid-in Capital	10,000	6,000	6,000
Retained Earnings	20,000	14,000	14,000
Unrecorded Excess of Market Value over Historical Cost			74,000
Total Equities	$55,000	$37,000	$111,000

Answers to Questions and Exercises

True/False

1.	T	6.	T	11.	F	16.	T	21.	F	26.	F
2.	T	7.	T	12.	F	17.	F	22.	T	27.	T
3.	T	8.	F	13.	F	18.	F	23.	T		
4.	T	9.	T	14.	F	19.	T	24.	F		
5.	T	10.	T	15.	T	20.	F	25.	F		

Matching

1.	k	4.	a	7.	d	10.	c	13.	h
2.	b	5.	l	8.	g	11.	f		
3.	j	6.	e	9.	i	12.	m		

Multiple Choice

1.	b	5.	a	9.	a	13.	b	17.	d
2.	c	6.	b	10.	d	14.	b	18.	c
3.	b	7.	b	11.	b	15.	a	19.	c
4.	d	8.	d	12.	a	16.	d	20.	d

Exercises

1.

	Dr.	Cr.
January 18, 1995:		
Investment in Franklin Enterprises	40,000	
Cash		40,000
Purchased 10 percent of outstanding shares (market value method).		
February 12, 1995:		
Investment in Merritt Company	75,000	
Cash		75,000
Purchased 30 percent of outstanding shares (equity method)		
December 31, 1995:		
Investment in Merritt Company	1,500	
Equity in Earnings of Affiliate		1,500
Recognized 30 percent of Merritt Company income.		
Unrealized Holding Loss on Investments in Securities	5,000	
Investment in Franklin Enterprise		5,000
Recognized decline in market value of Franklin shares.		
January 15, 1996:		
Cash	500	
Dividend Revenue		500
Received Franklin Enterprises dividends.		
January 18, 1996:		
Cash	900	
Investment in Merritt Company		900
Received Merritt Company dividends.		
January 19, 1996:		
Cash	18,000	
Realized Loss on Sale of Investments	2,000	
Investment in Franklin Enterprises		17,500
Unrealized Holding Loss on Investments in Securities		2,500
Sold one-half interest in Franklin Enterprises.		
January 20, 1996:		
Cash	8,000	
Investment in Merritt Company		7,560*
Gain on Sale of Investment in Stock		440
Sold 10 percent interest of Merritt Company.		
*($75,000 = 1,500 – 900) × 10%.		
December 31, 1996:		
Investment in Franklin Enterprises	1,500	
Unrealized Holding Loss on Investments in Securities		1,500
Adjusted remaining shares of Franklin Enterprises to reflect market value.		

2. a.

	Dr.	Cr.
Common Stocks (Company S)	200,000	
Retained Earnings, January 1, 1995 (Company S)	300,000	
Equity in Earnings of Company S (Company P)	50,000	
Investment in Company S (Company P)		550,000

To eliminate the parent company investment account and
subsidiary's shareholders' equity accounts.
($550,000 = $500,000 + $50, 000).

b.

Accounts Payable	5,000	
Accounts Receivable		5,000

To eliminate intercompany accounts receivables and
payables on consolidated work sheet.

c.

Sales Revenue	15,000	
Cost of Goods Sold		15,000

To eliminate intercompany sales and purchases on
consolidated work sheet.

3. a.

Rich Corporation and Segrid Corporation
Consolidated Balance Sheet
January 1, 1995

Assets	(1) Purchase Method	(2) Pooling-of-Interest Method
Current Assets	$ 27,000	$ 27,000
Property, Plant, and Equipment	79,000	65,000
Goodwill	60,000	- -
Total Assets	$166,000	$ 92,000
Equities		
Liabilities	$ 38,000	$ 38,000
Common Stock ($2 Par Value)	8,000 a	8,000 a
Additional Paid-in Capital	100,000 b	12,000 c
Retained Earnings	20,000	34,000
	$166,000	$ 92,000

a. $2,000 + (3,000 × $2)
b. $10,000 + (3,000 × $30)
c. $2,000 + $2,000 + $10,000 + $6,000 – (4,000 × $2)

b.

	(1) Purchase Method	(2) Pooling-of-Interests Method
Precombination Projected		
Net Income	$9,500	$9,500
Additional Depreciation $39,000/5	(7,800)	—
Goodwill Amortization $60,000/40	(1,500)	—
Revised Net Income	$ 200	$9,500
Number of Common Shares Outstanding	4,000	4,000
Earnings Per Share	$ .05	$ 2.38

Chapter 14

Statement of Cash Flows: Another Look

Chapter Highlights

1. The statement of cash flows, its rationale, and a T-account approach for preparing the statement were introduced in Chapter 5. Subsequent chapters have described the impact of various transactions on the statement of cash flows. This chapter synthesizes these discussions.

2. Cash flows refer to cash and cash equivalents. Cash equivalents represent short-term, highly liquid investments for which a firm has temporarily placed excess cash. Generally, these investments qualify as cash equivalents only if their original maturities are three months or less.

3. The T-account procedures involves four steps:

   a. Obtain a balance sheet for the beginning and end of the period spanned by the statement of cash flows.
   b. Prepare a T-account work sheet. A master T-account is at the top of the work sheet. The master T-account has sections labeled Operations, Investing, and Financing. Enter the beginning and ending balances in cash and cash equivalents in the master T-account. Complete the T-account work sheet by preparing a T-account for each balance sheet account other than cash and cash equivalents and enter the beginning and ending balances.
   c. Explain the change in the master cash account between the beginning and end of the period by explaining, or accounting for, the changes in the other balance sheet accounts. Accomplish this step by reconstructing the entries originally made in the accounts during the period and entering them in appropriate T-accounts on the work sheet. By explaining the changes in these other balance sheet accounts, accountants explain the change in cash and cash equivalents.
   d. Prepare a statement of cash flows using information in the T-account work sheet.

4. In the statement of cash flows, the net change in cash is explained by providing information on the flow of funds from operations, investing, and financing activities.

5. The operations section begins with net income. Net income is then adjusted by noncash revenues, expenses, gains, and losses to produce cash flow from operations.

6. Certain items require amounts to be added back to net income in deriving cash flow from operations because they were deducted in determining income but did not require a cash outflow. Examples include

depreciation expense, patent amortization, realized loss on sale of marketable equity securities, and increases in deferred taxes.

7. Some items require amounts to be deducted from net income in deriving cash flow from operations because they required more cash than was deducted in determining income or because the total cash provided from the transaction is shown in the investing section of the statement. Bond premium amortization and gain on sale of equipment are examples of these deduction adjustments.

8. Other adjustments, either addbacks or deductions, are made to net income because of changes in the balances of operating accounts. For example, addback adjustments are made for decreases in prepayments, accounts receivable, and inventories and increases in accounts payable and other current operations payables. Deduction adjustments are made for increases in prepayments, accounts receivable, and inventories and decreases in accounts payable and other current operations payables.

9. The investing activities section of the statement summarizes cash flows from acquisition (outflows) and sales (inflows) of investments and property, plant, and equipment.

10. Borrowing and stock transactions are summarized in the financing section of the statement of cash flows. Examples of inflows included in this section would be short-term borrowing, long-term bonds issued, and preferred or common stock issued. Outflows would include dividend payments, retirement of long-term debt, and acquisition of stock.

11. Some financing and investing transactions do not involve cash. Significant investing and financing transactions are reported as supplemental information to the statement of cash flows. These transactions, while not reported as part of the statement of cash flows, are entered in the T-account work sheet to account fully for the changes in the balance sheet. Examples include acquiring the use of a building by signing a capital lease, recognition of an unrealized holding gain on an investment in securities, and recording the conversion of bonds payable into shares of common stock.

12. Interpretation of information in the statement of cash flows requires an understanding of economic characteristics of the industries in which a firm conducts operations and a multiperiod view. These issues may be illustrated using the relationship between net income and cash flow from operations and the relationship between cash flow from operating, investing, and financing activities.

13. Net income and cash flow from operations differ due to (a) adjustment to net income for noncash revenues and expenses and (b) changes in operating working capital accounts. The extent that a firm adjusts net income for noncash items depends on the nature of its operations. For example, capital intensive firms will likely show substantial addback to net income for depreciation expense. Adjustments for changes in working capital accounts depend in part on a firm's growth rate. Growing firms usually experience significant increases in inventories and receivables. Financing growth for these firms may come from operations (suppliers) or from financing by issuing short- or long-term debt or stock.

14. Insight into the relationship between cash flows from operating, investing, and financing activities generally can be gained using the product life cycle concept. Changing cash flow characteristics accompany the product introduction, growth, maturation, and decline phase of a product cycle. Analysts extend this concept to a multiproduct firm by identifying the average life cycle phase of a firm's products.

Questions and Exercises

True/False. For each of the following statements, place a T or F in the space provided to indicate whether the statement is true or false.

_____ 1. For the statement of cash flows, cash is defined as cash and cash equivalents (short-term, highly liquid investments).

_____ 2. Depreciation expense is a deduction adjustment from net income in deriving cash flow from operations.

_____ 3. The purchase of common stock of another company is a financing activity.

_____ 4. An increase in deferred taxes is shown as an addback in deriving cash flow from operations.

_____ 5. All accountants use the T-account approach to the statement of cash flows preparation.

_____ 6. Accumulated depreciation is added to net income in deriving cash flow from operations.

_____ 7. A decrease in warranties payable would be shown as a deduction from net income in deriving cash flow from operations.

_____ 8. Cash dividends received from a 40 percent owned affiliate company would be added to net income in deriving cash flow from operations.

_____ 9. A gain on the sale of marketable securities would be shown as a deduction from net income in deriving cash flow from operations.

_____ 10. Net income is adjusted downward for patent amortization to derive cash flow from operations.

_____ 11. Bond discount amortization is deducted from net income in deriving cash flow from operations.

_____ 12. Loss on sale machinery is added to net income in deriving cash flow from operations.

_____ 13. Sale of equipment without a gain or loss is not shown on the statement of cash flows.

_____ 14. A decrease in prepaid insurance would be shown as an addback to net income on the statement of cash flows.

_____ 15. An example of a deduction adjustment in net income in deriving cash flow from operations would be a decrease in accounts receivable.

_____ 16. An increase in inventory would be presented in the investing section of the statement of cash flows.

_____ 17. Decreases in accounts payable would be shown as an addback adjustment to net income in deriving cash flow from operations.

_____ 18. Equity in undistributed earnings of an affiliate would be deducted from net income in deriving cash flow from operations.

_____ 19. An acquisition of a building by incurring a capital lease obligation would be shown as supplemental information to the statement of cash flows.

_____ 20. Acquisition of treasury stock should be presented in the investing section of the statement of cash flows.

_____ 21. The conversion of long-term bonds into common stock is an example of a noncash financing and investing activity.

_____ 22. Short-term bank borrowing and long-term bonds issued would both be presented in the financing activities section of the statement of cash flows.

_____ 23. Dividends paid would not be presented in the statement of cash flows.

_____ 24. Cash proceeds from the sale of a building would be presented in the investing section of the statement of cash flows.

_____ 25. A purchase of a long term investment in stock of another company would be presented in the financing section of the statement of cash flows.

Matching. For each transaction below, indicate the line(s) of the statement of cash flows where the effect would be presented and place the letter(s) for your answer in the space provided. Place an S for a noncash transaction that would require supplemental disclosure. Place an X if the transaction is not shown on the statement. Ignore income tax effects.

Operating Section of the Statement
a = Net income.
b = Addback to net income in deriving cash flow from operations.
c = Deductions to net income in deriving cash flow from operations.
Investing Section of the Statement
d = Proceeds from dispositions of noncurrent assets.
e = Acquisitions of noncurrent assets.
Financing Section of the Statement
f = Increases in debt or capital stock.
g = Dividends.
h = Reductions in debt or capital stock.

_____ 1. Borrowed cash from the bank by issuing short-term note payable.

_____ 2. Amortization of patent recorded.

_____ 3. Sale of equipment for cash with a loss recognized.

_____ 4. Preferred stock is issued for cash.

_____ 5. Depreciation recorded on equipment.

_____ 6. Investment in stock of another company.

_____ 7. Discount on bonds payable is amortized.

_____ 8. Increase in the balance of accounts payable.

_____ 9. Land is acquired by giving cash.

314

_____ 10. Equity in undistributed earnings of affiliate is recognized.

_____ 11. Deferred income tax payable is increased for the year.

_____ 12. Acquisition of a building and land by entering into a lease meeting the capital lease criteria.

_____ 13. Paid dividends for the year.

_____ 14. Warranties payable increased during the year.

_____ 15. Preferred stock is converted into common stock.

_____ 16. Treasury stock is purchased for cash.

_____ 17. Long-term investments are sold for cash with a gain recognized.

_____ 18. Treasury stock is sold for an amount greater than its repurchase price.

_____ 19. Salaries are paid during the year.

_____ 20. New equipment is purchased by issuing a long-term note payable.

_____ 21. Accounts receivable increased during the year.

_____ 22. Land was acquired by issuing preferred stock.

_____ 23. Unearned revenue was reduced during the year.

_____ 24. Prepaid rent was increased during the year.

_____ 25. Retirement of long-term debt at maturity by using bond sinking fund.

Multiple Choice. **Choose the best answer for each of the following questions and enter the identifying letter in the space provided.**

_____ 1. The statement of cash flows is typically prepared

    a. Before the balance sheet is prepared.
    b. After the balance sheet but before the income statement.
    c. After income statement is prepared but before the balance sheet.
    d. After both the balance sheet and income statement are prepared.

_____ 2. Each of the following is an addback to net income in deriving cash flow from operations except:

    a. Depreciation expense.
    b. Amortization of patent.
    c. Loss on the sale of marketable securities.
    d. All of the above.

_____ 3. An acquisition of a patent would be presented in the statement of cash flows

    a. As an addback to net income in deriving cash flow from operations.
    b. As a deduction from net income in deriving cash flow from operations.
    c. In the investing section.
    d. None of the above.

_____ 4. An amortization of a bond discount would be presented in the statement of cash flows

   a. As an addback to net income in deriving cash flow from operations.
   b. As a deduction from net income in deriving cash flow from operations.
   c. In the financing section.
   d. None of the above.

_____ 5. An acquisition of treasury stock would be presented is the statement of cash flows

   a. As an adjustment to net income for the difference in price paid versus the original issue price.
   b. In the financing section.
   c. In the investing section.
   d. None of the above.

_____ 6. Equity income from an affiliate would be presented in the statement of cash flows

   a. As an addback to net income in deriving cash flow from operations.
   b. As a deduction from net income in deriving cash flow from operations.
   c. In the investing section.
   d. None of the above.

_____ 7. Each of the following is an addback to net income in deriving cash flow from operations except

   a. Decrease in deferred income tax liability.
   b. Decrease in prepaid insurance.
   c. Decrease in accounts receivable.
   d. Increase in accounts payable.

_____ 8. Each of the following is a deduction from net income in deriving cash flow from operations except

   a. Increase in accounts receivable.
   b. Loss on sale of equipment.
   c. Amortization of bond premium.
   d. Decrease in accounts payable.

_____ 9. Each of the following is a deduction from net income in deriving cash flow from operations except

   a. Decrease in warranties payable.
   b. Increase in inventories.
   c. Increase in accounts payable.
   d. All of the above.

_____ 10. Each of the following is an addback to net income in deriving cash flow from operations except

   a. Gain on sale of building.
   b. Loss on sale of building.
   c. Decrease in inventories.
   d. All of the above.

_____ 11. Each of the following is an addback to net income in deriving cash flow from operations except

    a. Loss on sale equipment.
    b. Equity in affiliate's losses.
    c. Amortization of bond premium.
    d. All of the above.

_____ 12. Each of the following is a deduction to net income in deriving cash flow from operations except

    a. Gain on sale of building.
    b. Gain on sale of equipment.
    c. Gain on sale of marketable securities.
    d. All of the above.

_____ 13. Each of the following would be presented in the investing section of the statement of cash flows except

    a. Acquisition of equipment.
    b. Acquisition of building.
    c. Proceeds from sale of equipment.
    d. All of the above.

_____ 14. Each of the following would be presented in the investing section of the statement of cash flows except

    a. Proceeds from sale of equipment.
    b. Proceeds from sale of long-term investment.
    c. Proceeds from sale of marketable securities.
    d. All of the above.

_____ 15. Which of the following would be presented in the investing section of the statement of cash flows?

    a. Acquisition of equipment through a capital lease.
    b. Acquisition of treasury stock.
    c. Retirement of long-term debt.
    d. None of the above.

_____ 16. Which of the following would be presented in the financing section of the statement of cash flows?

    a. Long-term bonds payable issued.
    b. Long-term notes payable issued.
    c. Short-term notes payable issued.
    d. All of the above.

_____ 17. Which of the following would be presented in the investing section of the statement of cash flows?

    a. Retirement of long-term debt.
    b. Retirement of preferred stock.
    c. Acquisition of treasury stock.
    d. None of the above.

_____ 18. Which of the following transactions should be disclosed as a noncash investing and financing activity?

    a. Acquisition of building for cash.
    b. Common stock issued upon conversion of bonds.
    c. Acquisition of equipment by issuing a long-term note payable.
    d. Both b and c.

_____ 19. Which of the following transactions would be presented in the financing section of the statement of cash flows.

    a. Dividends paid.
    b. Dividends received.
    c. Interest paid.
    d. None of the above.

_____ 20. Which of the following would not be shown on the statement of cash flows?

    a. Stock dividends paid.
    b. Early retirement of debt.
    c. Reissue of treasury stock.
    d. None of the above.

_____ 21. Characteristics of growing firms include the following except

    a. Significant increase in inventories.
    b. Reporting a deduction adjustment to net income for deferred taxes change in the statement of cash flows.
    c. Significant increase in accounts receivables.
    d. All of the above.

_____ 22. The following statements point out the proper interpretation of information in the statement of cash flows except

    a. Capital-intensive firms will likely show a substantially smaller addback to net income for depreciation than would be shown by service firms.
    b. The product life cycle concept provides useful insights into the relation between cash flows from operating, investing, and financing activities.
    c. The adjustments for changes in operating working capital accounts depend in part on a firm's rate of growth.
    d. All of the above.

Exercises

1. Your client, LOL, Inc., provides you with the income statement and comparative balance sheet data below. The client indicates that long-term investments were sold during the year at book value and new property and plant were acquired costing $210,000. You are to prepare a T-account work sheet and reconstruct entries originally made and enter them in appropriate T-accounts. You do not have to prepare the formal statement of cash flows.

LOL, Inc.
Income Statement
For the Year Ended December 31, 1995

Sales	$880,000	
Other revenues	40,000	$920,000
Less:		
Cost of good sold	$260,000	
Selling expenses	26,000	
Depreciation expenses	84,000	
Income taxes	10,000	
Loss on sale of property and plant	24,000	404,000
Net income		516,000
Dividends		40,000
Income retained in business		$476,000

LOL, Inc.
Comparative Balance Sheet Data
as of December 31, 1994 and 1995

	1994	1995
Cash	$ 76,800	$ 322,600
Marketable equity securities (not cash equivalent)	20,000	19,000
Accounts receivable	98,000	246,400
Inventories	123,800	225,000
Long-term investments	174,000	160,000
Property and plant	425,000	480,000
	$917,600	$1,453,000
Acounts payable	$134,600	$ 200,000
Bonds payable	149,800	101,000
Accumulated depreciation	104,000	60,000
Capital stock	262,200	350,000
Unrealized holding loss on marketable securities	0	(1,000)
Retained Earnings	267,000	743,000
	$917,600	$1,453,000

2.   You are given below a list of several key transactions which may or may not affect the presentation of the statement of cash flows. You are to prepare the reconstructive work sheet entries (in journal form) to explain the change in cash and the other balance sheet accounts. Label each cash entry in a way which identifies the section of the statement of cash flows in which the item would appear. Explanations for the entries are not necessary. The first is answered as an example.

a. Internal records indicate $1,200 of depreciation is included in income determination for the period.

Example Answer
Cash (Operations-Addback)   1,200
  Accumulated Depreciation   1,200

b. The income statement indicates that net income of the period was $5,000.

c. Goodwill amortization amounted to $700 for the year.

d. Equipment was acquired for $15,000, giving a long-term capital lease.

320

e. Preferred stock totaling $3,000 was issued during the year.

f. The company declared and paid $2,000 of dividends to its shareholders during the year.

g. The company sold for $250 a piece of equipment originally costing $1,000 on which accumulated depreciation of $700 had been taken.

h. The company purchased treasury stock, $2,500.

i. Accounts payable decreased by $200 during the year.

j. The company borrowed $8,000 from the bank by giving a long-term note payable.

k. Accounts receivable decrease by $150 during the year.

l. Sold for $8,000 long-term investment in stock costing $7,000.

m. Wrote up long-term investment to reflect market value by $3,000.

n. Amortization of bond discount for the year was $75.

3.   Comparative balance sheets as of December 31, 1994 and 1995, and the income statement for this year ended December 31, 1995, for Lindsay, Inc., are presented below:

Lindsay, Inc.
Comparative Balance Sheets
December 31, 1994 and 1995

	December 31,	
	1994	1995
Cash	$ 50,100	$ 171,700
Marketable Securities (at market value)	33,500	13,100
Accounts Receivable, Net	48,000	90,000
Inventory	62,820	108,120
Total Current Assets	$194,420	$ 382,920
Investment in Carter Co.	122,440	133,960
Plant Assets	610,200	730,600
Accumulated Depreciation	(30,000)	(32,500)
Total Assets	$897,060	$1,214,980
Accounts Payable	$ 32,440	$110,892
Warranties Payable	10,000	9,000
Total Current Liabilities	$ 42,440	$ 119,892
Bonds Payable	100,000	230,000
Discount on Bonds Payable	(4,600)	(4,300)
Deferred Income Taxes	1,020	1,692
Preferred Stock	60,000	-0-
Common Stock	160,000	220,000
Unrealized Holding Loss on Marketable Securities	-0-	(2,300)
Retained Earnings	538,200	649,996
Total Liabilities and Stockholder's Equity	$897,060	$1,214,980

Lindsay, Inc.
Income Statement
For Year Ended December 31, 1995

Sales	$ 485,614
Gain on Sale of Marketable Securities	4,800
Gain on Sale of Land	21,400
Equity in Carter Co. Earnings	11,760
	$ 523,574
Cost of Goods Sold	296,814
Depreciation	2,500
Other Expenses	96,464
	$ 395,778
Net Income	$ 127,796

Additional information:

1. Lindsay, Inc., declared and paid $16,000 dividends during the year.

2. Land with a book value of $42,600 was sold during the year.

3. Equipment costing $163,000 was purchased during the year.

4. Bonds Payable were issued at par.

5. Lindsay, Inc., sold marketable securities costing $18,100 for $22,900.

6. During the year, Lindsay wrote down marketable securities by $2,300 to reflect their market value. At the beginning of the year the cost of marketable securities were equal to their market value.

7. During the year, Lindsay, Inc,. received $240 dividends from Carter, Co., a 30 percent owned company.

8. During the year, the preferred stockholders elected to exercise their conversion privilege. The conversion ratio was one preferred stock ($10 par) for two common shares ($5 par).

   a. Prepare a T-account work sheet for the preparation of a statement of cash flows.

   b. Prepare a formal statement of cash flows for the year ended December 31, 1995.

Answers to Questions and Exercises

True/False

1.	T	6.	F	11.	F	16.	F	21.	T
2.	F	7.	T	12.	T	17.	F	22.	T
3.	F	8.	T	13.	F	18.	T	23.	F
4.	T	9.	T	14.	T	19.	T	24.	T
5.	F	10.	F	15.	F	20.	F	25.	F

Matching

1.	f	6.	e	11.	b	16.	h	21.	c
2.	b	7.	b	12.	s	17.	d,c	22.	s
3.	d,b	8.	b	13.	g	18.	f	23.	c
4.	f	9.	e	14.	b	19.	x	24.	c
5.	b	10.	c	15.	s	20.	s	25.	s

Multiple Choice

1.	d	5.	b	9.	c	13.	d	17.	d	21.	b
2.	d	6.	b	10.	a	14.	d	18.	d	22.	a
3.	c	7.	a	11.	c	15.	d	19.	a		
4.	a	8.	b	12.	d	16.	d	20.	a		

Exercises

LOL, Inc.
T-Account Work Sheet
Cash

✓	76,800			

Operations

Net Income	(a)	516,000	148,400	(h)	Increase in Accounts Receivable
Depreciation expense	(b)	84,000	101,200	(i)	Increase in inventories
Loss on Sale of Property and Plant	(e)	24,000			
Increase in Accounts Payable	(j)	65,400			

Investing

Sale of Long-Term Investments	(c)	14,000	210,000	(d)	Acquisition of Property and Plant
Sale of Property and Plant	(e)	3,000			

Financing

Issue Capital Stock	(l)	87,800	40,000	(f)	Dividends
			48,800	(k)	Retire Bonds Payable
		322,600			

Marketable Equity Securities

✓	20,000	1,000	(g)
	19,000		

Accounts Receivable

✓	98,000	
(h)	148,400	
	246,400	

Inventories

✓	123,800	
(i)	101,200	
	225,000	

Long-Term Investments

✓	174,000	14,000	(c)
	160,000		

Property and Plant

✓	425,000	155,000	(e)
(d)	210,000		
	480,000		

Accounts Payable

	134,600	✓
	65,400	(j)
	200,000	

326

Bonds Payable				Accumulated Depreciation		
(k)	48,800	149,800 ✓		(e)	128,000	104,000 ✓
		101,000				84,000 (b)
						60,000

Capital Stock				Unrealized Holdings Loss on Marketable Securities		
		262,200 ✓				
		87,800 (l)		(g)	1,000	
		350,000			1,000	

Retained Earnings		
(f)	40,000	267,000 ✓
		516,000 (a)
		743,000

2.

			Dr.	Cr.
a.	Cash (Operations—Addback)		1,200	
	Accumulated Depreciation			1,200
b.	Cash (Operations—Net Income)		5,000	
	Retained Earnings			5,000
c.	Cash (Operations—Addback)		700	
	Accumulated Amortization (or Goodwill)			700
d.	Equipment		15,000	
	Capitalized Lease Obligation (Noncash Financing and Investing Transaction)			15,000
e.	Cash (Financing—Issue Preferred Stock)		3,000	
	Preferred Stock			3,000
f.	Retained Earnings		2,000	
	Cash (Financing—Dividends)			2,000

327

		Dr.	Cr.
g.	Cash (Investing—Sale of Equipment)	250	
	Accumulated Depreciation	700	
	Cash (Operations—Addback Loss)	50	
	Equipment		1,000
h.	Treasury Stock	2,500	
	Cash (Financing—Reacquisition of Stock)		2,500
i.	Accounts Payable	200	
	Cash (Operations—Deduction)		200
j.	Cash (Financing—Issue Note Payable)	8,000	
	Long-Term Note Payable		8,000
k.	Cash (Operations—Addback)	150	
	Accounts Receivable		150
l.	Cash (Investing—Sale of Long-Term Investments)	8,000	
	Cash (Operations—Deduction of Gain)		1,000
	Long-Term Investments		7,000
m.	Long-Term Investments	3,000	
	Unrealized Holding Gain on Investments (Noncash Financing and Investing activities)		3,000
n.	Cash (Operations—Addback)	75	
	Discount on Bonds Payable		75

3. a

Lindsay, Inc

T-Account Work Sheet

Cash

✓ 50,100			

Operations

Net Income	(1) 127,796	21,400 (4)	Gain on Sale of Land
Depreciation	(2) 2,500	4,800 (7)	Gain on Sale of Marketable Securities
Inc. in Accts. Pay.	(13) 78,452	11,520 (9)	Equity in Undistributed Earnings
Bond Disc. Amort.	(15) 300	42,000 (11)	Increase in Accounts Receivable
Inc. Deferred Income Taxes	(16) 672	45,300 (12)	Increase in Inventory
		1,000 (14)	Decrease in Warranties Payable

Investing

Sale of Land	(4) 64,000	163,000 (6)	Acquisition of Equipment
Sale of Marketable Securities	(7) 22,900		

Financing

Issue Bonds Payable	(6) 130,000	16,000 (3)	Dividends

171,700	

Marketable Securities			Accounts Receivable	
✓ 33,500	18,100 (7)		✓ 48,000	
	2,300 (8)		(11) 42,000	
13,100			90,000	

Inventory			Investment in Carter Co.	
✓ 62,820			✓ 122,440	
(12) 45,300			11,520	
108,120			133,960	

Plant Assets			
✓	610,200	42,600	(4)
(5)	163,000		
	730,600		

Accumulated Depreciation			
		30,000	✓
		2,500	(2)
		32,500	

Accounts Payable			
		32,440	✓
		78,452	(13)
		110,892	

Warranties Payable			
(14)	1,000	10,000	✓
		9,000	

Bonds Payable			
		100,000	✓
		130,000	(6)
		230,000	

Discount on Bonds Payable			
✓	4,600		
		300	(15)
	4,300		

Deferred Income Taxes			
		1,020	✓
		672	(16)
		1,692	

Preferred Stock			
(10)	60,000	60,000	✓
		-0-	

Common Stock			
		160,000	✓
		60,000	(10)
		220,000	

Unrealized Holding Loss on Marketable Securities		
(8)	2,300	
	2,300	

Retained Earnings			
(3)	16,000	538,200	✓
		127,796	(1)
		649,996	

b.

Lindsay, Inc.
Statement of Cash Flows
For Year Ended December 31, 1995

Operations:

Net Income	$127,796	
Noncash Revenues, Expenses, Gains, and		
Loans Included in Income:		
Gain on Sale of Land	(21,400)	
Gain on Sale of Marketable Securities	(4,800)	
Depreciation	2,500	
Equity in Carter Co. Undistributed Earnings	(11,520)	
Increase in Accounts Receivable	(42,000)	
Increase in Accounts Payable	78,452	
Increase in Inventory	(45,300)	
Decrease in Warranties Payable	(1,000)	
Bond Discount Amortization	300	
Deferred Income Taxes	672	
Cash Flow from Operations		$ 83,700

Investing:

Sale of Land	64,000	
Acquisition of Equipmen	(163,000)	
Sale of Marketable Securities	22,900	
Cash Flow from Investing		(76,100)

Financing:

Issue Bonds Payable	$ 130,000	
Dividends	(16,000)	
Cash Flow from Financing		$114,000
Net Change in Cash		$121,600
Cash, January 1, 1995		50,100
Cash, December 31, 1995		$171,700

Chapter 15

Significance and Implications of Alternative Accounting Principles

Chapter Highlights

1. The independent accountant expresses an unqualified opinion on a firm's financial statements by stating that the statements follow generally accepted accounting principles (GAAP). In the United States, Congress has ultimate authority to specify acceptable accounting principles. Congress has delegated this authority to the Securities and Exchange Commission (SEC). The SEC generally accepts pronouncements of the Financial Accounting Standards Board (FASB) as constituting acceptable accounting principles. In reality the SEC and the FASB communicate continuously as reporting issues arise. The FASB follows a process in selecting accounting principles that incorporates deduction from a broad theoretical framework (conceptual framework) and induction from the information needs and preferences of its various constituencies.

2. Firms in the United States have varying degrees of flexibility in choosing their accounting principles:

    a. In some instances, the firms have wide flexibility in choosing among alternatives, such as in selecting a depreciation or an inventory method.
    b. In other situations, specific conditions dictate the methods used; thus, there is little flexibility. An example is the accounting for investments in the common stock of other firms.

3. While a particular firm does not have unlimited flexibility in the selection of accounting methods, the partial listing below of some of the more significant currently acceptable accounting principles should give an impression of the wide flexibility that does exist.

    a. Depending upon the situation, a firm may recognize revenue at the time goods are sold or services rendered (accrual basis accounting), when cash is collected (long-term installment sales), or as production progresses (long-term contracts). Most firms recognize revenue at the time they sell (deliver) goods or render services.
    b. A firm may recognize bad debt expense in the period that revenue is recognized (allowance method) or if the amount uncollectible is unpredictable, in the period that specific accounts are determined to be bad (direct write-off method). GAAP requires firms with predictable uncollectible accounts to use the allowance method. Income tax laws require firms to use the direct write-off method.
    c. Firms record their inventories using one of several bases: acquisition cost, lower of acquisition cost or market, standard cost, or in some situations, net realizable value. If cost is used, firms may select from several acceptable cost-flow assumptions. Allowable cost flow assumptions include LIFO, FIFO, or

weighted average. Firms have some latitude in selecting a cost flow assumption for financial and tax reporting. However, a firm must use LIFO for financial reporting if it uses LIFO for tax reporting.

d. A firm accounts for investments in common stock using either the market value method or the equity method or it prepares consolidated statements. The accounting method used depends primarily on the percentage of outstanding shares held.

e. For financial reporting, firms may depreciate fixed assets using straight-line, double-declining-balance, sum-of-the-years' digits, or units of production method. Firms will use different estimated service lives depending on intensity of use, maintenance, or repair policy. Income tax laws specify the depreciation method and service lives for various types of depreciable assets. Income tax laws do not require conformity between financial and tax reporting for depreciable assets.

f. Firms account for the acquisition of another firm using either the purchase method or the pooling-of-interests method. Accounting standards specify the conditions that a firm must meet to use the pooling method. If the conditions are not met, then the acquisition must be accounted for using the purchase method. Firms account for corporate acquisition for income tax purposes using methods that parallel those for financial reporting. However, the criteria for financial and tax reporting differ, causing the possibility that the accounting differs for corporate acquisition in these two sets of reports.

g. A firm may set up as an asset and subsequently amortize the rights to use property acquired under lease (capital lease method) or give no recognition to the lease except at the time that lease payments are due each period (operating lease method). Whether a firm uses the capital or operating lease method for financial reporting depends on criteria such as the life of the lease relative to the life of the leased asset and the present value of the lease payments relative to the market value of the leased property. The criteria for a capital versus an operating lease for tax purposes differ somewhat from those used for financial reporting. Thus, firms may account for a particular lease differently for financial and tax reporting.

h. The items above do not represent an all-inclusive list of acceptable accounting principles. The list is intended merely to give the reader an idea of the alternatives that do exist in different situations. Firms must disclose their accounting principles in a note to the financial statements.

4. Effective interpretation of published financial statements requires sensitivity to the generally accepted accounting principles that firms use. Comparing the reports for several companies may necessitate adjusting the amounts for the different accounting methods used. Even though two firms may be alike in nearly all respects, they may present materially different reports due to their use of different accounting methods.

5. If investors accept financial statement information in the form presented without adjusting the information for the different accounting principles being used, one of two firms otherwise identical might receive a disproportionate amount of capital funds. Thus, the use of alternative generally accepted accounting principles could lead to a misallocation of resources in the economy. If investors make the necessary adjustments in analyzing the financial statements of various firms and invest accordingly, perhaps the concern over the variety of acceptable accounting principles is excessive. If the investors do make such adjustments, then increased disclosure of the procedures followed may be more important than greater uniformity in accounting principles.

6. The question of determining the effect of alternative accounting principles on investment decisions has been the subject of a great deal of research and extensive debate. Some argue that the current flexibility permitted firms in selecting accounting principles misleads investors and results in a misallocation of resources. Others present evidence to the contrary.

7. There are several possible objectives for financial reporting, each of which might dictate the selection of a different combination of generally accepted accounting principles.

    a. One criterion for assessing the usefulness of accounting information is the <u>accuracy</u> of the presentation of the underlying events and transactions. In applying this criterion, the firm would select those principles which most accurately measure the pattern of an asset's services still available at the end of the period. This objective has an important limitation. Since flows of past and future benefits are difficult to measure, accountants differ in their opinion as to which principles provide an accurate presentation for a particular firm.

    b. In choosing between alternative but generally accepted methods of accounting, a firm might choose those methods which minimize asset totals and reported cumulative earnings, thereby providing the most <u>conservative</u> measure of net income and assets. The use of conservatism as a reporting objective is intended to reduce the possibility that users of financial statements will develop overly optimistic assessments of a company. It is conceivable, though, that statement readers might be misled by earnings reports based upon conservative principles especially if earnings reported on a less conservative manner might have led to a different investment decision effect.

    c. An objective having the opposite effect of conservatism is <u>profit maximization</u>, which is an extension of the notion that the firm is in business to generate profits. Using this criterion as a reporting objective suggest that the firm should select accounting principles which maximize cumulative earnings and asset totals, keeping within the confines of generally accepted accounting principles.

    d. A final objective of financial statement reporting might be <u>income smoothing</u>, which suggests the selection of accounting methods that result in the smoothing of earnings over time. Advocates of this objective suggest that if a firm minimizes fluctuations in earnings, it will reduce the perceived risk of investing in its shares of stock and, all else being equal, obtain a higher stock price.

8. In selecting accounting procedures for income tax purposes, firms should choose those methods that minimize the present value of the income tax payments over time. The operational rule, sometimes called the least and latest rule, is to pay the least amount of taxes as late as possible within the law. The means of accomplishing this objective are to recognize expenses as quickly as possible and to postpone the recognition of revenue as long as possible. This policy may need to be adjusted somewhat if the tax rates are expected to change in future years or if the firm has had losses in earlier years and can carry those losses forward to offset taxable income of the current year.

9. The growing internationalization of business increases the need for comparable financial statements of firms operating in different countries. The International Accounting Standards Committee (IASC) is a voluntary association of professional accounting bodies from around the world. The IASC has issued several pronouncements attempting to harmonize international accounting principles. Although not binding, these pronouncements have helped reduce the diversity of accounting principles across countries.

Questions and Exercises

True/False. For each of the following statements, place a T or F in the space provided to indicate whether the statement is true or false.

_____ 1. Generally accepted accounting principles require that revenue is usually recognized at time of sale.

_____ 2. The close relation between financial and tax reporting in some countries impedes the effectiveness of the IASC.

_____ 3. The SEC has very little input into the deliberations of the FASB.

_____ 4. There is a great deal of flexibility in choosing depreciation methods for financial reporting purposes.

_____ 5. There will most likely be a deferred tax liability resulting from the handling of depreciation for financial reporting and taxes.

_____ 6. It is unlikely that any single generally accepted accounting principle could accomplish both the financial reporting objectives of conservatism and profit maximization.

_____ 7. Percentage of completion method must be used for all long-term construction contractors.

_____ 8. Assuming no change in income tax rates, use of the ACRS depreciation method for tax purposes instead of the straight-line method will significantly improve the present value of tax savings from depreciation over the life of an asset.

_____ 9. A firm accounts for investments in the preferred stock of other firms using either the market value method or the equity method, or else it prepares consolidated statements.

_____ 10. If the FIFO inventory method is employed for tax purposes, it must also be used for financial reporting purposes.

_____ 11. When the amount of uncollectible accounts can be reasonably estimated, the direct write-off method is not allowed for financial reporting.

_____ 12. If a firm wants a conservative yet acceptable set of financial statements, it should use the ACRS method of depreciation.

_____ 13. The methods of accounting for income tax purposes and financial accounting purposes can never be different.

_____ 14. It has been proved conclusively that firms using a conservative group of accounting principles will be undervalued by investors in the stock market.

_____ 15. The "least and latest rule" is an operational rule used to select the methods that minimize the present value of the stream of income tax payments.

_____ 16. A firm always has a wide flexibility in its selection of accounting methods.

_____ 17. All leases, for lessees, are treated as operating leases, but for lessors, are treated as capital leases.

_____ 18. The accountant must use the accounting principles that lead to the most accurate set of financial statements.

336

_____ 19. All methods allowed for tax reporting purposes are also allowed for financial reporting purposes.

_____ 20. The pronouncements of the International Accounting Standards Committee (IASC) are binding on member countries.

_____ 21. The production method is used more frequently than any other depreciation method due to its smoothing effect upon net income over time.

_____ 22. Research has proved conclusively that investors adjust for the use of different accounting procedures in analyzing the financial statements of various firms, and thus the concern over the variety of principles available to firms is unwarranted.

_____ 23. The development of accounting principles has been shown to be essentially a political process due to the active participation by both Congress and the SEC.

_____ 24. Over the entire life of a firm, the LIFO inventory method will show the same cumulative profits as the FIFO method.

_____ 25. The general rule in selecting accounting methods for tax purposes is to postpone revenue recognition and recognize expenses as soon as possible. If tax rates are expected to rise significantly, the reverse of this rule may be appropriate.

_____ 26. When the income reporting for tax purposes is greater than the net income reported for financial statement purposes, Prepaid Income Tax must appear on the balance sheet.

Matching

1. From the following list of objectives for financial accounting and tax reporting, select the objective which is most closely associated with each of the accounting and valuation methods that follows and place the letter for that principle in the space provided. An objective may be used more than once, and more than one objective may be applicable to each method.

a. Conservatism	d. Profit Maximization
b. Accurate Presentation	e. Tax Minimization
c. Income Smoothing	f. None of the Above

_____ 1. Completed Contract Method

_____ 2. Capitalization of prepaid advertising costs

_____ 3. ACRS Method

_____ 4. Straight-Line Method

_____ 5. LIFO Method

_____ 6. Lower-of-Cost-or-Market Method

_____ 7. Operating Method (accounting for leases) by lessor

_____ 8. FIFO Method

_____ 9. Double Declining-Balance Method

_____ 10. Capital Lease by lessee

_____ 11. Direct Write-Off Method

_____ 12. Expensing of R & D Costs

_____ 13. Percentage of Completion Method

_____ 14. Weighted-Average Inventory Method

_____ 15. Percentage of Sales Method for uncollectible accounts

Multiple Choice. **Choose the best answer for each of the following questions and enter the identifying letter in the space provided.**

_____ 1. Which financial accounting objective listed below would seem to be the closest to the objectives of tax reporting?

    a. Conservatism.
    b. Fair Presentation.
    c. Accuracy.
    d. Profit Maximization.

_____ 2. For which account below would the use of lower-of-cost-or-market be acceptable?

    a. Inventory.
    b. Land.
    c. Prepaid Rent.
    d. It would be acceptable for all accounts above.

_____ 3. The use of a straight-line method of amortization would be acceptable for which of the following?

    a. Building.
    b. Patent.
    c. Goodwill.
    d. All of the above.

_____ 4. Liberal Company and Low Gear Company are identical in all respects except that Liberal Company uses FIFO and Low Gear Company uses LIFO in costing its inventories. Prices have been rising steadily over the last several years. Which statement below would be incorrect in comparing the financial statements of these two companies?

   a. The inventory for Liberal Company would be higher than the inventory for Low Gear Company.
   b. The retained earnings for Liberal Company would be higher than the retained earnings for Low Gear Company.
   c. The net income in the current year for Liberal Company would be higher than the net income for Low Gear Company.
   d. The tax liability for Liberal Company would be less than the tax liability for Low Gear Company.

_____ 5. Which generally accepted accounting principle would be appropriate if the firm's objective was to present accounting information in a conservative manner?

   a. Lower-of-cost-or-market.
   b. Expensing of exploration costs when incurred.
   c. Amortization of organization costs over minimum time period.
   d. All of the above would be appropriate.

_____ 6. Which account below may appear on a company's balance sheet when the income for financial and tax reporting are different?

   a. Income Tax Expense.
   b. Deferred Income Tax Liability.
   c. Sales Tax Expense.
   d. All of the above.

_____ 7. In order to minimize the present value of income tax payments, which alternative course of action should a firm take?

   a. Use the LIFO inventory method instead of FIFO in periods of rising prices.
   b. Depreciate fixed assets on the straight-line method rather than the ACRS method.
   c. Capitalize exploration costs instead of expensing them.
   d. All of the above.

_____ 8. The Not Too Hot Radiator Company has decided to use straight-line depreciation in its financial statements and to use ACRS on its tax return. Which sentence concerning Not Too Hot's financial statements would be correct?

   a. The net cash flow from operations will be less than what it would have been if straight-line had been used for tax purposes as well as financial statement purposes.
   b. The income tax expense presented on the income statement in the early years of the assets' useful lives will be less than the tax payments to the federal government.
   c. Deferred Income Tax Liability will be shown as a liability on the balance sheet.
   d. All of the above statements are correct.

_____ 9. If a firm desired to smooth its income as a means of minimizing large fluctuations in the price of its stock, which method below would be employed to help accomplish this objective?

a. Weighted average for inventory.
b. Percentage of completion method for long-term construction contracts.
c. Straight-line amortization of patents.
d. All of the above might smooth income in certain circumstances.

_____ 10. The method of accounting for exploration costs of a mineral resource that would best attain the objective of income tax accounting would be to

a. Expense in total when incurred.
b. Capitalize only those costs related to mineral deposits.
c. Capitalize all costs associated with productive as well as nonproductive mineral deposits.
d. None of the above.

_____ 11. Which of the following instances is not an example of a firm having wide flexibility in the choice of alternative methods for financial reporting?

a. Accounting for depreciation.
b. Accounting for the investment in common stock.
c. Accounting for inventories.
d. None of the above.

_____ 12. For financial reporting, when is revenue normally recognized?

a. At point of sale.
b. While cash is being collected.
c. After all cash has been collected.
d. At the end of each year.

_____ 13. Which method below is normally considered to be acceptable for financial reporting?

a. ACRS.
b. Lower-of-cost-or-market for inventories.
c. Direct write-off of uncollectible accounts.
d. Capitalization of R & D Costs.

_____ 14. Which of the following has been delegated legal authority by Congress to prescribe accounting principles?

a. SEC.
b. FASB.
c. AAA.
d. IRS.

_____ 15. Which of the following must generally be used for financial reporting if it is used for income tax reporting?

    a. FIFO.

    b. LIFO.

    c. NIFO.

    d. Installment sales method.

Exercises

1. Indicate the accounting principal below that would most likely lead to profit maximization for financial reporting.

    a. FIFO, LIFO, or weighted-average method, when prices are <u>falling</u>.

    b. Straight-line, sum-of-the-years digits', or ACRS method in the first year of an asset's life.

    c. Percentage of completion method or completed-contract method in the first year of the contract.

    d. Effective interest or straight-line method in the last year of an outstanding bond, which was issued at face value.

    e. Double-declining-balance, straight-line or ACRS method in the last year of an asset's life.

    f. Expensing versus capitalization of prepaid advertising in the year prepaid.

    g. Direct write-off or allowance method in the first year of a new company.

    h. Point of sale or installment sale method in the year of sale.

2. Now answer Exercise 1 above, if the methods are being considered for tax reporting and the purpose is to minimize taxes.

3. Indicate the generally accepted accounting principle or method, which is being described below.

   a. Bad debts are recognized when specific accounts are determined to be uncollectible.

   b. A depreciation method that is not acceptable for financial reporting purposes.

c. A way of valuing inventory which recognizes the reduction of value below original cost.

d. The preferable method for amortizing bond discounts.

e. The method which accounts for a lease just like a purchase.

f. The required accounting for investments in common stock when the ownership is less than 20 percent.

g. The inventory method which must be used for financial reporting purposes whenever it is used for tax reporting purposes.

h. The method of recognizing income from long-term construction contracts which results in the most fluctuations in earnings over several periods.

4.   On January 1, 1995, the Lariscy Company is organized and 100,000 shares of $100 par value stock are issued at par. Following is the company's balance sheet for January 1, 1995.

Assets		Equities	
Cash	$ 2,500,000	Common Stock	$10,000,000
Land	3,500,000		
Equipment	4,000,000		
Total Assets	$10,000,000	Total Equities	$10,000,000

Merchandise inventory is purchased and sold during 1995 as follows:

Date of Purchase	Units Purchased	Unit Price	Units Sold
January 3	10,000	$100	9,500
June 6	18,000	110	16,000
November 10	20,000	120	17,000
	48,000		42,500

Merchandise sales totaled $11 million during 1995. In addition, long-term contracts were signed to produce machinery for the Capitalized Corporation. None of the machinery was completed during 1995, but on the basis of the percentage of work completed $1 million of profits have been earned.

All of the merchandise sales were made on account, and at year-end there was a balance in Accounts Receivable of $2 million. The experience of other firms within the industry indicates that on the average 5 percent of all credit sales will not be collected. During the year, $50,000 of accounts have been determined to be uncollectible.

The land was acquired for $2 million for speculative purposes. Lariscy Company believes that there is oil on the property and has spent $1 million on exploration costs.

The equipment was bought on January 1 and is being used in a building which has been leased by the Lariscy Company for 30 years. The estimated life of the equipment is 20 years, and its expected salvage value is $500,000.

To promote the company in its first year of operation, Lariscy spent $2 million on an extensive advertising campaign. Three-fourths of the advertising expenditure is expected to benefit the company in future years. Other operating expenses for 1995 were $1.2 million. Assume a tax rate of 40 percent. Also, assume that any method used for financial accounting purposes will also be used for tax purposes (with the exception of depreciation).

The president believes it is important to maximize reported profits in order to maximize the earnings per share for the stockholders. The controller is concerned about misleading potential investors by reporting possibly overstated profits. He would rather take a conservative approach, at least until the firm has proven itself. You are to prepare comparative income statements for the first year of operation, selecting those methods that would be most appropriate to (a) maximize profits for the president, and (b) show conservative profits for the controller. Also, (c) specify what you would do with each item in order to minimize income taxes.

5.   Presented below are the financial statements and footnotes for Holstrum Company for 1995. Following the statements are several questions for you to answer based upon the information given below.

Holstrum Company
Balance Sheets
December 31, 1994 and 1995

	12/31/94	12/31/95
Assets		
Current Assets		
Cash	$ 80,000	$ 52,000
Accounts Receivable (net)[1]	120,000	150,000
Inventory	80,000	60,000
	$ 280,000	$ 262,000
Property, Plant, & Equipment		
Land	$ 300,000	$ 340,000
Building[2]	750,000	700,000
Accumulated Depreciation	(100,000)	(120,000)
	$950,000	$920,000
Total Assets	$1,230,000	$1,182,000
Liabilities and Shareholders' Equity		
Current Liabilities		
Accounts Payable	$ 60,000	$ 70,000
Notes Payable[3]	100,000	-0-
Dividends Payable	20,000	-0-
	$ 180,000	$ 70,000
Stockholder's Equity		
Common Stock, par value	$ 200,000	$ 200,000
Retained Earnings	850,000	912,000
	$1,050,000	$1,112,000
Total Liab. and Shareholders' Equity	$1,230,000	$1,182,000

Holstrum Company
Income Statement
For the Year Ended December 31, 1995

Sales		$950,000
Cost of Goods Sold		400,000
Gross Profit		$550,000
Operating Expenses		
Depreciation	$ 50,000	
Selling & Administrative	210,000	
Bad Debts Expen	50,000	310,000
Operating Income		$240,000
Nonoperating Items		
Loss from Fire	$ 15,000	
Interest Expense	5,000	20,000
Income before Tax		$220,000
Income Tax		78,000
Net Income		$142,000
Earnings per Share		$ 14.20

Holstrum Company
Retained Earnings Statement
For the Year Ended December 31, 1995

Retained Earnings 1/1/95	$850,000
Net Income	142,000
	$992,000
Dividends Declared	80,000
Retained Earnings, 12/31/95	$912,000

Footnotes:

(1)   All sales are on account and no accounts were written off as definitely uncollectible during the year.

(2)   On 1/1/95 part of the building was destroyed by a fire. No other additions or retirements took place during 1995 in the building account.

(3)   The notes were paid off on July 1, 1995.

Questions:

a. How much cash was collected on account during 1995?

b. Which method of accounting for bad debts was being used by Holstrum Co?

c. If the balance in the Allowance for Doubtful Accounts was $15,000 on January 1, 1995, what would be its balance on December 31, 1995?

d. Was there any land purchased or sold during 1995? If so, how much?

e. What was the book value of the building destroyed by the fire?

348

f. If the company was able to salvage some of the building after the fire, what were the proceeds from salvage for the company?

g. Holstrum is using brand new equipment and furniture. Was it purchased or leased? Why?

h. How much inventory was purchased during 1995?

i. How much was paid on account for inventory purchases? Assume all purchases are made on account.

j. What interest rate was being paid on the notes outstanding on 1/1/95?

k. How many dollars in dividends were paid to stockholders during 1995?

l. How may shares of stock were outstanding on 12/31/95 and what was the par value of the stock?

m. What was the effective tax rate in 1995?

n. How much cash was provided from operations?

Answers to Questions and Exercises

True/False

1.	T	6.	T	11.	T	16.	F	21.	F	26.	F
2.	T	7.	F	12.	F	17.	F	22.	F		
3.	F	8.	T	13.	F	18.	F	23.	F		
4.	T	9.	F	14.	F	19.	F	24.	T		
5.	T	10.	F	15.	T	20.	F	25.	T		

Matching

1.	a,b,e	4.	c,d	7.	f	10.	f	13.	c,d
2.	d	5.	a,e	8.	d	11.	f	14.	c
3.	e	6.	a,c	9.	a	12.	a,e	15.	a,c

Multiple Choice

1.	a	4.	d	7.	a	10.	a	13.	b
2.	a	5.	d	8.	c	11.	b	14.	a
3.	d	6.	b	9.	d	12.	a	15.	b

Exercises

1. a. LIFO.
   b. Straight-line (ACRS not allowed for financial reporting purposes).
   c. Percentage of completion.
   d. Neither, since the bond was issued at face value there is no discount or premium to amortize.
   e. Double declining balance (ACRS not allowed for financial reporting purposes).
   f. Capitalization.
   g. Direct write-off (if allowed).
   h. Point of sale.

2. a. FIFO.
   b. ACRS.
   c. Completed contract.
   d. Neither, since there is no discount or premium to amortize.
   e. Straight-line.
   f. Expensing.
   g. Allowance (if allowed).
   h. Installment sale.

3. a. Direct write-off.
    b. ACRS.
    c. Lower-of-cost-or-market.
    d. Effective interest.
    e. Capital lease.
    f. Market value.
    g. LIFO.
    h. Completed contract.

4.

Lariscy Company
Comparative Income Statements Based on
Different Accounting Principles
For the Year Ending December 31, 1995

(a and b)

	(a) Profit Maximization (President)		(b) Conservative (Controller)	
Revenue:				
Sale of Merchandise	$11,000,000		$11,000,000	
Profit on Long-Term Contract	1,000,000		-	
	$12,000,000		$11,000,000	
Expenses				
Cost of Goods Sold	$ 4,720,000	(1)	$ 4,830,000	(1)
Depreciation on Equipment	175,000	(2)	400,000	(2)
Bad Debts Expense	50,000	(3)	550,000	(3)
Advertising	500,000	(4)	2,000,000	(4)
Exploration Costs	-	(5)	1,000,000	(5)
Other Operating Expenses	1,200,000		1,200,000	
Total Expenses before Income Taxes	$ 6,645,000		$ 9,980,000	
Net Income before Income Taxes	$ 5,355,000		$ 1,020,000	
Income Tax Expense (at 40 percent)	$ 2,142,000		$ 408,000	
Net Income	$ 3,213,000		$ 612,000	
Earnings per Share (100,000 shares outstanding)	$32.13		$6.12	

Supporting Schedules

1. Profit Maximization Approach: FIFO

10,000 units	× $100	=	$1,000,000
18,000 units	× 110	=	1,980,000
14,500 units	× 120	=	1,740,000
			$4,720,000

    Conservative Approach: LIFO

20,000 units	× $120	=	$2,400,000
18,000 units	× 110	=	1,980,000
4,500 units	× 100	=	450,000
			$4,830,000

2. Profit Maximization Approach: Straight-Line Method

    $$\$4,000,000 - \$500,000)/20 = \$175,000$$

    Conservative Approach: Double-Declining-Balance Method

    $$(\$4,000,000 \times \tfrac{1}{20} \times 2) = \$4,000,000 \times .10 = \$400,000$$

    It would also be acceptable to use the sum-of-the-years' digits method for the conservative approach.

3. Profit Maximization Approach: Direct Write-off Method

    $50,000

    Conservative Approach: Allowance Method

    $$.05 \times \$11,000,000 = \$550,000$$

    On the average, the allowance method and the direct write-off method should yield similar results over several years. In year 1, the allowance method should be higher since few of the uncollectible accounts would have been written off under the direct write-off method. In subsequent years, the allowance method could be either higher or lower than the direct write-off method.

4. Profit Maximization Approach: Partial Capitalization

    $$\tfrac{1}{4} \times \$2,000,000 = \$500,000$$

    The remaining $1.5 million is capitalized and will be allocated to those periods that are expected to benefit from the expenditure.

    Conservative Approach: Expense all of the $2 million expenditure in the year incurred.

     5.   Profit Maximization Approach: Capitalization of $1 million.

         All exploration costs are capitalized as part of the cost of the expected mineral deposit. Whenever oil is discovered, the cost will be amortized based upon the estimated productive output of the wells.

         Conservative Approach: Expense all of the $1 million expenditure.

(c) For tax purposes, in order to minimize income taxes:
    1.   LIFO would be used for inventory, which would then also have to be used for financial reporting (which would cause a problem for the president's attempt to maximize profits).

    2.   ACRS would be used for depreciation.

    3.   The allowance method for bad debts would be used (if allowed).

    4.   The entire amount of advertising and exploration costs would be deducted immediately.

5. a.

Accounts Receivable, 1/1/95	$ 120,000
Sales on Account	950,000
	$1,070,000
Less:	
Bad Debts	(50,000)
Cash Collections	(?)
Accounts Receivable, 12/31/95	$ 150,000

    The cash collections are $870,000
    ($1,070,000 - $50,000 - $150,000).

b. The allowance method since there was a bad debts expense for 1995 ($50,000) and no accounts were written off; the direct write-off method was not being used.

c.

Balance, 1/1/95	$ 15,000
Plus: Bad Debts Expense for 1995	50,000
	65,000
Less: Write-offs during 1995	-0-
Balance, 12/31/95	$ 65,000

d. The land account increased by $40,000 during 1995. Most likely this increase represented a purchase.

e. Building, 1/1/95		$750,000
Building, 12/31/95		700,000
Cost of Building Destroyed		$ 50,000
Accumulated Depreciation, 1/1/95	$100,000	
Accumulated Depreciation, 12/31/95	120,000	
Increase for 1995	$ 20,000	
Depreciation for 1995	50,000	
Accum. Depreciation for Building Destroyed		30,000
Book Value of Building Destroyed		$ 20,000
f. Book Value		$ 20,000
Salvage		(?)
Loss from Fire		$ 15,000

The proceeds from salvage were $5,000.

g. Leased—since there are not accounts for equipment and furniture in the Property, Plant, and Equipment section of the balance sheet.

h. Inventory Balance, 1/1/95	$ 80,000
Plus: Purchase	?
Total Available	$
Less: Inventory Balance, 12/31/95	60,000
Cost of Goods Sold	$400,000

Purchases were $380,000 ($400,000 + $60,000 – $80,000 = 380,000).

i. Accounts Payable, 1/1/95	$ 60,000
Plus: Purchases on Account	380,000
Total to be paid	$440,000
Less: Accounts Payable, 12/31/95	70,000
Amount paid on account	$370,000

j. Interest Expense, 1/1/95 - 7/1/95 (6 months)	$5,000
Plus: Bad Debts Expense for 1995	50,000
	× 2
Annual Interest	$ 10,000
Notes Payable	÷ $100,000
Interest Rate	= 10%

k. Dividends Declared in 1995	$ 80,000
Dividends Payable, 1/1/95 (and paid in 1995)	20,000
Dividends Paid in 1995	$100,000

l. Net Income $142,000
    Shares Outstanding   ÷   ?
    Earnings per Share   =   14.20

    The number of shares outstanding was 10,000 ($142,000 ÷ $14.20).

    The par value of the stock was $20 per share
       ($200,000 par value for common stock ÷10,000 shares).

m. The effective tax rate was 35.5 percent ($78,000 ÷ $220,000).

n. Net Income $142,000
    Additions:
       Depreciation $50,000
       Loss from Fire   15,000
       Reduction in Inventory   20,000
       Increase in Accounts Payable   10,000   95,000

    Deductions:
       Increase in Accounts Rec.   (30,000)
    Cash Provided by Operations $207,000

Chapter 16

International Financing Reporting

Chapter Highlights

1. Business firms desiring to sell goods or services in countries other than their home country must decide (a) if the good or service will be made in its home country and exported abroad or made abroad through a subsidiary and (b) should the firm structure transactions so that all cash flows occur in the currency of the home country or should the firm use the currency of the foreign country to denominate all cash flows?

2. The manner in which a firm structures its foreign operations affects its exposure to exchange rate changes. An exchange rate is the price of one country's currency in terms of another country's currency.

3. Exchange rates reflect the forces of demand and supply and are affected by economic and political conditions and prospects within a country relative to those in other countries.

4. Domestic firms account for their foreign investments following the same accounting principles that they use for domestic investments: the market value method when the ownership percentage is less than 20 percent; the equity method when the ownership percentage is between 20 percent and 50 percent; and consolidation for majority-owned investments.

5. The foreign entities keep their accounting records in their local currencies. To apply the appropriate accounting method for these investments, the domestic firm must translate the foreign entity's financial statements from the foreign currency into the domestic currency. This process is known as foreign currency translation.

6. Firms could use either the historical exchange rate, the current exchange rate or some combination of the two in translating each account in a foreign entity's financial statement.

7. The historical exchange rate is the exchange rate in effect when a particular transaction first enters the accounting records. The current exchange rate is the exchange rate at the date of the balance sheet for balance sheet items and the average exchange rate during the current period for income statement items.

8. Changes in exchange rates do not affect the U.S. dollar-equivalent amount of accounts translated at the historical exchange rate. Exchange rate changes do cause the U.S. dollar-equivalent amount of items translated at the current exchange rate to change. The change in the reported amount of these items that result from a change in the exchange rate are referred to as a foreign exchange adjustment.

9. Firms may treat the foreign exchange adjustment as a foreign exchange gain or loss in computing net income or bypass the income statement by including the foreign exchange adjustment in a separate shareholders' equity account.

10. Generally accepted accounting principles require firms to identify the functional currency of each foreign unit. The functional currency is the currency in which the foreign unit conducts most of its activities. If the foreign operation is primarily self-contained within a particular foreign country, the functional currency for these foreign units is their local currency. If the foreign operation is primarily an integrated extension of the parent's operations in the United States, the functional currency for these foreign units is the U.S. dollar.

11. The foreign currency translation method required for self-contained foreign operations (foreign currency is the functional currency) is the all-current translation method. The all-current method translates assets and liabilities using the exchange rate on the date of the balance sheet and translates revenues, expenses, and net income using the average exchange rate during the period. The foreign exchange adjustment that results from applying the all-current method appears as a separate shareholders' equity account and does not affect net income each period.

12. The foreign currency translation method required for foreign operations highly integrated with the U.S. parent company (the U.S. dollar is the functional currency) is the monetary-nonmonetary method. The monetary-nonmonetary method translates monetary assets and liabilities using the current exchange rate and nonmonetary assets and liabilities using the historical exchange rate.

13. Monetary items represent claims receivable or payable in a fixed number of foreign currency units regardless of changes in exchange rates. Because firms translate monetary items using the current exchange rate, monetary items give rise to a foreign exchange adjustment when exchange rates change. The foreign exchange adjustment is included as an exchange gain or loss in measuring net income each period under the monetary-nonmonetary method.

14. Unlike monetary items, nonmonetary items do not result in a fixed future cash inflow or outflow. Nonmonetary items are translated using the historical exchange rate, which results in reporting them at the U.S. dollar-equivalent amounts regardless of changes in the exchange rate.

15. Financial reporting in countries outside of the United States is both diverse and changing rapidly. The diversity of reporting practices occurs because countries differ with respect to the relative role of government in the economy, the principal sources of capital, and the extent of international activity.

16. Accounting standards differ across countries depending in part on two factors: (a) whether a governmental agency sets acceptable accounting standards or whether a private-sector agency assumes responsibility for standard setting and (b) whether acceptable accounting standards for financial reporting closely conforms to the accounting methods required for income tax purposes or whether no such conformity exists.

17. Some of the factors that affect whether a governmental agency or a private-sector agency assumes the responsibility for standard setting are the role of government in the economy, the sources of capital, and the extent of international activity.

18. In Germany, the Federal Parliament sets acceptable accounting principles. The methods of accounting that firms use for financial reporting conform closely to those for tax reporting. The accounting profession in Germany plays only an advisory role to the government in establishing acceptable accounting principles.

19. In Japan, the Ministry of Finance establishes acceptable reporting standards for publicly traded companies, based on recommendations from the Business Accounting Deliberation Council. The Ministry of Justice also plays a role in setting accounting standards in Japan. With the exception of using the equity method or consolidation in filing with the Ministry of Finance, the accounting principles that Japanese

358

firms follow are similar in their tax returns, their filings with the Ministry of Justice, and their filings with the Ministry of Finance.

20. In the United Kingdom, the Accounting Standards Board, a private sector body, establishes accounting standards. The Companies Act of 1985 stipulates the general format of financial statements and requires an independent audit of publicly held companies. Accounting methods used for financial and tax reporting need not conform. The opinion of the independent accountant must state that the financial statements and notes present a "true and fair" view of operating results and financial position.

21. The International Accounting Standards Committee strives to reduce differences in financial reporting between countries by recommending preferred accounting methods for various items. Its pronouncements have tended to limit the range of choices of acceptable accounting principles but have not settled on a single reporting method for most items.

22. Foreign firms that sell debt or equity securities in the United States must file a Form 20F report with the Securities and Exchange Commission each year. The Form 20F report must include a reconciliation between the accounting principles of the foreign country and U.S. acceptable accounting principles for both shareholders' equity and net income.

Questions and Exercises

True/False. For each of the following statements, place a T or F in the space provided to indicate whether the statement is true or false.

_____ 1. Monetary items give rise to exchange gains and losses when exchange rates change.

_____ 2. Whether foreign exchange adjustments are reported as part of net income or are included in a shareholders' equity account, total shareholders' equity will be the same.

_____ 3. When a foreign operation is primarily self-contained within a particular foreign country, the functional currency for these foreign units is the U.S. dollar.

_____ 4. The all-current translation method is required for self-contained foreign operations where foreign currency is the functional currency.

_____ 5. The monetary-nonmonetary method translates monetary items using the current exchange rate.

_____ 6. In Germany, the accounting profession has the primary responsibility for establishing acceptable accounting principles.

_____ 7. Nonmonetary items do not give rise to exchange gains and losses when exchange rates change.

_____ 8. When a foreign operation is primarily an integrated extension of the parent's operations in the United States, the functional currency for these foreign units is their local currency.

_____ 9. The all-current translation method translates assets, liabilities, revenues, expenses, and net income using the historical exchange rate.

_____ 10. The monetary-nonmonetary translation method is required for foreign operations highly integrated with the U.S. parent company where the functional currency is the U.S. dollar.

_____ 11. In Germany, the methods of accounting used for financial reporting do not closely conform to those used for tax reporting.

_____ 12. The monetary-nonmonetary method translates nonmonetary items at the historical exchange rate.

_____ 13. The foreign exchange adjustment that results from applying the all-current translation method bypasses the income statement and appears as a separate shareholders' equity account.

_____ 14. In the United Kingdom, the Companies Act of 1985 stipulated the format of financial statements, required an independent audit of publicly held companies, and established acceptable accounting standards.

_____ 15. The historical exchange rate is the exchange rate in effect when a particular transaction first enters the accounting records.

_____ 16. The foreign exchange adjustment that results from applying the monetary-nonmonetary translation method is used in measuring net income each period.

Matching. **From the list of terms below, select that term which is most closely associated with each of the descriptive phrases or statements that follow and place the letter for that term in the space provided.**

a.	All-Current Translation Method	g.	Functional Currency
b.	Current Exchange Rate	h.	Historical Exchange Rate
c.	Exchange Rate	i.	International Accounting Standards Committee
d.	Foreign Currency Translation	j.	Monetary Items
e.	Foreign Exchange Adjustment	k.	Monetary-Nonmonetary Translation Method
f.	Form 20F Report	l.	Nonmonetary Items

_____ 1. Represents the price of one country's currency in terms of another country's currency.

_____ 2. The process by which a domestic firm translates the foreign entity's financial statements from the foreign currency into the domestic currency.

_____ 3. The exchange rate in effect when a particular transaction first enters the accounting record.

_____ 4. The exchange rate at the date of the balance sheet for balance sheet items and the average exchange rate during the current period for income statement items.

_____ 5. This item may be reported as a gain or loss in computing net income or may be reported in a separate shareholder's equity account.

_____ 6. The currency in which the foreign unit conducts most of its activities.

_____ 7. The foreign currency translation method required for self-contained foreign operations.

_____ 8. The foreign currency translation method required for foreign operations highly integrated with the U.S. parent company.

360

_____ 9. Represents claims receivable or payable in a fixed number of foreign currency units regardless of changes in exchange rates.

_____ 10. This group strives to reduce differences in financial reporting between countries by recommending preferred accounting methods for various items.

_____ 11. This form is filed with the Securities and Exchange Commission each year by foreign firms that sell debt or equity securities in the United States.

_____ 12. These items do not result in a fixed future cash inflow or outflow and are translated using the historical exchange rate which results in reporting them at their U.S. dollar-equivalent amounts regardless of changes in the exchange rate.

Multiple Choice. Choose the best answer for each of the following questions and enter the identifying letter in the space provided.

_____ 1. Which of the following statements is not true regarding the all-current translation method?

     a. This translation method is required when foreign currency is the functional currency.
     b. The translation of assets and liabilities uses the exchange rate on the date of the balance sheet.
     c. Revenues, expenses, and net income are translated using the average exchange rate during the period.
     d. The foreign exchange adjustment that results from applying the all-current method is reported on the income statement as an exchange gain (loss).

_____ 2. Under the monetary-nonmonetary translation method, monetary items are translated using which of the following rates?

     a. Average exchange rate during the current period.
     b. Exchange rate at the end of the current period.
     c. Historical exchange rate.
     d. None of the above.

_____ 3. In the United Kingdom, which of the following establishes acceptable accounting standards?

     a. Accounting Standards Board.
     b. Federal Parliament.
     c. Ministry of Finance.
     d. Business Accounting Deliberation Council.

_____ 4. Under the all-current translation method, assets and liabilities are translated using which of the following rates?

     a. Average exchange rate during the current period.
     b. Exchange rate at the end of the current period.
     c. Historical exchange rate.
     d. None of the above.

_____ 5. Which of the following statements is not true regarding the monetary-nonmonetary translation method?

    a. Monetary items are translated using the current exchange rate.

    b. Nonmonetary items are translated using the historical exchange rate.

    c. When exchange rates change, monetary items give rise to exchange gains (losses), which are included in measuring net income for the period.

    d. All of the above statements are true.

_____ 6. Under the all-current translation method, revenues and expenses are translated using which of the following rates?

    a. Average exchange rate during the current period.

    b. Exchange rate at the end of the current period.

    c. Historical exchange rate.

    d. None of the above.

_____ 7. Which of the following is not a monetary item?

    a. Cash.

    b. Accounts Receivable.

    c. Bonds Payable.

    d. Advances from customers.

The information which follows relates to Questions 8–13. Adams, Inc., maintains a foreign operation in Durban, South Africa. On January 1, Adams invests the necessary funds ($100,000) to build the plant facilities. The subsidiary will conduct all business and record all sales in terms of South African rand (R). During its first year of operations, the subsidiary generated earnings of R10,000 and paid no dividends to Adams. The exchange rate for U.S. dollars per South African rand was as follows during the year:

U.S. Dollars per South African Rand

January 1	$1:R2.00
April 1	$1:R2.38
October 1	$1:R2.63
December 31	$1:R2.78
Average for Year	$1:R2.50

_____ 8. Adams' January 1 investment of $100,000 was convertible (or equivalent) to how many South African rand?

    a. R50,000.

    b. R100,000.

    c. R200,000.

    d. R250,000.

_____ 9. The subsidiary's earnings of R10,000 during its first year of operations was equivalent to how many U.S. dollars?

  a. $ 2,500.
  b. $ 4,000.
  c. $ 6,250.
  d. $25,000.

_____ 10. Which of the following reflects the exchange rate of U.S. dollars to South African rand at the end of the year?

  a. $1:R2.78.
  b. $1:R2.50.
  c. $1:R2.63.
  d. $1:R2.38.

_____ 11. At the <u>end</u> of the year, R210,000 (the initial investment plus first year earnings) is equivalent to how many U.S. dollars?

  a. $ 75,540.
  b. $104,000.
  c. $278,000.
  d. $583,800.

_____ 12. Denominated in terms of U.S. dollars, Adams' investment in the foreign subsidiary (including the subsidiary's first year earnings) totals

  a. $100,000.
  b. $102,500.
  c. $104,000.
  d. $125,000.

_____ 13. Assume that at the end of the year, the dollar-equivalent amount of the subsidiary's net assets is $75,540 while, denominated in U.S. dollars, the subsidiary's net assets total $104,000. The difference of $28,460 ($104,000 - $75,540) can be described as representing

  a. A foreign exchange gain resulting from the increase in value of the South African rand relative to the U.S. dollar.
  b. A foreign exchange loss resulting from the decrease in value of the South African rand relative to the U.S. dollar.
  c. Neither of the above.

_____ 14. Which of the following is not a nonmonetary item?

  a. Accounts Payable.
  b. Prepaid Rent.
  c. Machinery and Equipment.
  d. Common Stock.

_____ 15. Assume the following regarding the U.S. dollar ($) and the South African rand (R): (a) on January 1, $1 was equivalent to R2.00 and (b) on December 31, $1 was equivalent to R2.50. Which of the following statements is true?

    a. The South African rand has dropped in value relative to the U.S. dollar during the year.
    b. On January 1, $.50 would be required to purchase one South African rand.
    c. On December 31, R2.50 would be required to purchase one U.S. dollar ($).
    d. All of the above statements are true.

_____ 16. Under the monetary-nonmonetary translation method, nonmonetary items are translated using which of the following rates?

    a. Average exchange rate during the current period.
    b. Exchange rate at the end of the current period.
    c. Historical exchange rate.
    d. None of the above.

Exercises

1.   Corley Corp. established a foreign subsidiary in Cape Town, South Africa, on January 1, Year 1. Corley invested $250,000 for all of the subsidiary's common stock. During Year 1, the subsidiary engaged in the following transactions:

a. Purchased property and equipment on January 2, Year 1, costing R50,000.
b. Purchased inventory on account totaling R80,000 during Year 1. (The inventory was purchased evenly throughout the year.)
c. Sold inventory costing R60,000 on account during Year 1 for R100,000.
d. Collected R85,000 from credit customers.
e. Paid R70,000 to suppliers of inventory.
f. Paid operating expenses of R20,000 during the year.
g. Recognized R5,000 of depreciation expense during the year.

The exchange rate between the U.S. dollar and the South African rand was $1:R2.00 on January 1. The average exchange rate during Year 1 was $1:R2.50 and the exchange rate on December 31, Year 1, was $1:R2.78.

Prepare a balance sheet for the South African subsidiary in South African rand and in U.S. dollars on December 31, Year 1, using (a) the all-current translation method and (b) the monetary-nonmonetary translation method. Include the foreign exchange adjustment in a separate shareholders' equity account under the all-current method and in net income and retained earnings under the monetary-nonmonetary method.

2. This exercise is a continuation of Exercise 1, Corley Corp. Prepare a statement of net income for the South African subsidiary in South African rand and in U.S. dollars using (a) the all-current translation method and (b) the monetary-nonmonetary translation method.

Answers to Questions and Exercises

True/False

1.	T	6.	F	11.	F	16.	T
2.	T	7.	T	12.	T		
3.	F	8.	F	13.	T		
4.	T	9.	F	14.	F		
5.	T	10.	T	15.	T		

Matching

1.	c	5.	e	9.	j
2.	d	6.	g	10.	i
3.	h	7.	a	11.	f
4.	b	8.	k	12.	l

Multiple Choice

1.	d	6.	a	11.	a	16.	c
2.	b	7.	d	12.	c		
3.	a	8.	c	13.	b		
4.	b	9.	b	14.	a		
5.	d	10.	a	15.	d		

Exercises

1.

	All Current Method		
	Rand	Exchange Rate	Dollars
Assets			
Cash	R445,000	$1:R2.78	$160,072
Accounts Receivable	15,000	$1:R2.78	5,396
Inventory	20,000	$1:R2.78	7,194
Property & Equipment (net)	45,000	$1:R2.78	16,187
Total Assets	R525,000		$188,849
Liabilities and Shareholders' Equity			
Accounts Payable	R 10,000	$1:R2.78	$ 3,597
Common Stock	500,000	$1:R2.00	250,000
Foreign Exchange Adj.			(70,748)*
Retained Earnings	15,000	$1:R2.50	6,000
Total Liabilities and Shareholders' Equity	R525,000		$188,849

*Calculation of Foreign Exchange Adjustment:

	Rand	Exchange Rate	Dollars
Net assets position 1/1, Year 1	R500,000	$1:R2.00	$250,000
Increase in net assets during Year 1 from net income	15,000	$1:R2.50	6,000
Net assets position 12/31, Year 1	R515,000		$256,000
	R515,000	$1:R2.78	185,252
Foreign Exchange Adjustment			$ 70,748

The parent company had a foreign exchange loss because the South African rand decreased in value relative to the U.S. dollar.

	Monetary-Nonmonetary Method		
	Rand	Exchange Rate	Dollars
Assets			
Cash	R445,000	$1:R2.78	$160,072
Accounts Receivable	15,000	$1:R2.78	5,396
Inventory	20,000	$1:R2.50	8,000
Property & Equipment (net)	45,000	$1:R2.00	22,500
Total Assets	R525,000		$195,968
Liabilities and Shareholders' Equity			
Accounts Payable	R 10,000	$1:R2.78	$ 3,597
Common Stock	500,000	$1:R2.00	250,000
Retained Earnings	15,000		(57,629)
Total Liabilities and Shareholders' Equity	R525,000		$195,968

2.

All Current Method

	Rand	Exchange Rate	Dollars
Sales	R100,000	$1:R2.50	$ 40,000
Cost of Goods Sold	(60,000)	$1:R2.50	(24,000)
Operating Expenses	(20,000)	$1:R2.50	(8,000)
Depreciation Expense	(5,000)	$1:R2.50	(2,000)
Income	R 15,000		$ 6,000

Monetary-Nonmonetary Method

	Rand	Exchange Rate	Dollars
Sales	R100,000	$1:R2.50	$ 40,000
Cost of Goods Sold	(60,000)	$1:R2.50	(24,000)
Operating Expenses	(20,000)	$1:R2.50	(8,000)
Depreciation Expense	(5,000)	$1:R2.00	(2,500)
Foreign Exchange Loss			(63,129)*
Income	R 15,000		$ (57,629)

*Calculation of Foreign Exchange Adjustment

	Rand	Exchange Rate	Dollars
Net monetary assets, 1/1 Year 1	R500,000	$1:R2.00	$250,000
Increase in net monetary assets from Sales	100,000	$1:R2.50	40,000
Decreases in net monetary assets:			
Purchase of property & equipment	(50,000)	$1:R2.00	(25,000)
Purchase of inventory on account	(80,000)	$1:R2.50	(32,000)
Payment of operating expenses	(20,000)	$1:R2.50	(8,000)
Net monetary assets 12/31, Year 1	R450,000		$225,000
	R450,000	$1:R2.78	161,871
Foreign Exchange Loss			$ 63,129

The foreign subsidiary was in a net monetary asset position during the year. Because the South African rand has decreased in value relative to the U.S. dollar, the value of the net monetary assets (denominated in U.S. dollars) has decreased and a foreign exchange loss is recognized.